BLACK POLITICAL LIFE IN THE UNITED STATES

Edited by LENNEAL J. HENDERSON, JR.

BLACK POLITICAL LIFE
IN THE UNITED STATES

CHANDLER PUBLICATIONS IN
POLITICAL SCIENCE

Victor Jones, *Editor*

BLACK POLITICAL LIFE
IN THE UNITED STATES

A Fist as the Pendulum

EDITED BY
Lenneal J. Henderson, Jr.

CHANDLER PUBLISHING COMPANY
An Intext Publisher
SAN FRANCISCO • SCRANTON • LONDON • TORONTO

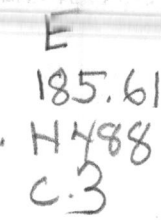

Library of Congress Cataloging in Publication Data

Henderson, Lenneal J   comp.
Black political life in the United States.

(Chandler publications in political science)
CONTENTS: Introduction, by N. Hare.—What is Black politics? A frame of reference for Black politics, by M. H. Jones. The Black man's role in American politics, by M. Dymally.—The history of Black politics. Up from slavery: from Reconstruction to the sixties, by C. Stone. The progressive parties and the Negro, by H. Walton, Jr. Minority politics in Black Belt Alabama, by C. V. Hamilton. The crisis of the Republic: reflections on race and politics, by M. Holden, Jr. [etc.]

1. Negroes—Politics and suffrage. I. Title.
E185.61.H488   323.1'1'96073   77-37515
ISBN 0-8102-0462-2

COPYRIGHT © 1972 BY CHANDLER PUBLISHING COMPANY
ALL RIGHTS RESERVED
INTERNATIONAL STANDARD BOOK NUMBER 0-8102-0462-2
LIBRARY OF CONGRESS CATALOG CARD NUMBER 77-37515
PRINTED IN THE UNITED STATES OF AMERICA

To my wife, Beverley, and my son, Anthony;
To my mother, father, sisters, and brothers,
and to Mrs. Williams;
To the National Conference of Black Political Scientists,
people in search of black political life.

Contents

List of Contributors ix
Preface xiii

1 Introduction Nathan Hare 1

PART ONE. WHAT IS BLACK POLITICS?

2 A Frame of Reference for Black Politics Mack H. Jones 7
3 The Black Man's Role in American Politics
  Mervyn Dymally 21

PART TWO. THE HISTORY OF BLACK POLITICS

4 Up from Slavery: From Reconstruction to the Sixties
  Chuck Stone 35
5 The Progressive Parties and the Negro
  Hanes Walton, Jr. 52
6 Minority Politics in Black Belt Alabama
  Charles V. Hamilton 66
7 The Crisis of the Republic: Reflections on Race and
  Politics Matthew Holden, Jr. 105

PART THREE. PROBLEMS AND ASPECTS OF BLACK POLITICS

8 The Negro Vote. Calvin Purdom   Chuck Stone 138

9 The Negro Elected Official in the Changing American Scene   *Kenneth B. Clark* 150

10 Negro Interest Group Strategies   *Harry A. Bailey, Jr.* 161

11 The American Crucible: Black Identity and the Search for National Autonomy   *J. Don Granville Davis* 173

12 Black Politics and the Kerner Report: Concerns and Direction   *Jewel L. Prestage* 186

13 Black Administrators and Higher Education
Roosevelt Johnson 200

14 Blacks and Conservative Political Movements
Hanes Walton, Jr. 215

PART FOUR. THE FUTURE OF BLACK POLITICS

15 Measuring Black Political Power   *Chuck Stone* 227

Black Political Life in America: A Bibliographical Essay
Lenneal J. Henderson, Jr. 253

Index of Persons 271

The Contributors

DR. HARRY A. BAILEY is chairman of the Political Science Department at Temple University in Philadelphia and has served as president of the Pennsylvania Political Science Association. He edited *Negro Politics in America* and co-edited *Ethnic Group Politics* with Ellis Katz.

J. DON GRANVILLE DAVIS is a lecturer in the Afro-American Studies Department at the University of California, Berkeley. He received A.B. and M.A. degrees from that institution and is now completing the requirements for the PH.D. He has been published frequently and is considered a leading specialist in black studies.

SENATOR MERVYN DYMALLY, born in Trinidad, is currently the only black member of the California State Senate, where he is chairman of the Democratic Caucus and of the Urban Affairs Committee. Senator Dymally is co-chairman of the National Conference of Black Elected Officials, chairman of the board of the Urban Affairs Institute, and editor-in-chief of *The Black Politician* magazine. He has also held the post of lecturer at the University of California, Davis, and at Whittier and Claremont colleges.

DR. CHARLES V. HAMILTON is Professor of Political Science at Columbia University. He received a PH.D. degree from the University of Chicago and a J.D. degree from Loyola University in Chicago. With Stokely Carmichael he co-authored the popular *Black Power: The Politics of Liberation in America*. He is a member of the editorial boards of several periodicals, including *The Black Scholar, The Journal of Black Studies*, and *Political Science Quarterly*.

DR. NATHAN HARE, publisher of *The Black Scholar* and author of *The Black Anglo-Saxons*, was the first person to be hired as a coordinator for a black-studies program in the United States when he went to San Francisco State College in the spring of 1968. Having earned a doctorate in sociology from the University of Chicago, he had taught previously at Howard University in Washington, D.C.

LENNEAL J. HENDERSON, JR., is Assistant Professor of Sociology and Government at the University of San Francisco, where he is also Director of Ethnic Studies. A doctoral candidate in political science at the University of California, Berkeley, he previously has taught in California at Saint Mary's College, Sonoma State College, California State College at Hayward, John F. Kennedy University and the College of Alameda; he has taught at Xavier University in New Orleans and at Howard University in Washington, D.C., as well. He is co-editor of *The Black Politician* magazine.

DR. MATTHEW HOLDEN is Professor of Political Science at the University of Wisconsin in Madison, where he is affiliated with the Center for the Study of Policy and Administration. He has previously taught at Wayne State University and at the University of Pittsburg. He is the author of *The Republic in Crisis* and is a member of the editorial board of *Afro-American Studies* magazine.

DR. ROOSEVELT JOHNSON is Director of Collegiate Assistance Programs at Saint Louis University. He has been a consultant in East Saint Louis to such projects as the Concentrated Employment Program and to the Human Relations Commission. He is a member of the Special Committee of the North Central (Illinois) Accrediting Association.

DR. MACK H. JONES is chairman of the Department of Political Science at Atlanta University. He is president of the National Conference of Black Political Scientists, an advisory editor for *Social Science Quarterly,* and a member of the editorial board of *Phylon* magazine.

DR. JEWEL L. PRESTAGE is chairman of the Political Science Department at Southern University in Baton Rouge, Louisiana. She is a member of the councils of the American Political Science Association and the Southern Political Science Association and serves also as a member of the editorial board for the "Studies in Race and Nations" of the Center on International Race Relations at the University of Denver.

CHUCK STONE has been editor of three prominent black newspapers—*The New York Age, The Washington Afro-American,* and *The Chicago Defender.* He has also served as executive assistant to the Committee on Education and Labor of the United States House of Representatives and director of public information and vice-chairman of the National Conference on Black Power. He has published three widely acclaimed books, *Tell It Like It Is, Black Political Power in America,* and *King Strut.* At present, he is Director of Minority Affairs of the Educational Testing Service in Princeton, New Jersey.

DR. HANES WALTON, JR., is Associate Professor of Political Science at Savannah State College in Georgia, where he has taught since 1967. He is the author of *The Negro in Third-Party Politics, The Political Philosophy of Martin Luther King, Black Political Parties, Black Politics: A Theoretical and Structural Analysis,* and *Political Theory and Political Broadcasting.*

Preface

THE PURPOSE OF this anthology is threefold: 1. It presents the perspectives of black scholars on black political life in the United States. 2. It presents a rich collection of significant literature and analysis for the growing discussions and debates about black politics. 3. It focuses on a few of the many aspects and implications of black politics for American politics, as well as for black people in American politics.

This anthology does not claim to cover all the present and future aspects of black politics. Nor does it claim final answers to the increasingly perplexing nature and problems of black political life in the United States. Its value lies in the fact that it presents more sides and aspects of black politics which must be read and understood by those who would be well-versed in black politics, particularly if they are to become directly involved in one aspect or another of black politics.

The perspectives of black scholars are presented in one anthology, first, because part of the debate about *the study* of black politics is whether or not being black or being white makes a significant difference in the motivations, assumptions, hypotheses, biases, and conclusions which finally become part of the research of this subject. Since there are several anthologies, articles, and books penned by white scholars on black politics, a comparison of those works with the works collected here may provide the reader with some clue or answer to this moot question. Certainly, who says what about black politics should become part of any consideration about *the study* of black politics. Second, by confining the selection of articles to black scholars, it may be possible to discern important variances and dissimilarities in perspective among them. This is vital because it is too often assumed that blacks are monolithic in their approach to the study of black politics.

Part of the consideration of the various perspectives of black scholars on black politics is historical. Several articles included in this anthology are very recent, some two or three years old, and others as much as ten years old. This is deliberate. The idea is to indicate what aspects of black politics have been uppermost in the minds of black scholars over a period of years. Interesting contrasts and differences will be observed in the terminology, methodology, and conclusions of black scholars during the past decade. That history of ideas is certainly important in appreciating how and why the perspectives of black scholars have changed (if they have) in these years.

Finally, several aspects of black politics are discussed in this anthology. It is hoped that this breadth will dispel the pervasive notion that black politics *only* means electoral politics—voting, political parties, elected officials. While the importance of electoral politics cannot be denied, it also should not be overstated or overemphasized.

As in the production of any work, many debts have been incurred. Thanks are due first to those black scholars who so generously contributed their work for publication. A special debt of appreciation is due the National Conference of Black Political Scientists and the Committee on the Status of Blacks in the Profession of the American Political Science Association for their many suggestions and personal inspiration. Mrs. Barbara Blake, Mr. Odell Johnson, Yasmeen, and Cynthia were meticulous and quick in the typing of the manuscript. Our editors, Jon Sharp and Victor Jones, were not only patient in awaiting the articles in the anthology but also helpful in their insightful suggestions about the organization of the articles, the coherence of their assembly, and, of course, guidelines for editing the articles. A special thanks is due to my black-politics class at Saint Mary's College of California; their help and inspiration were immeasurable. Finally, I wish to thank my wife, who kept me together while I put this together.

1

Introduction

Nathan Hare

BLACKS IN AMERICA are new in the arena of organized politics and the scientific study of politics and power. Yet black political scientists are, in at least one crucial sense, as many as two centuries ahead of their white counterparts. For one thing, they at least know who the enemy is, and to know the enemy, it has been said, is to be equipped to defeat him. This is only slightly oversimplified, in that it also is necessary, of course, to know how to defeat him—if not what we are defeating him for, which is where the new wave of black politicans and political scientists emerging in the aftermath of the Black Power cry and quickened by the black studies concept will have to come in. On them we must depend in the end for knowledge of the mechanisms and instruments of the seizure and distribution of power—the essence of politics, if not the most crucial element in all human encounter.

In the United States these days, real power continues to elude the black race, as such. This is only partly due to the nature of our political situation, where we constitute a visibly distinct minority on a stage white-washed with the veneer of majority-rule preachments. Those who rule in actuality are not necessarily those with the most votes, and the white oppressor rules currently almost everywhere, whether he constitutes a majority or not—in South Africa or Sweden, in Maine or Mississippi.

We need a new kind of politics, not only for blacks, but especially for blacks, one not so corrupt and seemingly incapable of reform. We need a politics generative of black statesmen with unselfish devotion to the interests of black liberation to replace the old-guard, token black politician dedicated more to the ends of white political parties and personal advantage and empowerment than to the interests of black liberation.

We must recognize that what is in the interest of blacks in a society officially self-admitted (the Kerner Report) to be racist is not likely to be in the interest of the white oppressors there. Hence, the black or oppressed sections of the population cannot trust the established order or system to provide us with the machinery required to liberate us. We must ourselves create that machinery. A society cannot be expected to change itself or to change predominantly from within. Change must be interjected by a dramatic force from without, designed to detonate the spark toward a new society, a new politics for interracial, democratic freedom.

Although blacks are not the only oppressed group in American society, we are the major group and our oppression is salient. And this is why the revolutionary force will come as a result of black people, in particular, taking on the task of working out a program for a politics of liberation. Other oppressed segments, including some whites, will play important roles in that change—indeed, it is the duty of decent whites to support the efforts of black freedom-fighters, inasmuch as the liberation of blacks is a prerequisite for the liberation of others in a society where black skin is branded. It is necessary that whites—and Chinese, Chicanos, native Americans, women, all—begin to understand this crucial fact, so we will not be thrown into unwarranted competition or permit our forces to be set against one another unnecessarily.

Some of this push toward a politics of liberation will come from routine infiltration into the existing, or institutionalized, political machinery (to be successful, a fighter must be skilled at in-fighting as well as long-range boxing). But we also must recognize that the total job cannot be accomplished merely by "working on the inside," or by "out-foxing" the oppressor at his own game any more than, as we have already begun to discover, by "out-wolfing" him.

Nevertheless, we should not turn our backs on all activity or participation in the established political order. There are good things to be derived from almost any kind of political endeavor, so long as we understand, in our effort to determine or control, its uses and misuses and relative limitations. For one thing, a political party—or even a political office or a nomination to fill that office—can be a platform from which to project our grievances in even obviously abortive campaigns. It also can be a means of exhorting our own black masses to action, or at least to raise issues and so to raise the general level of consciousness of ourselves as a people aware of its needs and of the elements of its exploitation. At the least, some participation in electoral politics as a strategy, if nothing more, can ultimately exhaust the black gullibility which remains so widespread and which we must lose before we can move to any genuinely revolutionary posture or position. By such experimentation the limits for our freedom of the political machinery institutionalized by our oppressor will eventually become apparent, as will the necessity for devising other avenues to black liberation.

We already have a new breed of black politicians emerging on the scene—Georgia legislator Julian Bond; California Assemblyman Willie Brown and California State Senator Mervyn Dymally; Mayor Richard Hatcher of Gary, Indiana; and United States Representative Shirley Chisholm of New York City, to name a few. We need more of them, but we must realize that they can do only so much alone. In tag-team style it is necessary for us to fight from without the ring, even as they and others yet to come continue the battle within.

We are caught now in the transition between the stage of revolutionary rhetoric and the stage of direct combat; and so we are confused and generally falling into conflict and ideological chaos, at once talking of revolution or of black nation-building and then simultaneously rushing to integrate ourselves with the established order. Our rhetoric and vision revolve narrowly around a concept of simple "survival," rooted in pessimism or else based on some strange courtship with death. Survival in the affairs of men should be pretty much taken for granted or met as the natural course of events. Threats to survival must, of course, be both anticipated and resolved, but survival alone must not become the long-term goal of a people in search of freedom. Where it is necessary to aim at the stars in hope of reaching the treetop, it surely is not sufficient to continue to make a struggle of merely standing up on the ground.

Now is the time to prove our ability to set ourselves up as a nation, starting with local black political councils, or entities by whatever name, selected or, perhaps in the beginning, necessarily volunteer or self-appointed, since many black people will fail to see their worth and potential power and so will disdain to participate. These entities in time will become the instruments for deciding just how and for what we must struggle politically as black people.

Say there is a grievance with a store or factory in the black community. The council would move to correct the grievance, perhaps moving mildly at first, then more radically, and finally in some way taking over the enterprise. In regard to police brutality, for another instance, the councils could form or constitute black police commissions to curtail and control police in the black community. Research would be done on every sector of society, and means would be devised for beginning to think of controlling the political and economic interests of black people.

In the end, if enough such councils or committees are organized through our efforts—first on the neighborhood level, then citywide, statewide, and, in turn, nationwide—there will emerge ultimately an independent political apparatus. This organization would probably be called something other than a black party, for it would be much more than that. It would be a black organization which could work out a national program.

At that point, of course, the oppressor will move to oppose it with both feet, even more than before, sending in spies and otherwise creating internal friction. Therefore, at one time or another, some group will have to come up with a program and establish a kind of dual national government, a black government with a Black Congress of elected delegates to make our own laws and pull together our own self-governing apparatus and machinery, including our own enforcement institutions. The Black Congress should be elected but from among the members of the local councils—by direct vote of the people, not through delegates—in every community, city, and state. We are talking about a congress, not a mere conference by that name.

We must move our struggle to a new level. Then we could, through the Congress, demand one-third of the total budget and one-third of the land surface of this country, or whatever is calculated to be just and proper on the basis of need and the laws of reparation. The days of the black caucus, which is essentially a protest group in nature—indeed, by definition—would be all over. Black power in this way would move from slogan to reality.

This is our first task, our duty and necessity, and all else will flow by a natural course from that. In the words of Kwame Nkrumah, "seek ye first the political kingdom and all things shall be added unto you." In this anthology on black politics there are the makings of a blueprint for a political kingdom for black people.

PART ONE
What Is Black Politics?

2

A Frame of Reference for Black Politics

Mack H. Jones

SINCE DAVID EASTON's eloquent argument two decades ago on the need for a conceptual framework to guide research in political science,[1] scholars in the field have been bombarded with theories, approaches, conceptual schemes, and—as one wag has aptly put it—"towards..." literature.[2] In the meantime, as the theoretical projectiles collect dust, disturbed only by the new approaches whistling by, research has continued along the atheoretical trail of institutional history.[3] Nowhere is this more evident than in the rapidly growing subfield of black politics. Much of what is done proceeds in an atheoretical manner, and when a theoretical network *is* evident, it is likely to be one with limited relevance for the black political experience.

The melting-pot theory of American pluralism seems to be the frame of reference most commonly used for analyzing and interpreting the black political experience in America,[4] although attempts have been made recently to carry over the modernizing traditional-systems model from the field of comparative politics.[5] In both instances, the researcher looks not to the black political experience for guidance in developing his conceptual scheme, but rather to the political experiences of other people. Such approaches posit a level of isomorphism between the black political experience and the experience of other groups which is denied by even a cursory examination.[6]

A frame of reference for black politics should not begin with superficial comparisons of blacks and other ethnic minorities in this country or elsewhere, because such an approach inevitably degenerates into norma-

---

Revised from a paper originally presented at the 1969 meeting of the Southern Political Science Association. Reprinted by permission of the author.

tive reformist speculation around the question of what can be done to elevate blacks to the position occupied by the group with which they are being compared. This, in turn, leads to the establishment of a linear model of ethnic or out-group politics and a Procrustean forcing of the black political experience into the contrived model, and in the process obfuscating, if not eliminating outright, the crucial variables in the black political experience. In developing a frame of reference for black politics, one should begin by searching for those factors which are unique to the black political experience, for this is the information which will facilitate our understanding of blacks in the American political system.

Joseph Roucek, some time ago, in an attempt to raise the study of the "race problem"[7] above normative reformist speculation, argued that the black-white problem should be looked upon simply as a question of power relations:

Majority-minority relationships are but another aspect of the universal struggle for power *modified only by the different conditions under which this struggle takes place on the local scene.*[8] (Emphasis added.)

This, of course, is a restatement of the ageless power theory and therefore nothing new, and, as its many critics assert, power theory does not explain very much. What it does and wherein its contribution lies is to point us in the right direction.

The important phrase of Roucek's proposition is "modified only by the different conditions under which this struggle takes place on the local scene." Accepting this proposition, it follows logically that black politics should be thought of as a manifestation of one dimension or extension of the universal struggle for power. The immediately preceding proposition accepted, the question becomes what are the conditions which modify the struggle on the local scene? Or, to put it differently, what are the factors which distinguish those activities subsumed under the rubric *black politics* from all the other power struggles occurring simultaneously and interdependently? Whatever these factors are, they distill the essence of the black political experience and hence ought to serve as the orienting concepts for a frame of reference.

What, then, are the modifying conditions? A recent attempt by Blalock to establish a set of empirical propositions explaining minority-group problems may be instructive at this point.[9] After considerable preliminaries, he advances the following:

GENERAL PROPOSITION: Men in superordinate positions act in such a manner as to preserve their position.

SPECIFIED CONDITION: In the United States, whites generally are in superordinate positions vis-à-vis Negroes.

LOWER ORDER PROPOSITION: In the United States, whites act toward Negroes in such a manner as to preserve their positions.[10]

While Blalock's propositions may appear to be commonplace or even trivial, the value in repeating them here may be demonstrated by observing that they are not reflected in many—perhaps a majority—of scholarly works dealing with the black experience.

Juxtaposing the contributions of Roucek and Blalock, we arrive at the conclusion that what we have is essentially a power struggle between blacks and whites, with the latter trying to maintain their superordinate position vis-à-vis the former. Since the political system is the arena in which societal conflicts are definitively resolved, black politics should be thought of as the manifestation of the power struggle between these two groups. However, we need to add one other specifying condition to further distinguish black politics from other extensions of the universal power struggle. That condition is the stipulation that the ideological justification for the superordination of whites is the institutionalized belief in the inherent superiority of that group.[11] This condition cannot be overemphasized. It says that it is not their late arrival, their patterns of migration, their numerical strength, nor their cultural patterns which, beginning with Jamestown and continuing to the present, have underlain the differential treatment of blacks; it says further that any attempt to explain the black political experience in terms of any one or any combination of these will be insufficient.

Anticipating the argument that it is too simplistic to say that black politics is a struggle between whites lined up on one side holding on to the coveted values of society and blacks trying to reverse the circumstances, let me hasten to point out that I fully understand (and will discuss below) that within both communities there are patterns of activity tending toward various goals. Nevertheless, the notion that the superordinate group, in the final analysis, seeks to maintain its position, as we shall demonstrate shortly, is useful.

So far I have argued that black politics should be thought of as an extension of the universal power struggle, modified only by the condition that whites occupy superordinate positions vis-à-vis blacks, that this position is based upon the institutionalized belief in the superiority of whites, and that whites act in a manner that will preserve their superordinate position. The orienting concepts, and therefore the frame of reference for black politics, must grow out of the above propositions. I will argue in the following paragraphs that a useful frame of reference may be constructed by using group theory as defined by Hagan[12] and by utilizing the terms of dominant and submissive groups as orienting concepts.

Why the group concept? Reduced to bare essentials, Hagan's thesis is that the optimum orienting concept for political science is *the group,* defined as *an activity of human beings.* Societal values are authoritatively allocated through the clashing of an infinite number of goal-directed patterns of activity. A frame of reference utilizing this nonreified notion of group is especially appropriate for studying black politics, because it is comprehensive enough to include all factors which are involved in the black political experience. Comprehensiveness is especially important when one wishes to study the politics of a people who are either on the periphery or outside the formal political structures, because traditional or more formalistic schemes of analysis—usually in-group oriented—may leave out much that is important.

To amplify this point, most of the serious works dealing with the black political experience may be best described as studies of leadership. Such works give disproportionate attention to the points at which black political activity intersects with the formal and legitimate structures in the political system. In the process, much of the fullness of black political activity, especially the clash of conflicting patterns of activity within the black community and the patterns of activity tending toward goals declared illegitimate by the cultural component of the American political system, is lost.[13] It is probably for this reason that none of the numerous leadership and community studies anticipated the black rebellions of the sixties. Further, given the recruitment pattern of black leadership—in which the white community has a disproportionate voice—such studies may be not only incomplete, but misleading as well. The group concept guards against unwarranted exclusiveness by telling us that we are concerned with all activity having impact on the allocation of the values involved in the black-white power struggle.

With the breadth of the area of inquiry established, it now becomes necessary to formulate guidelines or points of reference to facilitate the identification and interpretation of activities relevant to the black political experience. The concepts of dominant and submissive groups will serve our purpose.

The concepts of dominant and submissive groups distill the essence of the black political experience and give us an analytical tool which will allow us to isolate, categorize, and interpret the important variables in the black political experience. I am using the terms *dominant and submissive group* in much the same fashion as Wirth used *dominant-minority relations.* The appellation *submissive* is being used for two reasons. First, it indicates more clearly the psychological relationship between the two groups; and second, it guards against the inevitable confusion which occurs when the "minority" group is numerically in the majority.

The submissive group in the context of the American political system is a group of people who, because of their African ancestry are singled out from the other Americans for differential and unequal treatment. The justification for such treatment, de facto if not de jure, is the widely held belief in the inherent inferiority of persons of such ancestry. Moreover, this belief has been institutionalized and is subscribed to not only by members of the dominant group, but by members of the submissive group as well.[14] The dominant group is the residual category consisting primarily of persons of European ancestry. Its members enjoy higher status and greater privileges than members of the submissive group.

Dominant-submissive group situations may take varied forms ranging along a continuum beginning with a static situation in which both groups share strong feelings of legitimacy about the situation and therefore exhibit supportive behavior. The continuum, at the other pole, may be characterized by a situation in which members of the submissive group deny the legitimacy of the system and threaten to use and/or do use whatever means they deem necessary to accelerate the demise of the existing order. Thus, the first extreme may be represented by a system of tranquil slavery or a rigid caste system, while the other would involve out-and-out warfare between the two communities. Like all ideal types, these two extremes will rarely be found. Most dominant-submissive-group situations will be found somewhere between the two. The American pattern has been a fluid one, beginning somewhere near the first extreme and moving steadily, if slowly, toward the second.

At this point the questions may be legitimately raised, How do these concepts facilitate our understanding of black politics? How do they serve as orienting concepts? Let us deal with these questions. Students of dominant-submissive-group situations have observed that historically—across time and cultures—dominant groups have pursued certain policies in order to maintain their superordinate position vis-à-vis their submissive counterpart.[15] Similarly, submissive groups have availed themselves of certain policies in order to maximize their position. Or, to put it in group language, historically we have observed within dominant groups goal-directed patterns of activity designed to insure the superordinate position of the dominant groups; and at the same time within submissive groups we have observed patterns of activity designed to alter the situations. These concepts become useful to us because they provide categories for a rudimentary taxonomy. We can take the historically developed categories of activities found in dominant-submissive-group situations and apply them to observable patterns in the contemporary American dominant-submissive-group situation. To the extent that the categories are useful, we can move to the next stage of inquiry—searching for regularities in the interplay of these factors. To the extent that they are not previously used, and therefore not useful, the historically observed categories ought to put in sharp relief the differences between them and the patterns of activity in the contemporary American dominant-submissive-group situation. This in itself should bring us nearer to the point where we can advance explanatory propositions about the black political presence in the United States.

Figure 2:1 lists the patterns of activity which have been observed across time and cultures in dominant-submissive-group situations. Directional arrows are used to convey the notion that within each group participants in the several goal-directed patterns of activity seek, as an intermediate step, to have their policy orientations accepted as the goal of their respective groups, and ultimately as the authoritative policy of the society. At the same time, factions or those engaging in particular patterns of activity try to influence the disposition of the patterns in the opposite community in a fashion consistent with their policy positions. Thus, there are four dimensions to the dominant-submissive-group model. The first two involve intrafactional competition in each of the communities, the third involves competition across group lines, and the fourth is the synthesis of the other three. The synthesis, of course, is reflected in the authoritative policy decisions. That dominant-submissive-group situations have these four dimensions is worth keeping in mind as we turn to the question of its utility in understanding the black political experience in America.

Even a cursory investigation of American history indicates that patterns of activity tending toward the goals posited by the general model have been factors in the black political experience. The dominant group, during the formative years of the republic, pursued, almost categorically, a policy of continued subjugation. Following the Civil War the basic policy orientation of the dominant group exhibited three distinct patterns: continued subjugation, as indicated by restrictive statutes in many states and by paramilitary terror in both North and South; legal protection of members of the submissive group, as evidenced by the Civil War amendments; and population transfer, as demonstrated by the agitation to expel blacks to colonial enclaves. The contemporary dominant-submissive-group situation, as Figure 2:2 indicates, is characterized by several patterns of activity coinciding with the historically observed ones.

In the dominant group, cultural assimilation, the inferred goal of Pattern D1, is the most discussed policy orientation. The term *cultural assimilation* is used instead of unqualified *assimilation* because the widely held

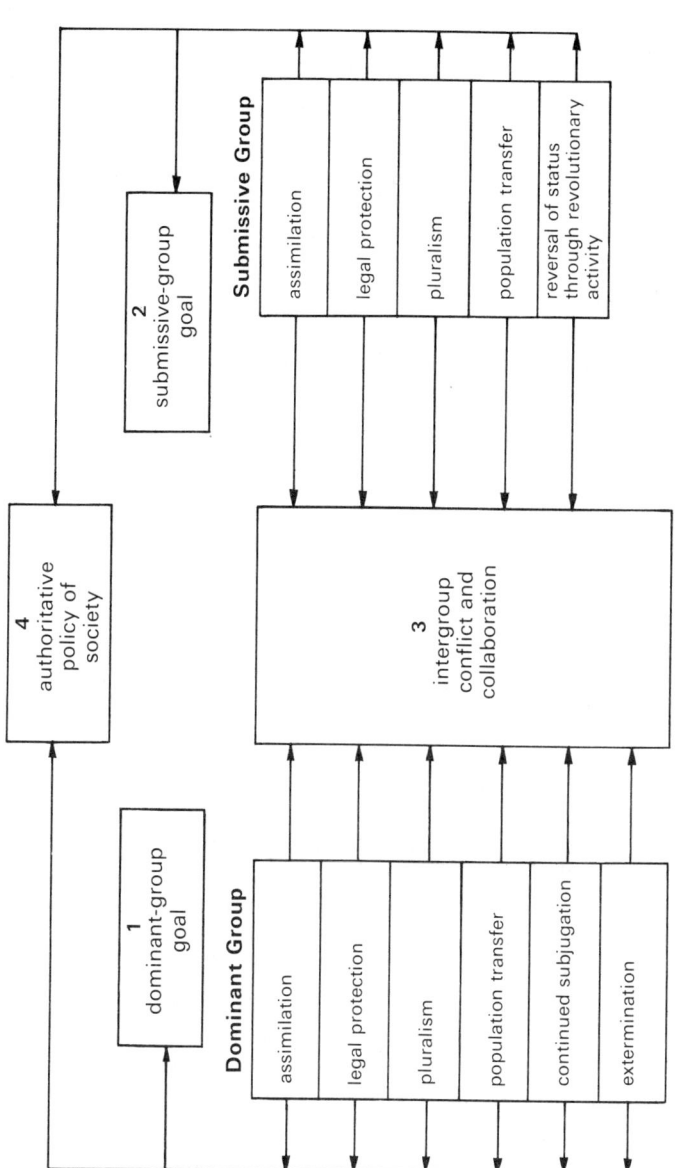

FIGURE 2:1. Goal-directed patterns of activity in general dominant-submissive-group situations. As the directional arrows indicate, each pattern of activity seeks to have its policy orientation accepted as the goal of its own group and of the society at large. At the same time, each pattern attempts to influence patterns across group lines in a manner consistent with its goals.

notion of white supremacy and its logical corollary, taboo against interracial sex, preclude any real assimilationist policy. Nevertheless, the official or acknowledged policy orientation of D1, which includes the major institutions of American life, such as churches, educational institutions, and industrial and commercial corporations, as well as scores of persons of high status and prestige, is a form of cultural assimilation.

Pattern D2, which tends toward legal protection and maintenance of white supremacy through separatism, subsumes individuals and reified groups who, while advocating minimal legal guarantees for members of the submissive group, oppose, but may grudgingly accept, civil-rights statutes or ordinances, once all legal and quasi-legal obstructionist ploys have been exhausted.

The third pattern in the dominant community includes the activity of individuals and reified groups who proclaim, without inhibition, their belief that whites are the natural masters of blacks and who categorically oppose movements toward sociopolitical equality for members of the submissive group. The fourth pattern, which tends toward extermination, is distinguished from D3 primarily by its willingness, if not alacrity, to use force to thwart advancement of the submissive group.

It should be noticed that the listing and brief discussion of observable tendencies in the dominant group do not include patterns tending toward a policy of population transfer. This is not because such a pattern is not observable but because population transfer does not appear to be the primary goal of any pattern of activity. It appears, however, in the policy orientations of all the patterns from D2 through D4, either as an attempt of members of the dominant group to accelerate the migration of blacks from certain areas or in the form of members of the dominant group's transferring themselves from among their submissive counterparts.

In the submissive group, Faction S1, the integrationist, appears to be the major faction. Individuals subsumed under this label are likely to initiate and/or support strong civil-rights legislation or other measures designed to improve the socioeconomic position of members of the submissive group *so long as these measures involve increased interaction with members of the dominant group.* Conversely, S1 opposes activity tending toward separatism, without regard to the source of initiation. The major civil-rights organizations and many black business and fraternal organizations, as well as most blacks of high status are in this pattern.

The second pattern, S2, engages those who accept the principle of gradualism in dominant-submissive relations. Individuals and reified groups who are involved in this pattern of activity tending toward legal protection are less likely than S1 persons to introduce measures and programs on their own, but are more inclined to accept the lead, and

Dominant Group

pattern		policy
D1	integration	cultural assimilation (permitted) [*continued subjugation*]*
D2	white separatism	legal protection [*continued subjugation*]
D3	restrained white supremacy	continued subjugation
D4	white terrorism	extermination

Submissive Group

pattern		policy
S1	integration	cultural assimilation (forced)
S2	accommodation	legal protection
S3	black consciousness	cultural pluralism
S4	black nationalism	population transfer (peaceful)
S5	revolution	reversal of status

*The policy orientation *continued subjugation* is enclosed in brackets to indicate that each dominant-group faction—rhetoric notwithstanding—in varying degrees tends toward continued domination of the submissive community.

FIGURE 2:2. Goal-directed patterns of activity in the American dominant-submissive-group situation.

therefore the policy cues, of factions of the dominant group. Although S2 types do not have ready access to impersonal channels of communications and, consequently, are less well known than those in other submissive-group patterns, they are a recognizable force in most black communities, as anyone who has done fieldwork—not to mention lived—in a black community will bear witness. Suffice it here to say that one of the two black daily newspapers in the United States and the president of what is reputed to be the largest black church organization in this country both consistently articulate views tending toward legal protection.

The third pattern within the submissive community, designated as *black consciousness,* stresses internal improvement within institutions already controlled by and neighborhoods densely populated with members of the submissive group. Extraordinary emphasis is placed upon the need to strengthen the self-image of its members before parity with the dominant community can be realized. Activities of individuals and groups subsumed hereunder move toward a policy of cultural pluralism which must be distinguished from the separatism of D2.

If realized, the separatism of D2 would result in two communities, with the dominant group having the authoritative voice in both. The activity of S3, if rhetoric is to be given credence, tends toward a goal which, if realized, would be two mutually respecting communities interacting on those issues which were of common interest, while guaranteeing the subcommunity control over matters deemed especially important to its own survival as a people. There are, of course, numerous empirical referents, both historical and contemporary, for this pattern of activity.

S4, the black nationalist pattern, stresses the need for members of the submissive group to disabuse themselves of all feelings of belonging to the American government and substitute instead the notion that they are part of a different—a black—nation. Population transfer is the basic policy orientation of this faction, which includes well known entities such as the Nation of Islam as well as lesser known ones like the New Republic of Africa. Included also are those persons who are currently involved in the resettling of blacks in Africa.

Since revolutionary activity as a policy, like the extermination policy of D4, contravenes legal proscriptions, there is little to be said about it here. However, recent events, including the Ahmed Evans affair in Cleveland in which a ghetto "riot" was deliberately launched, suggest that there are patterns within the black community tending toward the reversal of status through revolutionary means.

The foregoing cataloging of the patterns of activity within the two communities is admittedly sketchy. No attempt has been made to define them sharply. Such definitions, of course, are essential if this analytical framework is to be put to the test of the final arbiter—the field. However, this article is meant only to suggest the utility of such a scheme. Thus, I hope, the lack of precision will be indulged, if not excused. Whatever the verdict, let us explore further the usefulness of this frame of reference.

The dominant-submissive-group model, as discussed above and presented graphically in Figures 2:1 and 2:2, brings into focus the dynamics of black politics in America. By categorizing the various patterns of activity in terms of their policy orientations, it calls attention to areas of possible collaboration and conflict among the several factions both within and across group lines. This, in turn, should facilitate our understanding of why certain alliances and schisms develop within and across groups. Further, it promises to sharpen our understanding of black leadership—a much-discussed but rarely understood phenomenon. It should allow us to rise above common-sense explanations—Uncle Tom or selling out—of black leadership. And finally it should permit us to refine our stock of ambiguous concepts—status and welfare goals, race man, militant, and the like—which constitute the working language of this area of inquiry.

For purposes of illustration, we may begin by exploring its usefulness in understanding collaboration and conflict across group lines. We may begin with the assertion that each group will be inclined to form alliances with other factions to the extent that it perceives compatibility of goals. The power to initiate action rests with each of the several factions. In terms of day-to-day strategies, perceptions of short-term goals are likely to be more important than perceptions of long-term goals. By this I mean to suggest that factions are likely to forge temporary alliances with other factions in situations of the moment, even if they perceive their ultimate goals to be incompatible. Let me illustrate. Factions D1 and S1, both of which may be designated as the respective establishment factions, are given disproportionate attention. Both tend toward assimilation as a goal. The rhetoric of the two are more alike than not. Since the two, according to their rhetoric, are pursuing the same goal, it becomes understandable that they often appear as partners in an alliance. Often it appears that members of S1 accept the good faith of D1 and consequently assume as their primary role prodding S1 along toward more rapid assimilation. This close relation between the two is the father in the submissive group of many theories of conspiracy and notions of selling out.

However, when we consider our proposition that members of the dominant group always try to maintain their superordinate position, along with the disparate power of the two factions, another explanation begins to surface. Since D1 has dominant power over S1, the demands or initiatives of S1 are often shaped to conform, more or less, to the policy pursuits of D1. Moreover, the success and, to a great extent, the survival of the submissive-group faction depends upon what the dominant-group faction does. For example, witness Whitney Young of the National Urban League asking the national government for "some victories." So long as one accepts the notion that the two partners are tending toward the same goal, this relationship between the two appears to be a logical and perhaps a prudent one.[16] However, those in the submissive community who do not accept the notion of a confluence of interest between the two tend to resort to "Uncle Tom" or "selling out" explanations. A careful look at the assumptions and goals of the two factions, as the dominant-submissive scheme demands, suggests a different explanation.

For further illustration let us explore another pattern of interaction. Initiatives of S3 (black Consciousness) such as autonomous black-studies departments, black dormitories on "white" campuses, and strengthening the old schools and building new ones in black areas, to be controlled by blacks, are likely to meet greater opposition from S1 than from any other faction in the model. For example, it was the NAACP which brought suit to prevent the establishment of racially restrictive black institutions in American universities. The dominant-submissive-group model suggests an explanation for that. The area of conflict based upon the goals of the several factions is greater, at least on the surface, between S1 and S3 than between, say, S1 and D2 or D3.

Similarly, the fact that S3 (black consciousness) and D2 (white separatism) and D3 (self-acknowledged white supremacism) find themselves increasingly on the same side of the school integration controversy (in Georgia, Governor Lester Maddox and the black-consciousness faction are in concert on the closing of black schools, for example) is readily understandable in terms of our model.

The foregoing discussion suggests the utility of the dominant-submissive-group model as a frame of reference for understanding black politics in America. What remains to be accomplished is a more systematic delination of goal-directed patterns of activity within the communities. Once this has been done, we can use it as a classificatory scheme to sift and group political happenings in the lives of black people on both national and local levels. This, in turn, ought to facilitate the discovery of regularities in the patterns of interaction between and among those engaged in the several patterns of activity both within and across group lines. The discovery of such regularities would make possible the classification of subsystems according to the patterns of regularities observed. Once such classifications have been established, it may be possible, by using some variant of group vector analysis as adumbrated by Monypenny[17] to determine the probability of achieving certain kinds of change in certain kinds of communities, depending upon the mix and relative strengths of dominant- and submissive-group factions.

NOTES

1. D. Easton, *The Political System* (New York: Knopf, 1953).
2. For a discussion of the proliferation of "approaches," see S. Hoffman, "The Long Road to Theory," *World Politics* 11 (1959): 346–377.
3. This notion is borrowed from N. Long, "Indicators of Change in Political Institutions," an unpublished paper read at the Annual Meeting of the American Political Science Association, 1969.
4. For example, see J. Wilson, *Negro Politics* (New York: The Free Press, 1960), pp. 25–34.
5. See H. Holloway, *Politics of the Southern Negro: From Exclusion to Big City Organization* (New York: Random House, 1969), especially Chapter 1.
6. As early as 1945 L. Wirth called our attention to the distinction between racial and ethnic minorities and intimated the inappropriateness of trying to explain the black experience by referring to the history of ethnic minorities in "The Problem of Minority Groups," in *The Science of Man in World Crisis* ed. R. Linton, (New York: Columbia University Press, 1945), pp. 338–372.
7. J. Roucek, "Minority-Majority Relations in Their Power Aspects," *Phylon* 17 (1956): 24–30.
8. Roucek, "Minority-Majority," p. 30.
9. H. Blalock, *Toward a Theory of Minority Group Relations* (New York: Wiley, 1967).
10. Blalock, *Toward a Theory*, p. 191. It is not clear whether Blalock advances these propositions as valid ones dealing with black-white relations in America or whether they are cited simply as examples of the kinds of assertive statements we need to develop. Whatever his intentions, I accept the propositions as valid statements.
11. This point, I suppose, is now beyond dispute. Long a theme of political essays, it is now commonplace in respectable social-science literature and, as a recent development, in government reports.
12. See Hagan, "The Group in Political Science," in *Approaches to the Study of Politics* ed. R. Yong (Evanston: Northwestern University Press, 1958).
13. For a brief, yet adequate, discussion of the function of the cultural component in a society, see R. T. Holt, "A Proposed Structural-Functional Framework for Political Science," in *Functionalism in the Social Sciences*, ed. D. Martindale (Philadelphia: American Academy of Political and Social Science, 1965), pp. 84–110.
14. This assertion is consistent with two major works by clinical psychologists, one by a white team and the other by blacks. They are, respectively, A. Kardiner and L. Ovesey, *The Mark of Oppression* (New York: World, 1951), and W. Grier and P. Cobbs, *Black Rage* (New York: Basic Books, 1968).
15. A popular text asserts that dominant communities have followed six major types of policies in dealing with minority groups, which I have used in Figure 1. See G. Simpson and Milton Yinger, *Racial and Cultural Minorities* (New York: Harper & Row, 1965), pp. 3–26.
16. The perception of the confluence of interests and, therefore, complementarity of goals of S1 and D1 appears to be on the wane. Many blacks have begun to question the

good faith of D1. The fact that the Legal Defense Fund of the NAACP and the Civil Rights Division of the U.S. Department of Justice no longer are fellow plaintiffs but adversaries in certain desegregation suits is an indication of this development.

17. See F. Monypenny, "Political Science and the Study of Groups. Notes to Guide a Research Project," *Western Political Science Quarterly* June 1954.

3

The Black Man's Role in American Politics

Mervyn Dymally

SOMEBODY ON THE inside said once that politics is the art of the possible. But for the black outsider in America politics in the United States has been the art of the impossible.

It has been the art of the impossible because it has been the art of trying to make a fundamental change in a political system by using the structures and instruments that were designed to perpetuate that system.

It has been the art of the impossible because it has been the art of trying to make a social revolution with moderate tools that were invented to prevent social revolutions.

It has been the art of the impossible because of the nature of politics, which is the art of making some things impossible for outsiders. And because of the extremity of the black man's situation, which cannot be changed unless all things are made possible, the black man's role in American politics continues to be impossible.

Because of the black man's situation, which is radical by any definition, and because of the nature of American politics, which is moderate-to-conservative by any definition, the black man in America has been condemned to seek radical ends within a political framework which was designed to prevent sudden and radical social and economic changes.

For almost one hundred years now, the black outsiders of America have been squirming within the halters of this maddening paradox. During this period, some representatives of the outsiders in the councils of the insiders have made striking gains *as individuals*. But black people as a group have not been able to change their status or their social and economic conditions with political instruments. And the question we

---

Reprinted from *The Black Politician*, Fall 1969, by permission of the author and the publisher.

must grapple with now is whether it will ever be possible to achieve fundamental social and economic change by the practice of politics, as defined by the insiders.

The question now—and the question is radical because the times are radical and because our situation is radical—is whether politics is relevant to our contemporary crisis, which cannot be resolved without political programs of depth and dimension never before attempted in America.

Is the old politics—the politics of deals and trades and patronage, the politics of place and privilege and individual advancement—is the old politics relevant to the issues of bread for millions and housing and education for the poor?

Is politics relevant to the question of the redistribution of income and resources and the restructuring of the fundamental institutions of this society?

Is politics relevant to black reality?

Beyond all that, beyond the specific problems of black people, we must ask whether politics is relevant to white people.

Is it relevant to the emptiness and hysteria and the unresolved social and economic problems in the white community?

Can the old politics create white individuals who will not need racial scapegoats to solve their social, economic, and racial anxieties?

Watts and Newark and Detroit put these questions on the agenda of American life. In a very real sense, these rebellions were devastating critiques of the American Way of Politics. In rebellion, the black people of America have said that politics in America has failed them and that it is necessary now to create a new politics, a kind of politics that can address itself to the real problems of this profoundly *racist* society.

It is against this background that we must view the question of the black man's role in American politics. And in the light of these events and the history these events reflect, we must say frankly that black people have no role in contemporary politics.

Black people are the outsiders—the disinherited—of the American political system. As human beings, they live outside white America in numerous black colonies. And as voters and political persons, they inhabit the margins on the periphery of the system. Even the persons who represent these outsiders in the councils of the insiders occupy a marginal position—as the Congressman Adam C. Powell and the Senator Thomas J. Dodd cases indicated.

From time to time, the inhabitants of these black colonies have played crucial roles as representatives of persons inside the system. More significantly, they have crucially affected the system by their presence on the periphery. In other words, they have acted on the system from a distance.

Indeed, one might say that the political history of America is a series of approaches and withdrawals from the pressing reality of the black outsiders on the margin. In summation, then, the role of the black man *outside* American politics is the dual role of a political representative for insiders and a protagonist from the outside of the whole political system.

In considering this dual role, we have to deal with what J. D. B. Miller, the political theorist, calls the politics of the center and the circumference. We have to deal, in other words, with a quasi-colonial relation. As Dr. Kenneth Clark noted in his book *Dark Ghetto*, "The dark ghettos are social, political, educational and—above all—economic colonies. Their inhabitants are subject people, victims of the greed, cruelty, insensitivity, guilt, and fear of their masters." What I am concerned to emphasize here is that these colonies are controlled politically from the outside. Ultimate policy-making power lies in the hands of people who have their own representatives, some of them black, on the spot with power to see that the will of the white center is obeyed in the black circumference. We must note also that the inhabitants of the circumference do not deal with each other directly. "Black people and white people," as Gunnar Myrdal in *American Dilemma* notes, "deal with each other, like two foreign countries, through the medium of plenipotentiaries."

I say this with bluntness to emphasize the fact that when we talk about black politics we are not talking about ordinary politics. And we are not talking about ordinary politics because the American political system has not created a single social community in which the reciprocal rules of politics would apply.

Conventional politics cannot solve this problem, because conventional politics is *a part* of the problem.

It is part of the problem because the political system is the major bulwark of racism in America.

It is a part of the problem in the sense that the political system is structured to repel fundamental social and economic change.

We hear a great deal about the deficiencies, real or imagined, of certain black leaders, but not enough attention, it seems to me, is paid to the framework within which they operate. That framework prevents radical growth and innovation—as it was *designed* to prevent radical growth and innovation.

What we have to deal with here is what Arthur Schlesinger, Jr., called the *paradox of power*, the fact that power within the system is necessary to do certain things but that power within the system makes it impossible to do most things. When John F. Kennedy became President, he was no political novice. But he didn't realize, Schlesinger tells us, "how beautifully the [government] structure was organized to prevent anything from happening."

From the very beginning, the American political structure has been beautifully organized to keep anything from happening. We need not deal here with the theory that the constitutional convention was a conspiracy against the revolutionary ideals of the Declaration of Independence. But it is obvious from a cursory examination of that document that the Founding Fathers were animated by a desire to protect property and privilege from sudden social experiments. The theory of checks and balances, for example, is based on the theory that privilege must be protected from people. Thomas Jefferson, a large and wealthy slave-owner, protested against the anti-people biases of the new government. But he did not prevail; an additional safeguard, of course, was the two-part system, which was designed, in part, to filter out radicalism and to force dissent to express itself within two moderate channels. Insofar as the black man is concerned, one can say of the two parties what a political insider said to Lord Bryce: They are like two bottles of the same size, the same color and the same shape, with the same label—both of them empty.

The criticisms I make here of politics in America could be extended to most political structures—certainly, most political structures in the West. Governments cannot operate without support, which means in practice that they must identify with certain interests in society. And this means in America that government has usually identified with the interests of big white people.

Nothing illustrates this better than the central events in the political history of the black man. Contrary to the generally accepted idea, that history began not in slavery but in indentured servitude. The first black immigrants in English America landed at Jamestown in August 1619. They came, these first black men and women, the same way many, perhaps most, of the first white men came—under duress and compulsion. They found a system which permitted poor people to pay for their passage by working a stipulated number of years as indentured servants.

In Virginia, then, and in other colonies, the first black immigrants fell into a well-established socioeconomic groove which carried with it no implications of racial inferiority. During this transitional period of forty years or more, a period of primary importance in the history of America, the first black immigrants mingled with whites on a basis of substantial equality. Blacks and whites worked in the same fields, lived in the same huts, and fraternized in the same places.

Some, perhaps most, of the first black immigrants worked out their terms of indentured servitude and were freed. Within a short time, they were accumulating property, money, and other indentured servants. The record indicates that these black settlers were accorded substantially the same rights as freed whites. They voted in eleven of the thirteen original colonies. And some of them became the first black office-holders in America by filling the minor posts of beadle and surety.

All this changed dramatically with the opening of the New World and the introduction of sugar planting in the West Indies. This new situation created a demand for men that could not be satisfied by the casual kidnapping of poor blacks in Africa and poor whites in Europe. Beginning around 1660, the leading men of the colonies passed laws that made black people servants for life. This was a fatal and perhaps irreparable break in the sense of community between black and white Americans. It was the starting point, the first turn, on the road to the long, hot summers of recent years and the dangers beyond.

This ominous decision was later made a part of the charter of America at the Constitutional Convention, where northern delegates gave in to southern threats and wrote slavery into the Constitution. Within a few years, slavery had become a cancer in the heart of the American political system, with incalculable results that are still resounding in the streets of America today.

During the whole of the slave period, black people had no political history, in the narrow sense of the term *political*. But it is impossible to understand the political history of that period without reference to the black man. Although black men were disenfranchised in both the North and the South, black people voted in every election, influencing the political process by their presence and by the cause they embodied. Some black people voted with their feet, by escaping in the tens of thousands from the South. Others acted on the political process as nonviolent abolitionist demonstrators. It is a matter of record that great black abolitionists like Frederick Douglass and Henry Highland Garnet participated in the founding of the Liberty and Free Soil parties, both of which were forerunners of the Republican party. Still another form of political action for the four million slaves was violence, as evidenced by the Nat Turner rebellion of 1831.

When all these currents linked up with that great American agitator, Yankee self-interest, the stage was set for the Civil War, Emancipation, and Reconstruction.

It was during this period that black people came on stage and spoke lines in their own names for the first time. And it was during this period that the seeds were sown for the political crisis of today.

The period began with a promising political revolution. Largely as a result of the radical political vision of two Republican leaders, Representative Thaddeus Stevens of Pennsylvania and Senator Charles Sumner of Massachusetts, the freedmen were enfranchised, and federal troops were sent into the South to protect them in the exercise of the fundamental rights of American citizens. With the passage of the Fourteenth and Fifteenth Amendments and a civil-rights act which was a great deal stronger than the act passed in 1965, Reconstruction came to a legal climax.

But this legislation, so similar to the legislation of our day, only touched the surface of the problem. No one knew this better than the freedmen, who saw clearly that it was necessary to complete the political revolution by a social revolution. And what this meant, in the context of that day, was "forty acres and a mule." Thaddeus Stevens, an old, white man from Pennsylvania, who was the most powerful politician in Washington and who was perhaps the most relevant politician in the political history of black Americans, made a valiant effort to give the radical Reconstruction program the economic thrust it lacked. But he was thwarted by the Paradox of Power. After repeated attempts to push a radical land-reform bill through Congress, Stevens announced that the dream was stillborn. He had "fondly dreamed," he said in a House speech, "that when any fortunate chance should have broken up, for a while, the foundations of our institutions, and released us from obligations the most tyrannical that ever man imposed in the name of freedom, that American institutions would have been so remodeled, as to have freed them from every vestige of human oppression, or inequality of rights, or recognized degradation of the poor, and the superior caste of the rich." "But, alas," he said, "bowing to the inherent limitations of the system, this bright dream has vanished like the baseless fabric of a vision."

The failure of that dream—the refusal of the political leaders of America to ground political freedom on economic freedom—doomed Reconstruction and paved the way to our present crisis.

Before the curtain that had lifted for a moment dropped, black men and their white allies carried the South and the black man to heights of democracy that have not been equaled in this republic. During the heyday of Reconstruction, from 1867 to 1877, black men served in the legislature of every southern state. And in South Carolina during this period black men were a majority in the legislature in every session save one. Black people also sent twenty representatives to the United States House of Representatives and two black men were elected to the United States Senate from the State of Mississippi. There were also treasurers, secretaries of state, and superintendents of education in Mississippi, South Carolina, Louisiana, and Florida. And for a brief period the brilliant black politician P. B. S. Pinchback served as Governor of the State of Louisiana.

Despite mistakes, which were inevitable under the circumstances, black people made large strides toward renovating the political structures of the South. People who say that black power is simply white power in blackface ought to think long and hard about the Reconstruction period. Black people had considerable power in South Carolina, Mississippi, and Louisiana, where they constituted a majority of the population and a majority of the registered voters. The record indicates that the black Reconstruction governments gave poor and middle-class white people rights aristocratic whites had denied them. *Not only that: black people, in perhaps their greatest contribution, created in the South what had never existed before —a public school system supported by public taxation for every citizen, regardless of color.*

Perhaps the most important development of this period was the expansion of the political horizons of black people. Since politics was real, since it was an activity that corroborated reality and promised to change reality, black people gave to politics the kind of attention their children and grandchildren would give to entertainment and religion. Black people lived in that faraway and mystical period in a primary relation with power. They turned out in the thousands for political meetings, and they followed politics day by day, month by month, throughout the year.

Reconstruction was a supreme lesson, the right reading, one which might still mark a turning point in our history. For ten years in this country, for one hundred and twenty months, men tried democracy. Black people and white people married each other in the South—and the world did not end. Little black boys and little white girls went to school together—and the Confederate dead did not rise—did not, in fact, even make a sound at all, although the Ku Klux Klan said they were turning in their graves. All over the South in these years blacks and whites shared streetcars, restaurants, hotels, honors, dreams. The sun rose and the sun set, and the Constitution of the United States had some meaning from Maine to Mississippi—for ten long years.

Reconstruction was a lesson, first of all, for black politicians. It demonstrated clearly the need for bold, honest, and imaginative leadership. And it established, beyond doubt, the black man's right to participate in power.

On the debit side, it can be said that many of the black leaders of Reconstruction were too anxious to prove that they could live up to the Anglo-Saxon image. They were too anxious to prove that they could do what white politicians could do. Even more decisive was the failure of the black leaders of Reconstruction to mobilize a black power-base and to remain in close touch with the cotton-roots of their constituencies. Too many men, then, as now, were living too far away from the people they said they were representing.

We need not concern ourselves here with the myth of corruption men used to overthrow these governments. The black leaders of Reconstruction were overthrown because they were not corrupt.

In a very significant failure of the American political system, the Reconstruction governments were overthrown by an open and violent revolution. And this open and violent revolution was legitimized by the Compromise of 1877, a political bargain which gave Rutherford B. Hayes the presidency in exchange for a suspension of the constitutional safeguards which protected black people in the South.

Backed by every structure of power in the North, the South pushed black people back toward slavery by a white terrorist campaign which claimed the lives of tens of thousands of people. And this campaign of terror was sanctioned by the Supreme Court, which sucked the meaning out of the Fourteenth Amendment and invalidated the Reconstruction civil-rights laws.

Black people protested. They organized protests and called on the President. But nobody was listening, and nobody really cared! The Democratic party was openly hostile then, and there was no real alternative for black people, who continued to vote Republican out of habit and out of despair.

Black people were driven from power in the South by terror and fraud. But individual Republicans managed to hold onto power for several years in several states. And black voters sent representatives to southern legislatures and congressmen to Washington, until the dawn of the twentieth century.

As the years wore on, the area of black expressiveness narrowed, and by World War I it was considered subversive for black men to hold public office.

The violent overthrow of Reconstruction set the stage for the Great Migration to the North, which began around 1913 and continues today. Like the various immigrant groups, black people were soon organized into political machines. But these machines were composed of mutually hostile groups pursuing a politics of patronage and stalemate. Within the boundaries of this situation, black people would veto openly hostile policies; but they could not translate voting power into fundamental group gains. As a result, black people were penetrated by feelings of political powerlessness. Since politics had no relevance to their agony, since it was not an activity by which they could lift themselves, they began to look on it with indifference. Worse, some black people came to see politics as a marketing activity involving the trading of voters for petty political favors.

For all that, political involvement brought some gains, at least to individuals. In 1928, Oscar De Priest inaugurated a new era by becoming the first black congressman from the North and the first black congressman in America since the turn of the century. De Priest was elected as a Republican from the First Congressional District of Chicago. Six years later, Arthur Mitchell became the first Democratic congressman by winning an election in the same district.

After 1930, black politicians, Republicans and Democrats, were elected to the legislatures of most northern states and the border states of Kentucky and West Virginia. They also filled elective or appointive positions in the public service of every major city.

The disaster of the Depression widened the political alternatives in America. And, with the coming of the New Deal, black people deserted the Republican party and gave their votes and their hearts to the politics of the Democratic party. After World War II and the internationalization of the race problem, the political horizons of the black community widened, and black protest organizations began to mobilize mass pressures. The government responded to this new mood by intervening dramatically on behalf of black Americans. In the fifties and sixties, a series of Supreme Court decisions and civil-rights acts reopened the national compromise of 1877. Black people began to vote again in substantial numbers in the South. And in the South and North black people were named or elected to unprecedented political positions. By 1960 it was possible to speak of the beginning of the Second Reconstruction.

This period of political growth brought striking gains, particularly in the black middle class. But the record shows that black people as a whole lost ground relative to whites. In 1930 the rate of unemployment for blacks and whites, to use Department of Labor figures, was about the same. Thirty-five years later, the black rate was twice as high. Here are some of the cold facts reported by that department:

In 1948, the 8 percent unemployment rate for black teenage boys was actually less than that of whites. By 1964 the rate had grown to 23 percent, as against 13 percent for whites.

Between 1949 and 1959, the income of black men relative to white men declined in every section of the country. From 1952 to 1963 the median income of black families compared to whites actually dropped from 57 percent to 53 percent.

Since 1947, the number of white families living in poverty has decreased 27 percent, while the number of poor nonwhite families decreased only 3 percent.

The infant mortality of nonwhites in 1940 was 70 percent greater than whites. Twenty-two years later it was 90 percent greater.

Moreover, the isolation of blacks from white communities is increasing, rather than decreasing, as blacks crowd into the central cities and become a city within a city.

This is a record of failure *despite* political success. And it led to a general crisis of confidence in the fairness of the American political system.

"A voteless people," a national fraternity used to say, "is a hopeless people." We know now, from the example of Chicago, Newark, Harlem, Watts, and Detroit, that a voting people can also be a hopeless people. And I think it is incumbent upon all black Americans, in the light of this knowledge, to rethink their relation to American politics.

I have suggested here that conventional politics is designed to prevent fundamental needs of black people for a social revolution. If my hypotheses are correct—and I offer the whole history of America as evidence—it is incumbent upon us to either revitalize conventional politics or abandon conventional politics.

A new politics is necessary in America because the old politics has failed us. And I believe that the salvation of the black man in this country and the creation of democracy in this country depend, to a very great extent, on the creation of a new political vision in the black community.

I believe we must make a radical reevaluation of all our traditional political alliances in the light of the needs and the interests of the overwhelming majority of black people. Black representatives must dare now to redefine themselves in terms of the interests of their people. They must ask themselves who they are and who they really represent. And if their ultimate allegiance is to the black community and not to any special interests, they must dare to make that allegiance real by creating independent power-bases in the black community.

At the same time, black people must assume responsibility for financing the campaigns of black candidates. They must come together as a group and provide independent bases for a new and independent politics.

The most urgent need of this hour is the political education of black people. They must be made aware of their political and economic interests and the general nature of the problem. Beyond all that, it is necessary to make black people recognize their unity with others in the same situation. It may be necessary for some people to operate as liberals and moderates, Republicans and Democrats, but black people should realize that their real need is results, not names.

The so-called alienation of the urban black voter is based, I suspect, on a very sophisticated analysis of the American political system. Black people, by and large, don't believe politics can bring about a real—that is to say, effective—change in their basic situation. If the black masses are to rise to the requirements of this hour, they must be shown that politics is their affair and in their fundamental interests.

It has been said that the civil-rights movement must become political. I would add that the political movement must become a civil-rights movement. I believe the relevant black politician must carry off the difficult feat of blending the traditional political skills with the skills of the reformer. As individuals and as a group you have the responsibility of working to avoid another political crisis in this country.

There are two issues facing this country today:

1. We must end the war in Vietnam. We must withdraw our war troops in South Vietnam.

2. We must spend all our human and financial resources to solve the urban crisis facing our Afro-American, Mexican-American, and American Indian communities.

The report of the United States Commission on Civil Disorders is, in many ways, a bold document. Throughout its 250,000 words its message is agonizingly clear: America is and has always been a racist society. Bigotry penetrates every level and every region of the nation—middle class and lower class, North and South, business and labor, education, medicine, and journalism. The causes of the riots that occurred in dozens of American cities last summer were not hot-eyed hoodlums bent on destruction or organized conspiracies directed by a revolutionary force. The causes were ignorance, apathy, poverty. And, above all, a pervasive discrimination that has thwarted and embittered the American black man in every avenue of his life.

There is no time.

Today the central cities of this country are disaster areas. The debris is mounting, the walking wounded are everywhere. For months since the recent turmoil, you have been listening to the catalog of this crisis, much as eighteenth-century legislators in the plague cities studied the lists of the dead. It is true; death is everywhere: the death of the body, the death of hope. I am certain that we can turn the tide—God knows that we must at least try!

There is no time. There is no time to talk of half-measures, no time to prosecute wars, no time to lash back at the angry poor, no time to moralize about unreachable Utopia. There is not time. The seminars must end, the conferences conclude. Our wisdom must now be shaped into specific weapons of change. It is in this spirit—a spirit of crisis and a spirit of fragile hope—that I come to you.

Your challenge today and tomorrow is to make politics the art of the possible for the black man. For in the final analysis, as Emmett John Hughes pointed out, the art of politics is "the subtle and sensitive attuning and disciplining of all words and deeds—not to mend the petty conflict of the moment, nor to close some tiny gap in the discourse of the day—but to define and to advance designs and policies for a thousand tomorrows."

PART TWO
The History of Black Politics

4

Up from Slavery: From Reconstruction to the Sixties

Chuck Stone

> *I am just as much opposed to Booker Washington as a voter, with all his Anglo-Saxon reenforcements, as I am to the coconut-headed, chocolate-colored, typical little coon, Andy Dotson, who blacks my shoes every morning. Neither is fit to perform the supreme function of citizenship.*
>
> JAMES K. VARDAMAN,
> Mississippi senator, 1913–1919

WHITE AMERICA HAS never been quite able to escape the hangover from its obscene love affair with slavery.

As a nation, it has passed laws guaranteeing racial equality and issued proclamations, preached sermons, and published tracts pledging fidelity to the equality of man. Most of them have had little effect, and the sentiment expressed by Mississippi Senator Vardaman that black people are hardly "fit to perform the supreme function of citizenship" was harbored by most white Americans. Even today it could find hearty support.

The dominant fact of the political history of America's black people is slavery.

Every account of the black man in America begins with the subordination of the black man as an animal without privilege or respect. What distinguished him from all other immigrants was his black skin. The white indentured servant could eventually purchase his freedom and, with his white skin, merge into amorphous anonymity, undistinguishable from the most distinguished white statesman. This the black man could never do. His black skin set him apart, and it became the rationalization for white supremacy, the ethic upon which America was founded and built.

The Declaration of Independence was silent about the plight of black people. They, in fact, were not considered human. This was substantiated in Article I, Section 2, Paragraph 3 of the Constitution, which declared

---

From *Black Political Power in America*, copyright © 1968, by C. Sumner Stone, reprinted by permission of the publishers, The Bobbs-Merrill Company, Inc.

that the electorate "shall be determined by adding to the whole Number of free Persons, including those bound to Service for a Term of Years, and excluding Indians not taxed, three-fifths of all other Persons."

A slave was considered only three-fifths of a human being. While constitutionally slaves could not vote, several states nevertheless passed laws restricting suffrage to white males: Delaware in 1792; Kentucky in 1799; Ohio in 1803; New Jersey in 1807; Maryland in 1810; Louisiana in 1812; Connecticut in 1814 (the only New England state to do so); Tennessee in 1834; North Carolina in 1835; Pennsylvania in 1838; and Florida in 1845.

Probably the first confrontation between black men demanding their right to vote and the white officialdom of America occurred in 1778:

> The Negro's right to the franchise is said to have been established by the test case of Paul and John Cuffe in 1778. These two thrifty Negroes, of whom the former, Paul Cuffe, was a successful shipowner and far-ranging navigator, were called upon by the town of Dartmouth, not far from Boston, to pay a personal tax. They demurred, contending that inasmuch as they were not allowed to vote, they should not be held to pay taxes. After protracted argument, the town authorities admitted that taxpaying and the privilege of voting should go together.[1]

This was an exceptional case. Until their emancipation in 1863, black people were slaves, subhumans without the privileges, rights, or prerogatives of citizenship. While most slaves were treated with the same degree of kindness that one might treat a favorite dog, large numbers were brutalized unmercifully, flogged, beaten, or murdered at will.

The Abolitionists led the propaganda fight for black manumission; they carried on their fight mostly in the North before white audiences in an effort to win sympathy. Public opinion slowly began to stiffen against the excesses of slavery, and when the Civil War erupted, many white men viewed it as a necessary evil in the fight for freedom.

Abraham Lincoln, the sixteenth President, has been remembered kindly in history as the Great Emancipator, a benevolent, compassionate man who abhorred slavery. This is not completely true. Lincoln unlocked the chains of slavery only after he realized that his effort to preserve the Union had failed.

Whereas the Civil War began on April 11, 1861, when Fort Sumter in South Carolina was fired upon, Lincoln did not free America's three million slaves until January 1, 1863. He had hoped for some compromise to forestall the outbreak of hostilities between white brothers over black nonbrothers. Because this concern dominated his thinking, he waited until he was convinced no other solution was possible. As proof of his lack of compassion for the black slaves, Lincoln publicly took one of the most Machiavellian postures toward freedom ever uttered by an American

President. Responding to a public letter written to him by Horace Greeley, editor of the *New York Herald Tribune*, titled "The Prayer of Twenty Millions," Lincoln wrote:

> If there be those who would not save the Union unless they could at the same time destroy slavery, I do not agree with them. My paramount object in this struggle is to save the Union, and is not either to save or destroy slavery. If I could save the Union without freeing any slave I would do it, and if I could save it by freeing all the slaves, I would do it; and if I could save it by freeing some and leaving others alone I would also do that. What I do about slavery and the colored race, I do because I believe it helps to save the Union. . . .

The end of the Civil War on April 9, 1865, when the courtly southern gentleman General Robert E. Lee surrendered his sword to the commander of the Union forces, General Ulysses S. Grant, was the beginning of a new era of social strife almost as violent as the previous four years had been.

Lincoln's assassination placed in the presidency Andrew Johnson, a poor white from Tennessee who had fought his way to the top by overcoming opposition from upper-class whites. To Johnson, a member of the working class of whites, blacks were still an economic threat. When Congress passed a civil-rights act in 1866 he vetoed it. Congress passed a second civil-rights bill in 1867 over Johnson's veto. The act provided for negroes to be recognized as citizens of the United States and gave them the right to vote. The debate over the constitutionality of the act led to the framing of the Fourteenth Amendment to the Constitution, which passed both branches of Congress on June 13, 1866, and was ratified by two-thirds of the states by July 28, 1868.

This act had been passed in the first stage of the Reconstruction period, and it highlights the tensions between Congress and President Andrew Johnson.

Political reconstruction came in two stages. The first lasted from the end of the war until 1867. This was Presidential Reconstruction, carried out by the States, under Lincoln's and Johnson's supervision, with few conditions and not seriously interfered with by national agencies until the second stage approached. The second stage was Congressional Reconstruction, lasting from 1867 to 1876, carried on by the Republican politicians of the national legislature and forced on the unwilling South in detail by national agencies and national partisans.

From 1864 to early in 1867, under Presidential Reconstruction, the South was left free to resume fairly normal political activities. President Lincoln in a proclamation of December, 1863, set forth a plan for the rehabilitation of the seceded States. When ten per cent of the voting population of any State, "lately in rebellion," as determined by the election laws in force before the war, had taken an oath of allegiance, they might proceed to form a new State government, which, if republican in form, would be recognized and given protection under the Federal constitution.[2]

The South may have lost the war, but it was not going to surrender its traditions of white supremacy. In order to maintain some semblance of the old order, eight southern states passed what has come to be known as the "Black Codes." They required every black man to be in the service of some white, have both a lawful residence and a job, and carry an official certificate showing both. Vagrancy penalties were imposed on any person who could not support himself and his dependents, who refused to work for "usual and common" wages and specifically on negroes found unlawfully assembling. (The Union of South Africa was to adopt an identical system many years later, and it became known as "apartheid.")

Furthermore, some of the states continued to resist the Fourteenth Amendment.

Congressional exasperation with the paleolithic resistance of the southern states reached a boiling point in 1867, and in February, March, and April of that year, the first series of congressional reconstruction acts was passed. They declared that no legal governments existed in the former Confederacy and divided the region into five military districts under the command of generals of the Army. They were to direct a registration of voters which should include negroes and exclude ex-Confederates. These voters were to elect conventions in the former slave areas, and the conventions, in turn, were to adopt constitutions which, if acceptable to Congress, were to qualify the states for readmission as soon as they had accepted the Fourteenth Amendment. Congressional Reconstruction seemed designed to make the ex-slaves citizens who could participate in the process of governing. The shortcut to full equality was to be taken by means of the ballot boxes and the election of public officials.

Unhappily, there was a welfare mentality in Washington, D.C., that was a direct carryover from the white paternalism of slavery. This mentality resulted in the establishment of the Freedmen's Bureau to assist ex-slaves make the adjustment to their new status. The official title of the bureau, actually under the authority of the War Department, was The Bureau of Refugees, Freedman and Abandoned Lands.

The Bureau was an early WPA for negroes. Its purpose was to administer abandoned and confiscated plantations and act as a clearing house for the return of ex-slaves to pardoned ex-Confederates; provide clothing, shelter, medicine, and rations to the destitute, both blacks and whites. It is estimated by official sources that at that time the Bureau issued six million rations to freed slaves and two million rations to whites. Some of the more radical Republicans in Congress wanted the Freedmen's Bureau to redistribute land to ex-slaves, but the South vigorously resisted this move and the one commodity the blacks needed to achieve self-support —land—was never acquired.

The next step in the program of Congressional Reconstruction was the passage of the Fourteenth Amendment. This is generally believed to have been passed to guarantee Negroes the right to vote, but it actually had a larger purpose which is rarely recognized by historians. The Fourteenth Amendment disqualified for federal and state office any person who had engaged in insurrections against the nation—i.e., the Confederates—and made their amnesty conditional upon a two-thirds vote of Congress. In other words, southern states first had to call new constitutional conventions to elect new governments which were to enfranchise all negroes over twenty-one years of age and disenfranchise whites who had fought against the Union.

The South was aghast. According to an estimate in the Senate, 672,000 Negroes had been enfranchised, as against a total possible white electorate of 925,000. But some hundred thousand of these whites had been disenfranchised, and 200,000 disqualified for office.[3]

It was open season on democracy.

Northern whites made their pilgrimage to the South to help the negroes establish these new governments. Many arrived with nothing but a carpetbag containing all of their belongings, hence the word "carpetbagger," which meant a white northerner who had come to impose black supremacy on southern whites.

The constitutional conventions were held, and in all the southern states, with the exception of South Carolina, whites were in the majority. By 1868, seven states had completed ratification of the Fourteenth Amendment to be readmitted to the Union, and by 1870, the last three, Virginia, Mississippi, and Texas, joined them. The stage was now set for the election of public officials on a combined Negro-Radical-Republican slate.

The first year black men were to be elected to the Congress of the United States was 1870. From 1870 to 1901, a total of twenty black congressmen and two black senators were to help make the laws of the land. In some states, black men were school superintendents, state treasurers, secretaries of state, lieutenant governors, and in Louisiana, an acting governor, P. B. S. Pinchback.

South Carolina was the blackest of all. Perhaps because it was the only state to have a majority of black delegates to the constitutional convention, South Carolina was also the only state to have a black associate justice of the state supreme court, Jonathan J. Wright. He was also the first negro to be admitted to the Pennsylvania bar. In one year, 1872, the entire delegation to the U.S. Congress was composed of black men— Robert C. DeLarge, Joseph S. Rainey, and Robert B. Elliott.

A Reporter describing the first South Carolina legislature of the Reconstruction period wrote:

> The Speaker is black, the Clerk is black, the doorkeepers are black, the little pages are black, the chairman of the Ways and Means is black and the Chaplain is coal black. At some of the desks sit colored men whose types it would be hard to find outside of the Congo. . . . It must be remembered also that these men, with not more than half a dozen exceptions, have been themselves slaves, and that their ancestors were slaves for generations.[4]

This was the first manifestation of Black Power.

Black men were to play definitive roles during their brief sojourn in the political sun of democracy by helping to draw up budgets, passing laws that were the forerunners of much of our social-welfare legislation today, and administering governments.

The following men served in the House and the Senate between 1870 and 1901:

NAME	STATE	YEAR
U.S. SENATE		
1. Hiram R. Revel	Mississippi	1870–71
2. Blanche K. Bruce	Mississippi	1875–81
U.S. HOUSE OF REPRESENTATIVES		
1. Joseph H. Rainey	South Carolina	1870–79
2. Jefferson F. Long	Georgia	1870–71
3. Robert C. DeLarge	South Carolina	1871–73
4. Robert B. Elliott	South Carolina	1871–74
5. Josiah T. Wells	Florida	1871–76
6. Benjamin S. Turner	Alabama	1871–73
7. James T. Rapier	Alabama	1873–75
8. Alonzo J. Ransier	South Carolina	1873–75
9. Richard H. Cain	South Carolina	1873–75
		1877–79
10. John R. Lynch	Mississippi	1873–77
		1882–83
11. John A. Hyman	North Carolina	1875–77
12. Jeremiah Haralson	Alabama	1875–77
13. Robert Smalls	South Carolina	1875–79
		1882–83
		1885–87
14. Charles Nash	Louisiana	1875–77

15. James E. O'Hara   North Carolina   1883–87
16. Henry P. Cheatham   North Carolina   1889–93
17. John M. Langston   Virginia   1890–91
18. Thomas E. Miller   South Carolina   1890–91
19. George W. Murray   South Carolina   1893–97
20. George H. White   North Carolina   1897–1901

Of this group, two of the most outstanding were both from South Carolina, Robert Brown Elliott and Robert Smalls. An honor graduate of Eton, Elliott, who was born of West Indian parents in Boston, Mass., on August 11, 1842, was one of the most gifted and eloquent black politicians in American history. He held several political offices, being elected to the South Carolina legislative assembly at the age of twenty-six, to the Congress at twenty-eight; subsequently he became Speaker of the South Carolina legislature.

Elliott was a dark-skinned, heavy-set man who wore his hair in a bushy African style. During his service in Congress, he was one of that body's sharpest debaters, a fast thinker on his feet, and deeply committed to black equality. If some of the black Congressmen thought it best to maintain a discreet silence, Elliott did not. The Adam Clayton Powell of his day, he was quick to take on any display of bigotry on the House floor. Once, after a southern congressman had delivered a scurrilously racist attack, Elliott replied: "To the diatribe of the gentleman from Virginia, who spoke on yesterday, and who so far transcended the limits of decency and propriety as to announce upon this floor that his remarks were addressed to white men alone, I shall have no word of reply. Let him feel that a Negro was not only too magnanimous to smite him in his weakness, but was even charitable enough to grant him the mercy of his silence." This eloquent rejoinder brought applause from both the floor and the galleries.

Smalls, who served longer in Congress than any other negro Reconstruction congressman, was born a slave in Beaufort, S.C., on April 5, 1839. On May 13, 1862, he distinguished himself during the Civil War by smuggling his wife and three children on board the *Planter*, a dispatch and transport steamer, assuming command of the vessel, and, with the Confederate flag flying to get him safely past Confederate lines, sailing the boat into the hands of the Union squadron blockading Charleston harbor. This daring exploit earned him a commission as a pilot in the Union Navy from Lincoln. He subsequently became a captain, the only negro to hold such a rank during the Civil War. Smalls was an outstanding congressman who supported a wide variety of progressive legislation, such as a bill to provide equal accommodations for negroes in interstate travel and an amendment to safeguard the rights of children born of interracial marriages.

Another brilliant black politician was P. B. S. Pinchback, who held more political offices than any other black man, and who served in Louisiana as lieutenant governor, acting governor, congressman-elect, and senator-elect. He arrived in Washington, D.C., in January 1873, but the Senate refused to seat him. There were reports that the senators' wives did not want to associate with Mrs. Pinchback. Pinchback was a strikingly handsome brown-skinned man with sharp Arabian features whom white women found attractive. After wrestling with his case for three years, the Senate rejected Pinchback's claim to the Senate seat, and he returned to Louisiana.

While black men were being elected to Congress, to high state posts, and to an occasional local elective office (in 1870, Robert H. Wood was elected mayor of Natchez, Miss.), white southerners were organizing massive resistance campaigns. It was during these years that the Ku Klux Klan began an effort to intimidate negroes from voting and running for elective office. Not only were intimidation and force used against blacks, but business and social ostracism were used against whites who would not line up solidly against negroes in government. In Louisiana, the Democratic conservatives formed "White Leagues," ordered arms, and actually fought a pitched battle in New Orleans in which forty were killed and over a hundred were wounded. Had it not been for the presence of federal troops, the government of Louisiana would have fallen to white racists.

This is the most important fact of the Reconstruction era which sent black men to Congress and to the various state assemblies: the tranquilizing presence of federal troops. They kept law and order and protected the black man.

Then, in 1876, a man decided he wanted so desperately to be President that he was willing to scuttle democracy for it.

The presidential contest between the Republican Ohio Governor Rutherford B. Hayes and the Democrat Samuel J. Tilden ended in a deadlock because of disputed elections in South Carolina, Louisiana, and Florida where mixed radical governments and all-white Conservative governments had both been elected and each claimed to be the legitimate government.

Because of the deadlock, the decision was to be resolved by the House of Representatives. Hayes claimed the disputed states of South Carolina, Louisiana, and Florida. But the representatives of those three states, acting in concert with other southern representatives, were demanding a higher price for their votes than just the comfort of knowing they were responsible for the election of a President. They asked for a guarantee from Hayes that he would withdraw federal troops from the South and uphold the principle of States Rights—i.e., that he would let the South handle the negro problem in its own way. Hayes's representatives in the negotiations agreed. An agreement was finally worked out on February 26, 1877, whereby Hayes's representatives handed the southern representatives a note which read:

Gentlemen:
Referring to the conversation had with you yesterday in which Governor Hayes's policy as to the status of certain Southern states was discussed, we desire to say in reply that we can assure you in the strongest possible manner of our great desire to have adopted such a policy as will give to the people of the States of South Carolina and Louisiana the right to control their own affairs in their own way and to say further that we feel authorized, from an acquaintance with knowledge of Governor Hayes and his views on this question, to pledge ourselves to you that such will be his policy.

This paved the way for the Electoral Commission, composed of five senators, five Supreme Court justices, and five congressmen, to vote on the disputed election, and they did—strictly along party lines, eight to seven. On March 2, 1877, Hayes had won by one electoral vote.

Not necessarily a racist, but a man of honor, Hayes kept his word and pulled the federal troops out of the South. It was now "open season on niggers."

Southern states moved swiftly to wipe out all the political advances made by negroes. Several methods were devised to keep negroes from voting:

Polling places were set up at points remote from Negro communities. Ferries between black districts and political headquarters went "out of repair" at election time. . . . Without notice to the Negroes, the location of polling places might change, or the Negroes be told of a change which was then not carried out. The stuffing of ballot boxes and the manipulation of the count developed into fine arts.[5]

Backing up these various extralegal machinations were incredibly savage acts of white brutality against negroes attempting to vote or register as voters.

But southern white leaders refused to concede publicly that they needed to rely on violence to preserve political white supremacy in the South. "It is on this, sir, that we rely in the South. Not the cowardly menace of mask or shotgun; but the peaceful majesty of intelligence and responsibility, massed and unified for the protection of its homes and the preservation of its liberties," declared Henry W. Grady, one of the

South's foremost apologists for white racism, in a speech to the Boston Merchants Association in 1889.

This "peaceful majority of intelligence" to accomplish black disenfranchisement was twisted into ingenious exercises in officially approved frauds. One of the most complicated was South Carolina's "eight-ballot-box" election law of 1882, which required a special ballot box in every voting place for each office to be filled. The boxes were properly labeled, and election workers would read the titles when requested, but no one was permitted to speak to the voter or insert his ballot for him. So, if a ballot went into the wrong box, it was not counted. This gimmick was aimed particularly at the large number of illiterate negroes, but thousands of illiterate whites were also disenfranchised.

Meanwhile, a poor whites' agrarian revolution was taking place in the South. Its greatest number of election victories took place in 1890. But the movement collapsed in 1896, and the issue of "political niggerism" was resurrected to reunite the divided South.

The one issue on which all white men could agree was disenfranchising the negro. The southern states began to pass disenfranchising codes: poll taxes; the famed "grandfather clauses" (which ordained for the benefit of poor whites that permanent registrations were permitted for persons who had been able to vote prior to 1861 and for their descendants and for persons who had served in the federal or Confederate armies or in the state militias and their descendants); and naked terrorism, by far the most successful of all devices. Those negroes who did manage to survive the gamut of white obstacles to registering and voting were threatened with reprisals, fired from their jobs, intimidated on the streets, beaten at night by Ku Klux Klan nightriders, lynched, murdered, their families abused, and their houses burned to the ground. For a black man living in the South to attempt to register to vote was tantamount to a Jew living in Nazi Germany to try to live a normal life.

So successful was this organized conspiracy of massive southern white power that within a few years, most negro voters were purged from the registration lists in all of the southern states.

> For the 1896 national election, the last before the disenfranchising code, there were registered in the State [of Louisiana] 130,344 Negroes; Negro registrants were in the majority in 26 parishes. For the 1900 national election, two years after the adoption of the new constitution, there were registered only 5320 Negroes, and no parishes showed a majority of Negro registrants.[6]

What happened in Louisiana was repeated throughout the southern states, in some with more malice than in others. But all passed disenfranchising constitutions relegating the negro to the status of a noncitizen. A new era began, which Henry Lee Moon called "The Great Blackout."

Negroes as voters, negroes as politicians were to become the political freaks of American society.

Black political power was to become nonexistent from 1890 to the 1940's. The vast majority of negroes lived in the South, and their effective disenfranchisement, for all intents and purposes, demolished any potential political power the negro might have had. In 1900, for example, about 90 percent of America's negroes—7,922,969—lived in the South, while the other 10 percent—911,025—were scattered throughout the North, Midwest, and West.

The only political power negroes were able to claim during these years was gratuitous federal appointments in jobs reserved for negroes. One of the first such appointments occurred on April 16, 1869, when President Grant appointed Ebenezer Don Carlos Bassett as Minister Resident and Consul General to Haiti. He was the first negro to receive a diplomatic post. In 1877, Frederick Douglass was appointed a police commissioner by Grant, and, later in that year, Marshal of the District of Columbia by President Hayes. In 1880, former Mississippi Senator Bruce, the second negro to serve in the U.S. Senate, was appointed Register of the U.S. Treasury by President Garfield, and, in 1881, Garfield made Douglass Recorder of Deeds of the District of Columbia, a post that was to become almost the exclusive property of negroes. (It was a safe appointment. Negroes would be concerned with documents and archives and would have little time to be involved with the contemporary problems of their society.)

If, in 1967, the worst problem black people have is the overabundance of powerless national "negro leaders" who are regarded by white people as spokesmen (Whitney Young, Roy Wilkins, Bayard Rustin, etc.), this problem did not exist during and after the Civil War. There was a vacuum of negro leadership and an absence of black pride among negroes. Perhaps the most effective, the most brilliant, and certainly one of the most militant black spokesmen negroes had was Frederick Douglass, the father of the protest movement. Douglass' eloquent oratory, moving prose, and his constant organized activity on behalf of the enslaved black man made him a national figure. "I supposed myself to have been born in February 1817," he wrote in his autobiography, *Narrative*, in Talbot County, near Easton, in Maryland. "I hardly became a thinking thing when I first learned to hate slavery."

Douglass' mother was a slave and his father a white man.

Self-educated, he was soon employed as an agent of the Massachusetts Anti-Slavery Society. He toured the country speaking publicly against slavery, and his booming voice and dynamic personality left an ineradicable impression on white audiences.

In an era when the safest approach was to be an "Uncle Tom" or even not to speak out at all, Douglass was an uncompromising fighter. In today's boiling racial cauldron, he more than likely would have been a member of the Student Nonviolent Coordinating Committee rather than the Urban League. His famous Fourth of July speech, made in Rochester in 1852, has been quoted many times.

What to the American slave is your 4th of July? I answer: a day that reveals to him, more than all other days in the year, the gross injustice and cruelty to which he is the constant victim. To him, your celebration is a sham; your boasted liberty, an unholy license; your national greatness, swelling vanity; your sounds of rejoicing are empty and heartless; your denunciation of tyrants, brass fronted impudence; your shouts of liberty and equality, hollow mockery; your prayers and hymns, your sermons and thanksgivings, with all your religious parade and solemnity, are to him, mere bombast, fraud, deception, impiety, and hypocrisy—a thin veil to cover up crimes which would disgrace a nation of savages.

... You shed tears over fallen Hungary, and make the sad story of her wrongs the theme of your poets, statesmen, and orators, till your gallant sons are ready to fly to arms to vindicate her cause against the oppressor; but in regard to the ten thousand wrongs of the American slave, you would enforce the strictest silence, and would hail him as an enemy of the nation who dares to make these wrongs the subject of public discourse.

The timidity of many of today's black leaders can best be measured by the fact that very few would dare utter such militant thoughts.

Although there were other negro leaders active in the black rebellions of those days—Sojourner Truth, Harriet Tubman, Nat Turner, Denmark Vesey, and Gabriel Prosser—none of them were politicians. None of them were elected officials controlling the apparatus of government. Even the few black men in Congress were not able to develop a national black consciousness or a posture of national leadership, if for no other reason than black people were not ready for a national black political leader. With exceptions such as Nat Turner, Harriet Tubman, Sojourner Truth, and Frederick Douglass, the negro leaders of their time were passive, meek, and exceedingly solicitous of the white man's approbation.

There was another revolution taking place in America at the same time the political pogrom to decertify black citizens was achieving its goals, the Industrial Revolution. It, however, was a revolution that was going to bring the good life to white, not black Americans. It was a revolution that would attract millions of immigrants from Europe to this country to develop wealth, security, and fame while black people stood still and marked time in the backyards of their segregated hovels.

As the table below indicates, European immigration slowly diminished the proportion of negroes in the population from 14.1 percent in 1860 to 9.9 percent in 1920. The waves of Irish, Italians, Poles, Russian Jews, Scandinavians, and Germans seeking the good life heavily increased the white population.

Year	U.S. Population	Negro Population	Percentage
1790	3,929,214	757,208	19.3
1800	5,308,483	1,002,037	18.9
1810	7,239,881	1,377,808	19.0
1820	9,638,453	1,771,656	18.4
1830	12,866,020	2,328,642	18.1
1840	17,069,453	2,874,000	16.8
1850	23,191,876	3,638,808	15.7
1860	31,443,790	4,441,830	14.1
1870	39,818,449	4,880,009	12.7
1880	50,155,783	6,580,793	13.1
1890	62,947,714	7,488,676	11.9
1900	75,994,575	8,833,994	11.6
1910	93,402,151	9,827,763	10.7
1920	105,710,620	10,463,131	9.9
1930	122,775,046	11,891,143	9.7
1940	131,669,275	12,865,518	9.8
1950	150,697,361	15,042,286	10.0
1960	179,323,175	18,171,831	10.5

As the South became industrialized, negroes found few employment opportunities. There was almost no work to be had in the textile mills, and work in the iron foundries and furniture factories was limited to the least desirable jobs. On the farms, they could either work for white planters for subsistence wages or engage in one of several forms of farm tenancy from which the year's labor yielded a bare existence.

Negroes slowly began the great migration northward in search of better opportunities at the same time as Europeans were immigrating to America for the same purpose. World War I accelerated the movement of negroes to Northern cities. Gunnar Myrdal states in *An American Dilemma* that the biggest job gains for negroes did not occur during the New Deal, as so many historians have written, but during this period. "This should be emphasized: large employment gains for Negroes in the North—except for the present war boom—occured only during the short period from the First World War until the end of the 'twenties.' "[7]

As negroes crowded into the northern cities—New York, Chicago, Detroit, Philadelphia—they acquired smatterings of political consciousness. There were occasional breakthroughs during these years for limited political power.

One of the most astute black politicians of all time came into power during the 1920's. He was Robert R. Church, a wealthy Memphis businessman who managed to maintain his place on Tennessee's Republican

State Committee in the face of the "lily-white movement" of the Republican Party. Negroes credited Church with a series of appointments of negroes to federal office, various acts of charity (he donated a public park in the middle of valuable urban property in Memphis), and "perhaps most important of all, with invincible political cleverness." One of the vicious white racists of his time, Alabama Senator Heflin, paid unintended tribute to Church in the guise of an antinegro poem read during U.S. Senate investigations of patronage:

> Offices up a 'simmon tree,
> Bob Church on de ground;
> Bob Church said to de 'pointing power
> "Shake dem 'pointments down."[8]

Church understood the quid pro quo of politics and for years worked closely with Democratic boss Edward Crump by delivering the negro vote to Crump in exchange for patronage. Church was the black Frank Hague or Tom Pendergast of his day. There were others—Ferdinand Q. Morton of New York City, Oscar S. DePriest of Chicago (who as the sovereign of Chicago's black South Side was to be followed by William L. Dawson), and Texas' Norris Wright Cuney (who coined the phrase "lily-white").

It was sparse pickings for black politicians. Republicans were busy trying to divest black people of the independence that Lincoln had decreed for them. Naturally, most negroes voted Republican. From such political fidelity they expected a small amount of patronage that Republicans were not prepared to award to them. In the South, the Republican party took steps to purge its negro state committeemen in an effort to keep pace with the Democrats, whose all-white credentials were above segregationist reproach.

By the time Woodrow Wilson was elected President in 1912, the negro was the nation's forgotten man. In the previous year, 1911, a national convention of negro Democrats in Indianapolis "urged colored voters of the United States to note the conditions surrounding them, to cease following any one party to their detriment, and thus divide their votes." It was the hope of these negro Democrats that negro voters would begin to move away from the Republican party, for it had begun to treat them as shabbily as the Democratic party, which had never sought their electoral support. When Wilson won with a minority of the popular vote (Roosevelt, 4,216,020; Taft, 3,483,922; and Wilson, 6,286,214), some negroes exulted in the thought that their votes had been of significance. They expected both an increase in federal appointments and action at the executive level to end discrimination in some governmental departments. Their job was shortlived. Wilson actually did less for negroes than some of his Republican predecessors. His was a racist administration.

The impoverishment of negro political power is best reflected by the national negro leadership of the early twentieth century. After Douglass, there seemed to be no national spokesman to whom whites could turn to find out what the negro was thinking. But in 1896, they found one who would gladden their hearts. In his famous "Atlanta Compromise" speech at the Atlanta Exposition that year, Booker T. Washington, an educator who had founded the Tuskegee Institute, called for negroes to "drop your buckets where you are," return to the soil, become skilled tradesmen, and lead lives separate and apart from white people. Washington was such a devout Uncle Tom that he even advocated "the protection of the ballot . . . for a while at least, either by an educational test, a property test, or by both combined."

Washington quickly became *the* national negro spokesman, and he said precisely what America's whites wanted to hear and believe. Washington's brand of head-scratching, shoe-shuffling accommodation to segregation angered the more militant negro leaders, such as W. E. B. Du Bois. It was to meet the challenge of Washington's political subservience that the Niagara Movement, which led to the founding of the NAACP, was born.

Negroes were becoming politically involved in some northern cities. Negro candidates occasionally challenged white aldermen and white congressmen in the heavily negro districts in St. Louis, New York City, Chicago, Philadelphia, and Cleveland. Most of them failed. One who succeeded was Oscar S. DePriest, a wily back-room manipulator with a fiery personality who played the game of politics as shrewdly as the white man. He was successively elected Chicago's first negro alderman and then first negro congressman, in 1929. A Republican, DePriest was the first negro congressman since 1901. He became an immediate national hero to negroes, but because of the taint of the corrupt "Big Bill" Thompson machine, which had elected DePriest, most white-controlled "respectable" negro leaders shied away from him. DePriest's notable achievement was ignored by the NAACP, which awarded its Spingarn Medal that year to Mordecai W. Johnson, who was cited for his "successful administration of Howard University."

DePriest served in Congress for six years and then was defeated by a negro Democrat, Arthur W. Mitchell, who served for eight years.

The circumstances of the elections of other negro congressmen [will not be discussed here.] A summary of their terms of service, as of 1967, follows:

NAME	STATE	YEARS
1. Oscar S. DePriest	Illinois	1929–35
2. Arthur W. Mitchell	Illinois	1935–43
3. William L. Dawson	Illinois	1943–66*
4. Adam Clayton Powell	New York	1945–66**
5. Charles C. Diggs, Jr.	Michigan	1955–66*
6. Robert N. C. Nix, Jr.	Pennsylvania	1959–66*
7. Augustus Hawkins	California	1961–66*
8. John Conyers, Jr.	Michigan	1965–66*

* Elected in 1966 to the Ninetieth Congress.
** Elected to the Ninetieth Congress, but excluded on March 1, 1967.

The election of negro congressmen represented the only tangible evidence of black political power at the national level, and the small number constitutes an indictment of the black man's political acumen. Despite occasional negro federal appointments, an occasional negro alderman or city councilman, a judge or a member of the board of education, negroes were never able to gain the kind of political power the Irish, the Italians, the Jews, and the Poles had acquired in a comparatively short time.

Meanwhile, the negro continued to make almost no economic or political progress. Lynchings in the South, racial segregation in public accommodations and the public schools, tacit "gentlemen's agreements" between Northern real-estate brokers created and maintained ghettos as severely restricted as any in South Africa.

In 1947, President Truman appointed a Committee on Civil Rights, and it issued a report called "To Secure These Rights." This was a documented account of the deprivations negroes suffered in housing, employment, and education. A rate of unemployment two and one-half times that of whites and total segregation in the public schools of the South were two of the factors the report listed as most detrimental to negro equality. Taking its cue from this report, in 1952 the NAACP filed suit in a federal court to desegregate the public schools of the South. Few expected the U.S. Supreme Court to rule overwhelmingly in the NAACP's favor, but it did—unanimously—on May 17, 1954, declaring that "separate but equal" public schools were unconstitutional.

The first phase of the Negro Revolution, the litigative phase, was thus inadvertently launched. It was to be quickly followed by four successive stages: the sit-in phase beginning in Greensboro, N.C., on February 1, 1960; the massive demonstrations phase, beginning in April 1963 in Birmingham, Ala., and culminating in the August 1963 "March on Washington"; the insurrectionist or rebellion phase beginning in the summer of 1964 in Harlem and Bedford-Stuyvesant, N.Y., and spreading to Watts, Los Angeles, in the summer of 1965; and finally the black power phase, beginning in the summer of 1966 in Greenville, Miss.

During each phase, black political sensitivities were heightened and the rumblings of an aroused black political machine were heard in cities across the country.

NOTES

1. John Daniels, *In Freedom's Birthplace* (Boston: Houghton Mifflin, 1914), pp. 23-24.
2. Paul Lewinson, *Race, Class and Party* (New York: Grosset and Dunlap), p. 18.
3. Lewinson, *Race, Class and Party*, p. 41.
4. Quoted in Lewison, *Race, Class and Party*, p. 45.
5. Lewinson, *Race, Class and Party*, p. 64.
6. Lewinson, *Race, Class and Party*, p. 81.
7. Gunnar Myrdal, *An American Dilemma* (New York: Harper $_7$ Brothers, 1944), p. 295.
8. Lewinson, *Race, Class and Party*, p. 139.

5

The Progressive Parties and the Negro

Hanes Walton, Jr.

AS A RESULT of the Populist movement, some historians argue, the Bourbons and agrarian leaders attempted to remove, once and for all, the Negro from southern politics.[1] Other historians have suggested that the movement for disfranchising the Negro began before the Populist crusade and reached its peak after the movement had subsided. In other words, the Negro's participation in the Populist crusade only increased and gave impetus to the movement for final disfranchisement.

However, the fact is that between 1890 and 1910 drastic measures to curtail Negro voting were embodied in new constitutions adopted by eight southern states.[2] These statutory restrictions, engineered by southern states, went a long way in effectively eliminating the Negro as a political force in the South. Prior to 1890, a review of the state constitutions shows that no legal attempts were made to exclude the Negro from suffrage. Only illegal devices such as murder, fraud, and violence were used to restrain the Negro vote. But, together with these devices, the legal restraints, such as the poll tax, property qualifications, the "grandfather clause," the reading or interpretation test, and the disfranchisement for crimes, made Negro voting very difficult. Even those few Negroes who braved threats and various sorts of intimidation were now disfranchised by the law. And furthermore, most Negro leadership in the South had adopted Booker T. Washington's submissive philosophy and urged their followers to drop agitation for civil and political rights. Under such pressures, Negro voting dwindled to a mere nothing.

In addition, Negro votes were now shunned by both parties in the South. The Democratic party had always discouraged Negro enfranchis-

---

Reprinted from *The Negro in Third-Party Politics* (Philadelphia: Dorrance Publishing Co., 1969) by permission of the author.

ment, now the Republican party, seeking respectability and trying to become a "white man's party," avoided the Negro vote and supporters like the plague. The Republicans began to move immediately toward "lily-white" Republicanism.[3] This phrase "lily-white" was coined by Norris Wright Cuney, a Negro State Republican leader in Texas. He had fought off attempts by white Republicans, who were laboring under the stigma attached to them by the Bourbons as "nigger lovers," to remove Negroes from the party. Their efforts to do this came in the form of "White Republican Clubs," which grew slowly in the South from 1888 to 1892. After 1896, "lily-white Republicanism," encouraged by the "let-alone policy" of some Republican presidents, grew at such a rapid pace that the party, in a very short time, had eliminated all Negroes from its ranks in every southern state except Mississippi.[4]

Under such circumstances, the motivation to vote also declined: the Negro who desired to vote could only support those inimical to his interests. He no longer had a choice. However, this is not to say that the Negro as a political issue did not exert some type of influence. On the contrary, the Negro, even though disfranchised, played a major and important role in southern as well as national politics. Although this role has in many respects been more negative than positive, the Negro has continued to be a significant political issue and factor in both southern and national life. A case in point is the Progressive movement of 1912.

The Progressive movement of 1912 grew out of the soil that had been nurtured by the Populists, Knights of Labor, and other reform groups of the period. The impetus for this movement was not the evangelism of the Populists but the literary expressions of many journalists in the forms of exposés and reports.[5] These journalists were dubbed "Muckrakers" by Theodore Roosevelt, because of the corruption, scandals, graft, and general evils that they exposed in American big business and politics. These exposés were published in such magazines as *Cosmopolitan*, *McClure's*, and *Collier's Everybody's*, and in numerous books and newspaper articles.

As a result of these shocking and revealing exposés, many social, economic, and political reforms were instituted on the local and state levels. When Theodore Roosevelt came to power he instituted reforms on the national level, but only enough to keep the Progressive wing of the Republican party satisfied. Under William Howard Taft's administration, big business again gained the upper hand, reforms broke down, and the Progressive Republican League was formed. During the next year, it became a third party and nominated ex-President Roosevelt for the presidency.

Therefore, with the country split into basically three political groups, i.e., the Democrats, the Republicans and the Progressives, the Negro emerged as a vague "balance of power" force.[6] This was especially true in the North because of the heavy Negro migration from the South. This migration was occurring because of declining southern agriculture, increasing intolerance on the part of southern whites, and the search for a Negro "Mecca." Immediately after reaching this Negro "Mecca" in northern cities like New York, Chicago, and Philadelphia, Negroes allied themselves with the various political machines in the cities in which they lived. Such alliances brought many benefits, ranging from much-needed jobs to rise of Negro congressmen, like Oscar De Priest.[7] The ease with which Negroes allied themselves with these political machines encouraged the political bosses to add more of the newly arriving Negroes to the voting rolls. Therefore, the Negro voting strength in the North increased tremendously before the First World War. In a final analysis, these alliances added to the strength and vitality of the political machines, be they corrupt or otherwise.

In the 1912 campaign, the Democrats, led by their presidential candidate Woodrow Wilson, made an ambiguous appeal to the increasing northern Negro vote and the decreasing southern one. This appeal was due to the prodding of Oswald Garrison Villard, grandson of William Lloyd Garrison,[8] and it caused the NAACP to urge Negroes to support Wilson and the Democratic party.[9] This slight overture on Wilson's part, however, went unnoticed by southern Democratic newspapers.[10]

As for the Republican party, the Negro delegates to the national convention, having the "balance of power," rejected the nomination of Roosevelt and helped to nominate Taft. However, Taft, being weak, capitulated to the policies of the southern wing on the party, i.e., the "lily-white" Republicans. This decreased Negro party members' support and caused some disillusionment in the ranks of the party's Negro followers.

Roosevelt, having failed to gain the Republican nomination because of his shifting Negro policies,[11] accepted the Progressive party offer. He immediately made a personal appeal to both whites and Negroes, North and South, to join in his new political and social movement. "Many Negroes both in the North and in the South looked to him as their deliverer and hastened to join the Progressive ranks."[12] This appeal, however, failed to win back a majority of his Negro and white supporters. During his first term as President, he alienated whites by appointing a Negro, William Crum, as a Customs Collector in South Carolina, closing a post office in Indianola, Mississippi, when whites forced the colored postmistress to resign, and having Booker T. Washington to the White House as a dinner guest. In his second term, he alienated Negroes by capitulating to "lily-white Republicanism," dishonorably discharging three companies of Negro soldiers for participating in the Brownville riots and offering a quasi-defense of Negro lynchings.[13] Therefore, Roosevelt's newest appeal for support was viewed by many with skepticism.

Soon, however, southerners advised Roosevelt that the only way the Progressive party could grow in the South was to divest itself of the few Negro voters in the region. His chief southern adviser, John Parker of New Orleans, told him that "this should be a white man's party, recognizing the superior ability of the white man and his superior civilization. ... The South," he continued, "cannot and will not under any circumstances tolerate the Negro's" presence in the party.[14] In other words, a strong platform by the Progressive party, denouncing the Negro and Negro participation, was necessary for substantial southern support.[15]

At first, Roosevelt tried to side-step this issue. In his public speeches, he refrained from discussing the issue, hoping that this would be a successful strategy. Seeking to further improve his strategy of not antagonizing either whites or Negroes, he announced in mid-July that the problem of the composition of state delegations to the national convention would be left to the various states. This strategy, however, failed. Rival Negro and white Progressive groups were formed in Georgia, Alabama, and Mississippi, and Florida. Each group named a delegation to the national convention, and each claimed to be the legitimate representative of the party in his state. With the arrival of four Negro delegations from the deep South, at the convention on August 3, 1912, a conflict over seats ensued, and Roosevelt had to take a definite stand.[16]

This Roosevelt did, before the national convention convened. In a letter to Julian Harris of Atlanta, the son of Joel Chandler Harris, Roosevelt set forth his new position in regard to the Negro in southern politics.[17] This letter immediately appeared in many southern newspapers and was widely circulated in a campaign pamphlet entitled, *The Negro Question: Attitude of the Progressive party toward the Colored Race*. In this letter, Roosevelt expressed concern for the welfare of southern Negroes, and a friendly feeling, but unreservedly accepted "lily-white" Progressivism in the South.[18] On the other hand, he made it clear that the party would appeal for the support of the better class of Negro voters in the northern states, and that the Negro delegates from these states would be accepted at the national convention.

Therefore, shortly after the convening of the national convention on August 3 in Chicago, Roosevelt's philosophy began to take form. The nagging question facing the credential committees, i.e., whether the white or Negro delegation from the South should be seated, was quickly resolved in terms of the Roosevelt philosophy. The contest between the rival Florida delegations was so bitter that the state was allowed to go unrepresented.[19] The twelve Negroes from Alabama were denied seats but the white delegation was accepted. The Negro delegation from Mississippi was denied their seats by a 17 to 16 vote. Later the same day, the credential committee offered a resolution which was adopted by the convention stating that every Negro delegate from the lower south be excluded from the meeting. However, the northern Negro delegates were cordially welcomed by the convention and by Roosevelt.[20] He declared that these Negroes had "won the respect of their communities," and were "the peers of the northern white men"; and that this should serve as a source of inspiration to which the southern Negroes could aspire.

Furthermore, Roosevelt refused to allow the adoption of a resolution demanding equality for Negroes, and a law which guaranteed to protect the Negro's right to vote. This resolution, written by W. E. B. Dubois, who had at first supported Roosevelt's movement, was read at the Chicago convention by Dr. Joel Springram. It stated in part that:

> The Progressive Party recognizes that distinctions of race or class in political life has [sic] no place in a democracy. . . . The [Negro] deserves and must have justice, opportunity and a voice in their own government. The party, therefore, demands for the American of Negro descent the repeal of unfair discriminating laws and the right to vote on the same terms in which others vote.[21]

The defeat of this resolution by Roosevelt drew the ire of the northern Negro delegation. Many threatened to withdraw their support from the party. However, Roosevelt tried to win them back after the convention by having dinner with several Negro Progressives in Rhode Island. However, this simple gesture on his part failed. Moreover, southern newspapers published the story on the eve of the election, declaring that Roosevelt was for social equality between the races, and that he was in opposition to the policy of white supremacy.[22] Notwithstanding these declaration, many southern states had strong and vociferous Progressive party campaigns but made no appeal for the Negro vote.

In the election of 1912, the "Bull Moose" Progressives received 4,127,788 popular votes and 88 electoral votes. The party received nearly 28 percent of the total popular vote, with the highest percentage in any one state coming from South Dakota.[23]

As for Negro support, it is doubtful whether the southern Negroes, after receiving such rough treatment at the national convention, turned out favorably for the party. In the North, many Negroes, especially the militant ones, turned away from the party because of the treatment handed out to their southern brethren. On the whole, although the party did receive some northern and minor southern Negro support,[24] the majority of Negroes tended to vote Democratic.

Roosevelt's shabby treatment of the Negro and his actions in regard to the Negro question caused a race deadline to be drawn in the elections. This grew out of his desire to win, the need of Negro support, and a lack of understanding of the Progressive principles. He saw the party mainly as a vehicle to defeat Taft and to further his own political ambition, and not as an organization for major social reforms.[25] This can easily be seen in his refusal to accept the Progressive nomination in 1916 and in his endorsement of the Republicans.

The Progressives tried again in 1924. This time the party was headed by Robert M. La Follette, former Republican congressman from Wisconsin. His approach to society's problems was mainly pragmatic, and he sought to restore government to the people. La Follette's candidacy and his platform received endorsements from the Socialists, the Railroad Brotherhoods, the Farmer-Labor party, the Non-partisan League and the Executive Committee of the American Federation of Labor.[26] However, even with this varied and numerous support throughout the country, the Progressives' campaign was "conducted under insuperable odds." For instance, La Follette ran on the Farmer-Labor ticket in five states, on the Socialist in six, on the Progressive in forty-five and on the Independent in three states. This ballot confusion aided in deflecting votes and promoting vicious propaganda about him, describing him as a radical.

His campaign also had its effects upon Negro communities both North and South. In 1924 the Negro migration northward had reached tremendous proportions because of the deteriorating conditions in the South. With the meteoric rise of the Negro in the urban centers of the North, and the usurpation of his vote by the political bosses and machines, the Negro vote became a non-Negro vote. It no longer belonged to him but to the political machines. Commenting on this situation, James Weldon Johnson stated that "practically every Negro vote is labeled, sealed, delivered and packed away before every election.... The Republicans felt sure of it and the Democrats don't expect it."[27] Dubois, elaborating further, stated that "the basis of our trouble is that still to a large number of prominent Negroes, politics is simply a method of private gain. They sell their votes," he argued, "their opinion, their influence, and they think that this is what voting means."[28]

Therefore, when the Progressive party appeared in 1924, the Negro was faced with a dire situation. The Republicans had failed to pass the Dyer's anti-lynching bill, and the Democratic party had two wings. The northern wing recognized the Negroes' demands in many of the northern states and treated them with favor and respect. Nationally, however, the southern wing of the party, with its idea of white supremacy, controlled its politics. In addition, both parties at their national conventions had endorsed the Ku Klux Klan.[29] Thus, the NAACP and some Negro leaders urged Negroes, before the Progressive party's National Convention in August, to look to the third party with enthusiasm.[30] Dubois urged, "let the Negroes read with thoughtful care and deep understanding the manifesto of the third party."[31] Other leaders stated that "toward any third party advocates the intelligent Negro must be receptive, hoping they are not enemies, seeking to make them friends and trying to balance the prospects of good will in supporting them."[32] In sum, the Progressive party appeared to many Negro leaders as a way out of their dire situation.[33]

In July of 1924, the Conference for Progressive Political Action met in Cleveland, Ohio and two platforms were issued: one by La Follette and one by the Conference.[34] To this Conference the NAACP sent delegates, among them Oswald Garrison Villard and William Pickens, a brilliant graduate of Yale. These men endeavored to let the convention know that Negroes were interested in the merits of the party rather than in names, slogans and symbols.[35]

During the convention, "there were perhaps some unnecessarily cautious tactics to avoid wrangles over divisive domestic issues, and some very inconceivable efforts on the part of those who managed the convention to carry out preconceived ideas and prearranged programs." But there prevailed an atmosphere of honesty and sincerity.

For instance, it had evidently been decided before the Progressives went to Cleveland not to bring up the Klan issue, because, as it was claimed, such a religious and racial issue might becloud the more essential economic issues.[36] The Progressives there were mindful of the furious fight in the Democratic National Convention over the Klan and actual showdown on the issue was prevented by its exclusion. It was estimated, however, that about 10 percent of the Progressive delegates were favorable to the Klan,[37] but the Socialist wing of the Progressive party was actively and decidedly anti-Klan. It was this wing who, in a separate and subsequent meeting of their own, declared unequivocally against the Klan and in favor of the impartial recognition of Negroes in all labor unions.[38]

On the whole, the National Convention was a contradiction. It addressed itself to all the social, economic and political ills facing the country, except those of the Negro. The party's platform as well as the candidates represented the finest ideas in the American liberal tradition, but the Negro and related issues went unnoticed. Nothing specifically was uttered either at the convention or in the two platforms issued by the convention in regard to the Negro question.[39] When pressed by the

NAACP delegates, the Progressives merely said that "the Negro is an American citizen and is included in all that the Progressives seek for the American citizen." On the other hand, the "four Railroad Brotherhoods which dominated the convention did specifically exclude Negroes from their union rights." La Follette, however, refused to talk straight about the issue or problems.

Therefore, after the convention, Negro leaders and organizations expressed their ideas about the platforms adopted and the party. One observer stated that "La Follette's industrial program will help me as a laborer more than his silence on the Negro problem hurts me." Pickens, a delegate to the convention, felt that the Progressives' omission of the Negro problem from their platform was a blunder in practical politics. He argued that the party could not expect to win the Negro vote, if it knew its power, inclinations, and distribution, without some unmistakable recognition of Negroes in their election campaign.[40] The NAACP stated that La Follette's deliberate dodging of the Klan and the Negro issues was inexcusable. His program, the organization felt, was one of the best programs ever, but even if it were instituted, Negroes would still be disinherited from its benefits. The organization stated that although this had been brought to La Follette's attention, he had remained silent. Therefore, the NAACP concluded that he and his organization had no convictions as to the rights of "black folks."[41]

After such a declaration that the only political strategy left to them was to support their congressional candidates and forget about the presidential election. However, in October, La Follette changed his position regarding the Negro. He attacked the Klan and quoted Abraham Lincoln in defense of the Negro. In addition he also set up a Negro Progressive Bureau.[42] For most Negroes this gesture was one borne of necessity and the desire to win, rather than one of true principles.

Although the Progressives of 1924 received more popular votes than any other third party in history, La Follette's support from Negroes was very small. Negro leaders, such as Bishop Hurst of the New York A.M.E. Church, W.E.B. Dubois, James Weldon Johnson and William Pickens, a La Follette elector, actively and wholeheartedly supported his campaign. However, the majority of Negroes on election day reacted to machine politics.[43] In the following year, La Follette died, and the movement collapsed with his death.

In 1948 another Progressive party attempted to ascend to political power. The support for this movement came from many sectors and segments in the country. Among them were ex-New Dealers, the CIO Political Action Committee groups, a few Negro leaders and members of the American Communist party.[44] These supporters, sympathizers and backers launched a new third party, with Henry A. Wallace accepting the presidential nomination, on December 29, 1947. Senator Glen H. Taylor of Idaho accepted the nomination for the vice-presidency. The third party began to move immediately, and Wallace expressed himself in unequivocal terms on every major issue, including civil rights and civil liberties.

Prior to the acceptance of the Progressive Citizens of American (hereafter, PAC) nomination, Wallace made a tour of the South.[45] In this tour, Wallace defied "Jim Crow" laws and the southern system of segregation in general. Throughout the South he concentrated on the civil-rights issue, speaking to mixed audiences wherever possible. He called for an end to discrimination and unjust treatment of the Negro in the South and in the country as a whole. Southern whites reacted viciously and Wallace suffered many humiliations in trying to advance the cause of Negro equality.[46] He was booed, heckled, and pelted with eggs, but this didn't stop his call for social justice. He retorted by endorsing President Truman's Committee on Civil Rights and its report, "To Secure These Rights." In addition he called for immediate assimilation of the Negro into American society.

Wallace, after accepting the PAC's nomination, placed many Negroes on the executive committee of the party. Among them were Paul Robeson and Charles Howard. In the ranks of his supporters were such outstanding Negroes as Joe Louis, W.E.B. Dubois, A. Philip Randolph, and Walter White. However, Louis, Randolph, and others quit the party in late 1948. Louis, who in the early part of the campaign made contributions to the PAC, shifted on the eve of the election to Thomas Dewey, the Republican nominee.[47] During the early part of the PAC campaign, however, clamor for Negro support and votes came both from Negro leaders who had affiliated with the party and from the party leaders.

The Negro vote in the South, before Wallace's movement, had increased tremendously.[48] The Supreme Court decision of April 3, 1944, in the *Smith* vs. *Allwright* case destroyed the "white primary" system and removed a major obstacle to Negro voting. Since the banning of the white primary in 1944, some "liberal" southerners and some of the indigenous Negro leadership extended a cautious and helping hand to the aspiring Negro electorate. This drive to increase the Negro vote in the South had been largely self-generated, inspired and directed by the indigenous leadership. This combination of Negro leadership and "liberal" southerners had increased the Negro vote in the South to approximately one million by 1948.[49] With this vote the Negro was expected to achieve a miracle. He was "confronted with the problems of weighing the merits of the candidates on the vital issue of civil rights; of determining which candidate could most effectively implement such a program; and of evaluating the political parties and the forces they represent." In other words, the Negro voter in 1948 was faced with a dilemma, and this dilemma was increased by the actions of the Presidential candidates. Governor Dewey had a creditable record of appointment of Negroes to responsible positions, and pushed measures through the New York legislature for fair employment and educational opportunities. President Truman endorsed civil-rights legislation and advocated equality for Negroes. Wallace also endorsed civil-rights legislation and supported Negro candidates in various contests throughout the country. Moreover, he defended the rights of several Negroes in court action, like Rosa Lee Ingram and her two minor sons. She had been convicted of murdering a white tenant farmer and sentenced to death in the electric chair. Wallace's telegram on March 13, 1948, to Governor Thompson of Georgia aided in getting the sentence commuted to life imprisonment.[50] Thus, Wallace, by his militant and uncompromising stand against injustice and inequality, greatly enhanced his status among the Negro voters. Wallace's strong action for Negro rights caused many political forecasters, both white and black, to make vast predictions regarding Wallace and the Negro vote.

Some Negro leaders declared that Wallace would receive more than half (approximately 2 million) of the Negro vote.[51] Others declared that a vote for Wallace would be a futile protest, since his third party could not possibly be elected to implement his proposals and recommendations. White observers stated that "although southern Negroes were glad to see a white man take such a strong stand in their favor, many of their leaders felt that the head-on Wallace approach actually hurt rather than helped race relations. Moreover, there was no point in voting for a sure loser." On the situation in the North, Henry Lee Moon remarked: "In the North, where the black politicans are more integrated into the existing party machinery it is less likely that Mr. Wallace will muster a really substantial Negro vote."[52]

Noting these forecasts, and understanding the difficulties which confronted the Negro in the forties, the issue of discrimination took precedence over all others. Of course, Wallace was concerned with social welfare, anti-inflation, labor, housing legislation, the European Recovery Program and the Marshall Plan. But the elimination of race as a political issue through the attainment of equal rights for all citizens regardless of race, creed, or color was and still is the primary objective. Thus, Wallace appeared, at first, to be the Negro's major choice.

Then, however, President Truman gave his civil-rights program to Congress on February 2, 1948. This caused the southern wing of the Democratic party (Dixiecrats) to revolt. At the same time it gained the loyalty of many Negroes, who began to leave the ranks of the PAC. Moreover, Truman on July 26 established a Committee on Equality of Treatment and Opportunity in the Armed Services and a Fair Employment Practice Board. This caused A. Philip Randolph and Grant Reynolds to publicly call off their defiance-of-the-draft-by-Negroes campaign because they believed in Truman's sincerity to abolish discrimination in the armed services and in the federal government.[53]

This shift in attitude and policy by Truman caused a political shift in the Negro community. The Dixiecrats' revolt over Truman's civil-rights program hurt the Progressives more than it did the Democratic party, in terms of Negro support.[54] Immediately, large numbers of Negro voters realized that they could accomplish more by working and voting for the Democratic party, because it had a much greater possibility of carrying out its promises. Negroes all over the country bolted from the Progressive party ranks. Negro Progressive members like Randolph, White, and Cannon now endorsed the Democratic party. These events marked the beginning of the end for the PAC. Using hindsight, MacDougall claimed that this shift to the left was one of the "smartest, if not *the* smartest" of Truman's political maneuvers.

In the November elections, Wallace polled 1,157,063 popular votes, far below the predicted four million. Final returns from the major centers of Negro populations showed that, in spite of Wallace's concentrated appeal for their votes, Negroes backed Harry Truman as strongly as they had Franklin D. Roosevelt.[55] The national pattern of Negro voting was better than 75 percent in favor of Truman, and 4 percent in favor of Wallace. In the big city Negro wards, like Chicago, Pittsburgh, and Philadelphia, the Negro preference for Truman over Wallace was overwhelming. For example, in Philadelphia, in a district of 131,000 (51 percent Negro), Wallace received only 2,400 Negro votes.[56]

In William Dawson's district in Chicago, where Dawson himself received 92,000 votes, the Progressive party polled only 5,000. In Pittsburgh, only 2 percent of the Negro vote supported Wallace. The practically all-Negro Hill district in Pittsburgh gave Wallace 300, Dewey 3,000, and Truman the remainder of its 9,000 votes.[57] In Harlem, Wallace received 21,000 votes, Dewey 25,000, and Truman 90,000. In the South, Wallace received less than 1,000 Negro votes. On the West Coast the picture was generally the same. Negroes overwhelmingly supported the Democratic party.

The question now arises, why did Negroes fail to support Wallace's Progressive movement which was so strongly pro-Negro? Part of the answer revolves around Truman's strong stand on civil rights. He was the first President, with the possible exception of Lincoln and Roosevelt, who had sought to advance the cause of Negro equality. This, many Negroes felt to be admirable, and they couldn't let him down.

Secondly, since Truman belonged to a major party and Wallace to a minor party, Truman had the best chance of winning. A vote for Wallace would have been a futile and wasted one. The Negro's immediate needs in terms of decent treatment as an American citizen were so great that this fulfillment could not be postponed by protest-voting. Hence, a vote for Truman was the wisest alternative.

Thirdly, the Progressive party failed to handle the Communist issue wisely.[58] Combining the Negro's struggle for equality and the Communists' demands further alienated Negroes.[59] Negroes, both then and now, were trying to achieve their full status as American citizens, and this forced them to be nationalistic. The internationalistic attitude and world outlook of the PAC and the Communists were in conflict with the Negro objectives; furthermore, the Negro wanted to avoid being stigmatized as a Communist because it lessened his chances for full equality. Therefore, the upshot of this analysis is that Negroes were Progressives only because of the party's stand on the race issue and not in terms of general principles. When the Democratic party took a stronger stand on the race question, the Negro voters could easily desert the Progressive ranks. Opportunity drew Negroes to the Progressives; a better opportunity to improve their conditions took them away.

The PAC tried again in 1952 and 1956, but by this time all of its Negro supporters had left the party ranks.[60]

NOTES

1. Moon, *Balance of Power: The Negro Vote* (Garden City, N.Y.: Doubleday, 1949), p. 79.

2. Kirk Porter, *A History of Suffrage in the United States* (Chicago: The University of Chicago Press, 1918), p. 205.

3. Paul Lewinson, *Race, Class and Party* (New York: Oxford University Press, 1932), pp. 20–33.

4. Moon, *op. cit.*, p. 80. See Lewinson, *op. cit.*, Chapter 4.

5. Howard P. Nash, Jr., *Third Parties in American Politics* (Washington, D.C. : Public Affairs Press, 1959), pp. 217–218. See also, William B. Hesseltine, *Third-Party Movements in the U.S.* (New York: Van Nostrand-Reinbold, Anvil, 1962), pp. 67–68.

6. Moon, *op. cit.*, pp. 76–89.

7. Harold Gosnell, *Negro Politicians* (Chicago: University of Chicago Press, 1935), pp. 18–79. See Also Elbert Tatum, *The Changed Political Thought of the Negro, 1915–40*. (New York: Exposition Press, 1951).

8. Arthur S. Link, "The Negro as a factor in the Campaign of 1912," *Journal of Negro History* vol. 32 (January, 1947), p. 88.

9. "Editorial," *Crisis* (November, 1912), p. 29. There were several Negro Leagues and organizations which backed Wilson, like the National Colored Democratic League which

spent $52,256 to sway the northern Negro vote. See "Quo Vadis?," *Crisis* (November, 1912), pp. 44–45.
   10. Link, *op. cit.*, p. 93.
   11. Rayford W. Logan, *The Negro in the U.S.*, (New York: Van Nostrand-Reinhold, Anvil, 1957), p. 60.
   12. James Haynes, "Why the Negro Should be a Progressive," *Crisis* (November, 1912), p. 42. See also "The Negro Delegates," *Nation* (June 20, 1912), p. 606.
   13. Logan, *The Negro in the U.S.*, *op. cit.*, p. 61.
   14. Link, *op. cit.*, p. 94.
   15. A.S. Link (ed.), "Correspondence Relating to the Progressive Party's 'Lily-White' Policy in 1912," *Journal of Southern History*, vol. 10 (November, 1944), pp. 481–483.
   16. George Mowry, "The South and the Progressive Lily White Party in 1912," *Journal of Southern History*, vol. 6, 1940, p. 237.
   17. Link (ed.), "Correspondence . . . ," *op. cit.*, p. 482.
   18. Mowry, *op. cit.*, p. 242.
   19. Jane Addams, "The Progressive Party and the Negro," *Crisis* (November, 1912), p. 30.
   20. *Ibid.*
   21. "Quo Vadis?," *op. cit.*, p. 45.
   22. A.S. Link, "Theodore Roosevelt and the South in 1912," *North Carolina Historical Review*, vol. 23 (July, 1946), pp. 313–14.
   23. Svend Petersen, *A Statistical History of American Presidential Elections* (New York: Frederick Ungar, 1963), pp. 78–79.
   24. Link, "Negro as a Factor in the Campaign. . . . ," *op. cit.*, p. 98.
   25. Hesseltine, *Rise and Fall of Third Parties* (Gloucester, Mass.: Peter Smith, 1957), p. 23.
   26. Kenneth MacKay, *The Progressive Movement of 1924* (New York: Octagon Books, Inc., 1966), pp. 11–12.
   27. *Ibid.*
   28. "Editorial," *Crisis* (September, 1924), p. 200. See also James Weldon Johnson, "The Gentlemen's Agreement and the Negro Vote," *Crisis* (October, 1924), p. 260.
   29. MacKay, *op. cit.*, pp. 214–216.
   30. "Editorial," *Crisis* (August, 1924), p. 151, 153.
   31. *Ibid.*
   32. *Ibid.*
   33. *Ibid.*
   34. Kirk Porter and D.B. Johnson, *National Party Platforms 1840–1964* (Urbana: University of Illinois Press, 1966), p. 243.
   35. MacKay, *op. cit.*, pp. 217–218.
   36. William Pickens, "The Progressives' Political Action," *Crisis* (September, 1924), p. 211.
   37. *Ibid.*
   38. *Ibid.*
   39. Porter and Johnson, *op. cit.*, pp. 252–256.
   40. Pickens, *op. cit.*, p. 211.
   41. "Editorial," *Crisis* (August, 1924), p. 154.
   42. "Editorial," *Crisis* (October, 1924), p. 247.
   43. MacKay, *op. cit.*, p. 218.
   44. Karl M. Schmidt, *Henry A. Wallace: Quixotic Crusader, 1948* (Syracuse: Syracuse University Press, 1960), p. 5.

45. Curtis D. MacDougall, *Gideon's Army*, vol. 1 (New York: Marzani & Munsell, 1965), pp. 220-224.
46. "The South Gets Rough with Wallace," *Life* (September 13, 1948), pp. 33-35.
47. "Political Notes," *Time* (November 1, 1948), p. 24.
48. Henry Lee Moon, "The Negro in Politics," *New Republic* (October 18, 1948), p. 9.
49. *Ibid.*
50. MacDougall, *op. cit.*, vol. II, p. 389.
51. Daniel James, "Cannon the Progressive," *New Republic* (October 18, 1948), p. 14.
52. Moon, "The Negro in Politics," *op. cit.*, p. 9.
53. MacDougall, *op. cit.*, vol. II, p. 386.
54. Schmidt, *op. cit.*, p. 244.
55. "The Negro Prefers Truman," *New Republic* (November 22, 1948), p. 8.
56. *Ibid.*
57. *Ibid.*
58. Samuel W. William, "The People's Progressive Party of Georgia," *Phylon* (Third Quarter, 1949), p. 229. This account by William, a Negro party member, is more opinionated than factual, but is nevertheless illuminating.
59. Wilson Record, *The Negro and the Communist Party* (Chapel Hill: The University of North Carolina Press, 1951), p. 251.
60. Hesseltine, *Third-Party Movements in the U.S., op. cit.*, p. 95.

6

Minority Politics in Black Belt Alabama

Charles V. Hamilton

A COUNTY IN FLUX

IN 1960, THERE WERE nine Negroes for every white person in Macon County, Alabama. No Negro had ever held public office in the county; and, prior to 1954, no Negro had ever filed for such an office. For decades, Negroes had accepted political dominance by the whites. The smooth-working accommodation system conformed to the pattern many felt had been advocated by Booker T. Washington, the Negro founder of Tuskegee Institute. Whether this is an accurate representation of Washington's position is not important. The central point is that many—both Negroes and whites—believed it to be.

At exactly what point the opposition to the status quo began to form is difficult to say, but several events took place in the 1930s and 1940s that served as a forecast of things to come. One active Negro leader, who had been on the faculty of Tuskegee Institute for over 25 years, stated: "Booker T. Washington came to teach the Negroes how to make a living. I came to teach them how to live." This idea of "how to live" meant a definite change in the status quo; it meant full participation in the political and civic affairs of the community in addition to obtaining a formal education, buying a home and painting the fence. One white citizen stated that the real trouble started in 1944 when the college discontinued the practice of reserving special seats in the college chapel for the white townspeople.

During the early 1940s, getting registered was not easy although no great number of Negroes attempted to do so. One Negro theorized that

---

Minority Politics in Black Belt Alabama by Charles V. Hamilton, published as a Case Study by the Eagleton Institute of Politics, reprinted by permission of the author and the publisher.

the white officials did not want to give the Negroes the impression that registering to vote was a simple matter, because "it might give the Negroes funny ideas." The difficulties encountered gave some Negroes ideas of pursuing legal action. In 1945, William P. Mitchell, a Negro employee of the Veterans Administration Hospital, brought a suit in the federal district court alleging that he had been denied the right to register because of his race in violation of the Fourteenth Amendment to the United States Constitution. Mitchell lost the case on the lower level, but the appellate court reversed the decision. The case was finally dismissed in November, 1947, after a photostatic copy of Mitchell's registration certificate was "found" and presented to the court. The certificate was dated January 20, 1943, two and one-half years before the initial filing of the suit and after the case had been in the courts for over two years.

Throughout the 1940s and 1950s, Negroes found their way to the county courthouse to make application for voter certificates. Slowly the rolls increased. In 1940, there were approximately 29 qualified Negro voters, 115 in 1946, 514 in 1950, and 855 in 1954. A clear trend had been established that could result in political catastrophe for the white political officials if allowed to continue. Notwithstanding that the board of registrars became inoperative on January 16, 1956, and did not function again publicly until June 3, 1957, the number of registered Negroes had increased to 1,110 by January 1, 1959.

Many could easily see that political control of the city and the county was at stake. Approximately 1,800 Negroes were employed either at the federal Veterans Administration Hospital or at the private college, Tuskegee Institute. Their jobs required educational attainments above the average educational level of most Alabamians—white or Negro. There was erupting in some areas in the South a social revolution caused by the emergence of what some observers referred to as a "new Negro" who appeared to be the product of a combination of four factors: numerical strength, economic independence, educational ability, and a new sense of civic awareness and desire for civic participation.

Quite often the Negro leaders of the Tuskegee Civic Association (TCA), the local Negro political interest group, stated that they had no intention of establishing a "black oligarchy" any more than they intended to continue to live under a white one. This did nothing to calm the fears of those in power. The local whites were faced with the possibility of losing political power to a minority race that found itself in the unusual position of being, in fact, a majority. The whites would not relinquish their power positions, and the Negroes were giving increased evidence that they intended to share at least some of that power. The issue was clearly drawn.

Deprived of the ability to use the weapons of fear and economic reprisal, the white political officials in Macon County have relied on the delaying tactics of the county board of registrars or the complete inoperation of the board for long periods at a time to prevent the number of Negro voters from increasing. From January, 1959, to May, 1960, the county was without a board of registrars, the result of simultaneous resignations of the board members on December 10, 1958. For nearly eighteen months, no citizens could become registered voters.

THE REGISTRARS RESIGN

The resignation of two members of the Macon County Board of Registrars on December 10, 1958, (the third member had died in November, 1958), followed on the heels of hearings held in Montgomery, Alabama, on December 8 and 9 by the United States Commission on Civil Rights. The Commission had subpoenaed 27 Negroes from Macon County and three Macon County officials: Probate Judge William Varner and Registrars Grady P. Rogers and E. P. Livingston.

The Negroes testified on December 8 that they had made unsuccessful attempts to register. All the Negroes concluded their testimony by stating —upon questioning by the Commission—that they felt they were being denied the right to register because they were Negroes. The Commission called Judge Varner to testify. John Patterson, governor-elect then Alabama attorney general, served as counsel for the local officials. Judge Varner had received a subpoena from the Commission to appear and to bring certain records pertaining to the registration of qualified voters of Macon County. Patterson advised Varner that he should not remove the records from the Probate Office and that if agents of the Civil Rights Commission wanted to examine any records, they must do so in the office of the Probate Judge. Judge Varner brought the records, however.

On December 4, 1958, Grady P. Rogers received a subpoena to appear and to bring all records containing denials of registration and notice of such denials for all applicants denied registration for the years 1956, 1957, and 1958. Rogers stated that he did not have the records because they had been "impounded" by the County Solicitor of the Circuit Court. The action of the county solicitor was taken on December 8. Rogers refused to answer any questions relating to the registration of whites or Negroes in Macon County. His refusal was based on the grounds that his answers might tend to incriminate him and that he was a judicial officer and not subject to inquiry. The other registrar, E. P. Livingston, gave the same answer. Both refused to take the oath before the Commission.

The following day, December 10, 1958, Rogers and Livingston sent a joint letter to Governor James E. Folsom stating that they were resigning their positions as registrars for Macon County. They said they were doing so because they were being intimidated by the federal authorities.

GOVERNOR PATTERSON AND THE *TCA*

John Patterson was inaugurated Governor of Alabama on January 18, 1959. Many Negroes in Tuskegee felt that the Patterson administration would be one of the most racist-minded in Alabama's history. During his campaign for the governorship, he had repeatedly asserted that public school desegregation would not occur in Alabama during his term of office. He firmly avowed to close the public schools rather than integrate them. Patterson had announced that he would not invite the marching bands of the state Negro schools to participate in the inaugural parade, as had been the usual practice. He explained that he felt his record and his stand against the National Association for the Advancement of Colored People (NAACP) in Alabama would embarrass the Negroes. (Patterson had been attorney general at the time of the state suit against the Alabama NAACP seeking an injunction to halt its activities in the state.)

The attitude of many Tuskegee Negroes was further supported by the defeat Patterson suffered as a result of his previous contact with the Tuskegee Civic Association.

The TCA was a predominantly Negro organization (there were a few white members, none residents of Macon County) that had been engaged in local civic activities for more than twenty years. The membership of the group prior to 1957 never exceeded 200. It had the respect of the Negroes in the community, but it never had a mass base. Its major concern over the years has been to persuade Negroes to register and vote. For years the TCA held monthly meetings which were often attended by only ten to twenty persons. These meetings were essentially educational, devoted to discussion of such topics as "The Duties of Citizenship" and "The Duties of County Officials."

On June 25, 1957, when the Alabama Legislature was considering a bill to gerrymander all but ten Negro voters out of the city of Tuskegee (the bill was passed on July 13, 1957),[1] the TCA held a meeting which was attended by approximately 3,000 persons. At this meeting, the President of the TCA, Charles G. Gomillion, also a member of the faculty of Tuskegee Institute, called upon the persons present to "spend our money wisely," to "spend our money with those who would help us, not oppress us." This was, in effect, calling for an economic boycott of the white merchants in Tuskegee. A boycott as such was illegal in the state, so the word itself was never used.

On July 25, 1957, the TCA office was searched by state officials led by John Patterson. A second "raid" on the TCA offices was held on July 29, 1957. On August 15, Patterson obtained a temporary injunction against the TCA forbidding intimidation and coercion of customers of Tuskegee merchants. The restraining order was issued by the Fifth Judicial Circuit Court of Macon County. In the final disposition of the case on June 21, 1958, the same court held for the TCA, stating: "Thus far in this land, every person has a right to trade with whomever he pleases, and, therefore, the right not to trade with any particular person or business." In what was an unprecedented move, Negro attorneys for the TCA called John Patterson to testify, and many Negroes felt that this action personally insulted Patterson. The attitude of many Negro witnesses was one of great self-confidence in the face of examination by Patterson. During a recess in the sessions, one Negro woman went to Patterson and stated in a very audible tone that "some day there will be an attorney general for all the people of Alabama." After the decision, many Negroes expressed the feeling that "we really showed Patterson this time," and "if he ever gets to be governor, the TCA had better watch out."

This was the man to whom the TCA appealed to appoint a board of registrars beginning in January, 1959.

THE VOTER FRANCHISE COMMITTEE

The job of trying to get a new board for the county was conducted specifically by the Voter Franchise Committee (hereafter referred to as the committee) of the TCA under the chairmanship of William P. Mitchell. Mitchell was also executive secretary of the TCA. These functions occupied his spare time, for he was also a physical therapist at the Veterans Hospital. He had a reputation for being an exceptionally meticulous and tireless worker for the TCA. Most of the organization's voluminous correspondence received his personal attention.

Mitchell worked closely with Daniel Beasley, a long-time member of the committee and also an employee at the hospital. Beasley was a native of Macon County and was said to be the most popular employee at the hospital. He had the reputation of knowing virtually every one in Macon County, white and Negro, which was probably only a slight exaggeration. These characteristics later proved invaluable in obtaining signatures for petitions.

Mitchell and Beasley had worked together for years in getting Negroes to make applications for voter certificates. They conducted clinics in the TCA office to acquaint individuals with the three-page "voter registration questionnaire."[2] They kept records from 1951 of every Negro who appeared at the registrar's office, the number admitted, and the amount of time needed for each to complete the application. They either appeared personally or had some one stationed in the courthouse to record this information at every meeting of the board of registrars, as well as the time the board started work, the length of time it remained in session, and the days it was supposed to meet but did not. They subsequently checked on each individual to see if a certificate had been issued.

In this way, they were able to compile a detailed, seven-year record of Negro voter-registration in Macon County that was presented to the Civil Rights Commission. They were able to show that during the seven-year period, 1951 to 1958, 1,585 applications for voter certificates were made by Negroes. Only 510 certificates were issued—32 percent. They were able to show that for the 12½ year period prior to December 1, 1958, Macon County was without a board of registrars for three years and four months. All of this was largely a two-man operation. Between the two of them—Mitchell and Beasley—they knew all but a handful of the 1,110 Negro voters of Macon County as of January 1, 1959.

There were eight other members of the committee, but since there was no board of registrars, their work was reduced to a minimum. Mitchell continued to call monthly meetings of the committee at which he would review the month's work, receive suggestions and occasionally assign tasks to a few members. In the final analysis, virtually all the TCA business was handled by Mitchell, especially in Gomillion's absence. (Gomillion was on leave of absence from the Tuskegee faculty until September, 1959 to complete his graduate studies.)

STATE LAW: ". . . THE GOVERNOR . . . SHALL MAKE OTHER APPOINTMENTS . . ."

A few days after the board members resigned, Mitchell decided to write Governor Folsom asking him to appoint a new board of registrars of Macon County. Folsom had only a month remaining in office, and Mitchell felt that Patterson would "not be in a hurry" to appoint a new board. In addition, Folsom had been a much more liberal governor than Patterson was expected to be, and Mitchell stated that Folsom had always received a large number of Negro votes. Folsom might be inclined to appoint a board out of gratitude to the Negro voters or, which was more likely, in anticipation of running again for the governorship in 1962. The letter was written, but no answer was received from Folsom.

During the second week in January, 1959, Mitchell raised the question of the possibility of "making" Patterson appoint a board of registrars. The Alabama statute read:

> If one or more of the persons appointed on such board of registration shall refuse, neglect, or be unable to qualify or serve, or if a vacancy or vacancies occur in the membership of the board of registrars from any cause, the governor, auditor and commissioner of agriculture and industries, or a majority of them acting as a board of appointment, shall make other appointments to fill such board.

As far as was known, there was no precedent for a suit under this statute, and the courts might construe this duty of the state officials as discretionary. Mitchell was not convinced. He thought there might be a possibility of obtaining a writ of mandamus against the state board of appointment if it refused to appoint a board of registrars in "a reasonable time." The word "shall" in the statute stuck in his mind and he was to return to this tactic some months later.

PETITIONS AND LETTERS

The detailed data presented to the Civil Rights Commission made an impression on the Commission investigators; but, above all, the TCA was further convinced of the necessity for record-keeping in "building a case." Now, since there was no board, Mitchell decided to make a record of the systematic attempts to have one appointed. No one thought these efforts would bring direct, and certainly not immediate, results in terms of the appointment of a board, but this was to be all part of the process of "documenting" a case against the state officials. In addition to this, Mitchell and another member of the TCA's executive cabinet had appeared before twelve United States Senators in Washington, D.C., on July 30, 1957, to testify to the efforts made by Negroes in the county to become enfranchised. The Senate was considering a civil rights bill at that time. On August 28, 1957, Senator Paul Douglas wrote Mitchell: "It will be helpful . . . if civic-minded persons like yourself will continue to assemble the facts that will help to make the case for the next forward step. The final bill is better than seemed possible three weeks ago."

The second week in January, 1959, Mitchell and Beasley drew up a petition to be sent to the Governor and the other two members of the state appointing board. The petition, containing the signatures and addresses of twelve unregistered Negro citizens of Macon County, urged the state appointing board to appoint a board of registrars so the Negroes might register. Each person signed four copies: one was sent to the Governor, one to the commissioner of agriculture and industries, one to the state auditor, and one was kept in the TCA files. The copy to the Governor was sent by certified mail.

The first petitions were sent on January 20, 1959 in order to reach Patterson's desk the morning of his first day in office, January 21, 1959. Mitchell was careful not to mail them too soon, because he feared that Patterson could say he received them before he was officially governor of the state. Mitchell was assured from years of experience that such attention to detail was absolutely necessary in dealing with most Alabama officials. Shortly after the original idea of the petition came up, Beasley conceived the idea of sending the petitions each week with twelve different signatures until a functioning board had been appointed.

The petitions read the same:

We the undersigned residents of Macon County, Alabama respectfully request you, the Commissioner of Agriculture and Industries and the State Auditor, to appoint a board of registrars for Macon County in order that we may register as voters in said county.

The majority of the signatures throughout the year were secured by Beasley and another member of the committee, Frank Bentley. Virtually all the signers were employed either at the hospital or the college, and thus were safe from economic reprisals by the whites. (Most of the faculty of Tuskegee Institute supported the program and work of the TCA as dues paying members—one dollar per year—but there were only four on the nineteen-member executive cabinet and only one on the Voter Franchise Committee.) Beasley carried a set of petitions with him at all times, and obtaining twelve signers a week was not difficult. He would stop persons at the local Negro-owned drug store or supermarket. An occasional announcement was made at the weekly mass meetings, and this would result in several signatures, but no attempt was ever made to secure a large number of signatures at any one time by setting up a booth or by setting aside a specific time when individuals could come to the TCA office. When this suggestion was made, it was considered but not adopted. Some members of the committee felt it would be too cumbersome and might result in repeating signatures. As the months wore on, some of the signers, to Beasley's knowledge, did repeat as many as three and four times.

Along with the first set of petitions, Mitchell wrote Patterson urging him to appoint a board. Copies of the letter were sent to the state auditor and the commissioner of agriculture and industries.

When the Civil Rights Commission had begun its investigations in the fall of 1958, one of the main questions asked was whether Negro citizens had complained to the attorney general of Alabama. This had never been done. It was known that Attorney General Macdonald Gallion was Patterson's close associate and nothing would result from such action, but, again, it was a matter of "building a record." Fifteen local, unregistered Negro citizens were contacted by the TCA and asked to write Gallion urging him to investigate the denial of their right to vote in Macon County. The TCA was careful not to compose the letters. The individuals were to use their own stationery and their own language. In each instance, the person stated that he or she had attempted to register and had been unsuccessful and felt this failure to be registered was on account of race.

Gallion answered most of the letters, and his response was much the same in all instances:

January 23, 1959

This acknowledges receipt of your letter dated January 20, 1959 (postmarked 7:30 A.M. January 19, 1959), in which you make complaint of being denied voter registration in Macon County. This matter will receive the proper attention of this office.

To the knowledge of the committee, no investigations were ever made, and the fifteen persons were never contacted by the attorney general's office after the letters of acknowledgment.

Mitchell recalled past experience when a board had been appointed but no public announcement was made. As a result, the Negroes were not aware that a board of registrars had been functioning.[3] To guard against this, Mitchell asked a committee member to write the secretary of state, Mrs. Bettye Frink, asking her for the names of the members of the Macon County Board of Registrars. The Alabama statutes require the office of the secretary of state to keep such information. The thinking was that Patterson might have appointed a new board and simply had it recorded but not announced. The writer of the letter was not to identify himself with the TCA. On February 12, 1959, the following reply was received:

I have for acknowledgment your request for the names of the current members of the Macon County Board of Registrars. The records of this office do not disclose any resignations by any Members of the Macon County Board of Registrars nor any other change in that Board.

Yours truly, Bettye Frink, Secretary of State

This caused a great deal of concern among the committee members. At that time, the United States Justice Department had an injunction suit against Grady P. Rogers and E. P. Livingston and the state of Alabama under the provisions of the Civil Rights Act of 1957. The suit was attempting to enjoin the denial of the right to vote to Negroes in Macon

County on account of race. The main defense was that Rogers and Livingston had resigned, and the 1957 act permitted suits only against individuals, not against the state. The defendants argued that inasmuch as the board members had resigned, there was no one against whom a suit could be brought. Mitchell immediately sent a photostatic copy of the Frink letter to the Justice Department.

It was not known why Mrs. Frink had answered the letter in this way. She was a 25-year-old Birmingham housewife who was a political novice, but this was no acceptable explanation. Mitchell and Beasley stated that the women state officials had always been more responsive to TCA communications in the past. At any rate, the decision was made not to give the letter much publicity at the time in hope that a favorable relationship could be cultivated with Mrs. Frink in the future. Although she was not a member of the state appointing board, the TCA was always enthusiastic about receiving any kind of response from Montgomery.

Meanwhile, the weekly petitions continued, and Mitchell continued to make written requests of the Governor and the other two members of the appointing board. None of these was acknowledged.

In February, 1959, Mitchell decided to write the former registrar, Grady P. Rogers, who was the newly elected state representative for Macon County. The letter was sent by certified mail, and it had a "Tuskegee Civic Association" return address. It was returned marked "Refused."

After several weeks of this type of activity, some members of the committee became somewhat impatient. It was understood that Patterson would probably not deal with the complaints, but some Negroes were becoming increasingly concerned with the need for new tactics to "smoke him out." At this point, the possibility of a mass march on the state capitol was suggested. One member of the committee felt this would at least produce good newspaper coverage and compel Patterson to respond. Patterson had made very few public statements about the Macon County registrars situation and no statements whatsoever about the demands being made by the TCA. It was believed that Patterson would probably not respond unless he was faced with masses of Negroes camped on his doorsteps. There had been other mass meetings held by Negroes on the steps of the capitol building, and these meetings had received wide press coverage. A mass march would further help to publicize the registration stalemate, and, in view of the official silence confronting the TCA, extensive publicity of the Negroes' grievances could be a useful weapon. Mitchell gave the idea considerable thought, and it was discussed for several days afterward.

The idea was finally tabled. Another member of the TCA executive cabinet stated later that this was a form of action that the TCA did not condone. "Ours is not a mass action group," she said. "We just don't operate like that."

As an alternative, Mitchell suggested that a letter be sent to the Governor and the other two members of the appointing board requesting a conference with them. On May 11, 1959, the following letter was sent to Patterson, with copies to the state auditor, Mrs. Mary Texas Hurt Garner, and to the commissioner of agriculture and industries, R. C. Bamberg:

> This comes to request a conference with you and the other members of the state board of appointment regarding the matter of securing a board of registrars for Macon County. As you know, this county has been without a publicly functioning board of registrars since December, 1958. Please communicate with us as to your date of choice regarding a conference concerning this vital matter.

No answer was received, and two weeks later, Mitchell wrote Mrs. Garner and Bamberg by certified mail requesting a conference. Again, there was no response to these communications.

A COURT DECISION

On March 6, 1959, United States District Judge Frank Johnson, Jr., ruled against the federal government in the Justice Department's injunction suit against Rogers, Livingston, and the state. The suit charged that the disparity between the percentages of white and Negro voters in Macon County was "being perpetuated by racially discriminatory acts and practices" of the registrars who applied "different and more stringent standards" to Negro applicants. It named twelve college graduates and eight high school graduates the registrars refused to certify because of race or color. Governor Patterson called the suit "another example of the reprehensible and irresponsible attitude that the present administration in Washington is taking toward the states and state officials."

The court ruled that the two defendant-registrars had resigned in "good faith" and that neither a memberless board of registrars nor the state of Alabama constituted a "person" within the meaning of the Civil Rights Act of 1957. After dismissing the suit, Judge Johnson promptly warned registrars that the court would not "sanction the proposition . . . that registrars are free to resign at will, indiscriminately and in bad faith, and thereby cast off all their responsibilities."

The Justice Department appealed the case to the United States Fifth Circuit Court of Appeals and, because of a bill then pending in the Alabama Legislature to permit boards of registrars to destroy voting records, immediately sought an injunction prohibiting destruction of records pertaining to the twenty Macon County Negroes named in the suit. The request was denied, but the purpose was accomplished through the court's proviso that the state of Alabama give written assurance that these records would be preserved. Attorney General Gallion provided that assurance. A hearing on the suit was held in New Orleans in May, 1959, before the Court of Appeals, and the lower court's ruling was upheld. The Justice Department then appealed to the United States Supreme Court.

In the meantime, Judge Johnson's words rekindled a thought in Mitchell's mind—that of the possibility of bringing a mandamus action against the state appointing board. Perhaps, he thought, if it was possible to show that the failure to appoint a board was an act of bad faith, the court would compel the appointment of a board. Mitchell, and later Beasley who agreed with him, knew that Judge Johnson was talking about the act of resignation of board members and not the act of appointing a board, but this was a distinction without a difference. The idea was only dormant; it was not dead.

NEGROES SEEK APPOINTMENTS

On February 15, 1959, the *Birmingham News* carried a page one story entitled: "No One Wants to Serve—Macon Registrars Jobs Go Begging." The story read:

The state senator who represents Macon County says the current breakdown in voter registration machinery in Macon County may go on for months to come.

If that happens, no prospective new voter, white or Negro, can be registered unless perhaps he can get a court order to do it.

Veteran Senator L. K. Andrews, grimly apprehensive over the outcome, said the recent intervention of federal authorities has left white residents of the county more reluctant than ever before to serve on the Board of Registrars. And there's little likelihood that the three state officials who appoint the registrars would ever consider putting Negroes in the job.

"We'll have trouble getting people to serve," the legislator predicted. "I haven't had a single person ask me to help get him appointed since I was elected the last time. But by contrast I had numerous requests the first time."

The TCA set out immediately to remedy this situation. A meeting of the committee was held to discuss the best methods to persuade individuals to apply for positions on the board. It was known that in all likelihood no Negroes would be appointed, but the decision was made to ask

Negroes to apply notwithstanding. Then there was a lengthy discussion on the possibility of getting white citizens to apply.

As far as Negro applicants were concerned, the committee decided to seek persons who had been long-time residents of the county, either businessmen or retired persons, so there would be no question of their availability in terms of time off from work to serve. No persons on the hospital staff or employed by the college were considered. A list was drawn up and narrowed to six Negroes. All were registered voters who had been in the community for over twenty years and who had reputations as good, solid citizens. Mitchell arranged a meeting at the TCA office.

The prospective candidates were briefed on the reason for calling them together. Mitchell told them of the efforts to obtain a functioning board, a story he was to tell often and with much pride. They were informed of the need to have qualified persons apply for appointment. Every one immediately agreed to offer to serve on the board, but no one entertained the slightest expectation of appointment. One lady asked if she should admit that the TCA asked her to apply. This was discussed, and it was finally agreed that no criminal act was being performed, that there was no coercion, and it would be quite proper, should the matter come up, to state the facts. Notwithstanding this, it was agreed not to use TCA stationery (the letters might be refused again), and each letter was to be composed in the individual's own words.

All the letters were relatively short, stating that the person had been a qualified voter in Macon County for a certain number of years, either self-employed or retired, and would like to be considered for appointment to the Macon County Board of Registrars. No indication of race was given. Some of them indicated they believed in democracy, in "good government," and they would like this opportunity to be of public service. One letter referred to the news story of telling of the difficulty in finding persons to serve. All the letters were addressed to Patterson as chairman of the state appointing board, and they were sent by certified mail. Copies were sent to the other members of the appointing board.

Mitchell once again emphasized that while their action would probably not result in their appointment, this was all part of the process of refuting the claim that sincere efforts were being made by the state officials to appoint a board. It would further document the injustices encountered by Negro citizens in Macon County. Even though none ultimately expected to be appointed, several of them experienced excitement. Two persons admitted afterward that they had never written to a governmental official before, and it was "high time our people spoke up." The question of qualifications was raised, and one man in his late sixties quickly answered: "If Rogers is qualified, then we all are." The persons were assured that the nature of the duties did not, in the least, require extensive specialized training, only a normal intelligence. They all agreed to contact the TCA if and as soon as any response was forthcoming. There was an agreement not to publicize immediately the fact that these individuals had offered their services, but to wait and see what, if anything, resulted. Over a year later, in May, 1960, none of the applicants had been contacted.

WHITE CITIZEN OFFERS TO SERVE

Persuading white persons to apply for positions was obviously far different from and much more difficult than approaching Negroes. The thinking was that Patterson and the appointing board would probably not consider a white citizen unless this individual agreed not to alter drastically the status quo. So, if the committee approached a white citizen who agreed to register all citizens fairly, this would automatically kill his chances of being appointed. There was no doubt that, of the approximately 3,081 white persons in Macon County, at least two could be found who would be acceptable to the TCA, but the committee could not run the risk of asking persons whose views were largely unknown to it. Mitchell felt that if Patterson was at all inclined to appoint a particular white citizen, he would certainly not do so if he discovered that this person had been asked by the TCA to serve. Notwithstanding this, at least it would contribute to the "case we are building."

The situation in Tuskegee was such that even Beasley felt it virtually unthinkable to ask a white person to volunteer. Whatever working relationships he had developed before were nonexistent now. The "boycott" of white merchants made it very unlikely that any white businessman would consent to serve. Or, if he did, it was thought the price he might ask would be the end of the "boycott." The TCA was not willing to consider this.

The decision was reached to exert an effort to enlist white applicants living outside Tuskegee proper. One of the members of the committee who lived in the rural area of the county volunteered to contact a white citizen in his district whom he knew. For purposes of protection of the citizen, his name would not be made known even to the rest of the members of the committee. When it was discussed, the committee member who knew him said: "I think I can talk to him, and I think he would do it. He's been fair all along." The committee realized the possible consequences if it became known that a white person had been "fair all along." By itself, this was not dangerous, but, combined with the further intention to register Negroes without regard to race, it could be, some felt, quite damaging.

The committee member agreed to make the contact and report. A few days later, he brought the message: "He said he would."

Meanwhile, Beasley had approached a white grocer in the rural section of the county. This person had also agreed to apply and had asked Beasley to draw up a letter for him to sign. Immediately, a brief letter was written to the Governor offering to serve on the board of registrars. The letter indicated that the applicant was white and a grocery store owner in the county. It was felt that the mention of race would have weight at this point, but some Negroes were beginning to think that Patterson did not intend to appoint anyone to the board, white or black. But at least there were two white applicants.

A few days later, Beasley brought a set of petitions to the TCA office and stated that, unfortunately, the grocer had decided "not to have anything to do with it after all." Beasley said that the man "really was not prejudiced," but apparently felt he should not become involved. The committee was disappointed, but it still had the other promise.

At a committee meeting shortly afterwards, the report on the other white citizen was: "He said he did." It is not known if he was ever contacted, and several subsequent appointments did not include his name.

MASS MEETINGS

The TCA had been holding weekly Tuesday evening mass meetings since June 25, 1957. At first, these meetings served as a gathering place to hear about the "boycott." Inspirational speeches were made and the meetings were normally attended by 600 to 800 people. The various churches in the community were used as meeting places.

In January, 1959, the meetings were still being held, but attendance had dropped considerably. Instead of hundreds, the average meeting attracted from forty to sixty people, though attendance improved on a night when a noted speaker was scheduled.

The efforts to get a board of registrars were not dramatic enough, and many people could not identify personally with these efforts. As one Negro said: "Well, Mitchell and you all are handling that. There's nothing I can do right now but stay away from town, and I'm doing that." Announcements were made at the meetings of the work of the committee during the previous week, and Mitchell would ask unregistered persons who had not done so to sign the petitions.

The meetings gradually became less protest-oriented and came more and more to resemble lecture sessions. Eventually, the TCA began to refer to them frequently as "civic education meetings." Because of the very heavy religious influence in the community, some of the Tuesday evening gatherings, expecially when ministers were the principal speakers, appeared to be little different from Sunday morning church services. Each meeting was preceded by a half-hour devotional service, and a majority of the times a church choir furnished music. Occasionally, no reference was made to the work of the committee. An effort was made to have the meetings take on more characteristics of political rallies, but in vain.

BIRTH OF A BILL

One morning in May, 1959, Mitchell called a committee member at 7:30, a frequent practice. Usually he called to ask him to write letters or to do something at the TCA office, but on that morning he sounded more anxious. "I think we've overlooked something," he stated. "I think we should write Sparkman and Hill and Andrews." (These were the two Alabama Senators and Representative in the United States Congress.) He asked that letters be drafted setting forth the efforts the committee had made to reach the state officials and asking the assistance of the congressmen. Mitchell thought that one of them might attempt to persuade Patterson that the Macon County situation did not present Alabama in the best light nationally. Again, this was not done with any high expectations, but inasmuch as letters were being written, the United States Senators and Representative might as well be included on the list.

Replies came promptly. Hill wrote:

I have your letter of the 16th and in reply thereto let me say that the State Board of Appointment is established under the laws of the State of Alabama. The Board therefore derives its authority from the laws of the State of Alabama and operates under the laws and jurisdiction of the State of Alabama.
As a United States Senator, I have no voice or authority in the administration of State laws and the State Board of Appointment.

Sparkman replied:

I have your letter of May 16 regarding the Macon County Board of Registrars. As you know, this Board is set up under the laws of the State of Alabama. Accordingly, its membership, organization, and operation are controlled by state law. As a United States Senator, I have no authority in connection with the administration of the laws of Alabama.

Representative George Andrews did not answer.

Shortly after the responses from Hill and Sparkman, one committee member suggested to Mitchell that the TCA launch a nationwide campaign for a federal law regulating registration and voting. It was quite clear by this time that there were not going to be any major results on the state level. The decision was made to obtain 2,000 signatures on petitions urging Congress to pass a federal law regulating voter registration. The TCA would draft a proposed bill and submit it for consideration, and the committee planned to tie in its efforts on the local level with this new drive. Now would be the time to start revealing the case against Alabama. The state officials had been given their chance. Now the TCA would release all information to show the Congress and the nation the true injustices in black belt Alabama. From this point on, the TCA took on new life and, in a real sense, new meaning.

The petition read:

We, the undersigned, as citizens of these United States of America, in view of:

1. the many years of denials of the constitutional right to vote to many American citizens because of their race and color, and
2. the various and devious tactics employed by many local officials, especially in some southern states, to prevent the registration of potential voters on account of race and color, and
3. the failure of several southern state officials to remedy this situation, notwithstanding repeated and persistent requests from local citizens to have them do so, and
4. the great likelihood that such denials, tactics and state inaction will continue indefinitely, and
5. the fact that voting is one of the most basic of all constitutional rights, the absence of which weakens our nation as a representative democracy, do respectfully petition the Congress of the United States to give thorough consideration to and to pass an effective federal law regulating voter-registration.

At the mass meeting of May 26, 1959, Mitchell announced the plans. Fortunately, there was an exceptionally large audience because a noted Negro attorney from Montgomery and one of the leaders in the Montgomery bus boycott, Fred Gray, was the speaker. One hundred petitions had been mimeographed with space for 56 signatures. Each person was to sign three copies. The plan was to send one copy to Senator Paul Douglas, one to Representative James Roosevelt, and one copy to be retained in the TCA files. Douglas and Roosevelt were selected because it was felt they were definitely committed to the type of legislation the TCA was interested in, and, in view of their several outspoken statements in the past, the committee believed they would use the petitions to the fullest advantage. It was realized that there were other friendly congressmen, but the selection had to be limited. Several petitions could have been sent to several different congressmen, but the committee wanted

Douglas and Roosevelt to introduce the bill in their respective houses and, possibly, to lead the fight for its passage.

Approximately 350 signatures were obtained at the May 26 meeting. Several sets of petitions were sent to individuals and groups in thirteen states, North and South. The committee was always careful to spell out in its letters exactly why it felt a federal law was necessary. A "Fact Sheet on Voter Registration in Macon County, Alabama" was prepared setting forth statistics on Negro voter-registration and the various steps the TCA had taken to get the Governor to appoint a board. Mitchell constantly reminded his listeners of the importance of not giving the erroneous impression that this was a campaign for a bill that would apply only to Macon County. The point was always stressed that such a law was needed in many areas throughout the South.

From the start, the committee looked upon this new venture as having a two-fold purpose. First, if enough support could be obtained for the idea, the Governor might be pressured into appointing a board. Second, perhaps it was political naïveté, but the committee thought it had a chance to have a bill introduced and considered. Mitchell was fairly convinced that if the TCA publicized fully its fruitless efforts with the state officials, it would get a national hearing in the Congress.

Early in June, 1959, Mitchell wrote 35 United States senators and representatives advising them of TCA plans. Several encouraging replies were received.

Senator Joseph S. Clarke wrote:

Thank you for your letter of June 9, regarding the need for effective Federal legislation to protect voting rights as guaranteed by the Fifteenth Amendment. I am acutely aware of this need . . . the registration situation in Macon County is a national disgrace.

The late Senator William Langer said:

This will acknowledge and thank you for your letter of June 10, relative to a law to govern voter registration. You can depend upon my active support and I will do everything possible for it. It should have been passed 100 years ago.

Roosevelt and Douglas replied that they were ready to assist in whatever way possible. The national chairmen of the Democratic and Republican parties were sent letters describing the Macon County situation and indicating the TCA's intention to ask for a voter-registration law. Paul Butler answered that he felt such a law would have a "salutary effect," and Senator Thruston B. Morton declared that he favored the civil rights program outlined by the Eisenhower administration.

Petitions were given to many persons in the community who had them signed on their jobs and in their club meetings. Approximately 1,800 signatures were ultimately returned to the TCA office from local and national points.

A proposed bill was drawn up and sent along with another letter to the 35 congressmen on June 15, 1959. In addition, the petitions were sent to Senator Douglas and Representative Roosevelt. A mass meeting was planned for June 16 at which time the TCA would announce the sending of the petitions and the drafting of the bill. On June 16, the local TV station in Montgomery announced the plans and the mass meeting for that night. The principal speaker was a member of the committee and an instructor on the faculty of Tuskegee Institute. The TV news account stated that certain state legislators indicated that they would suggest a state investigation of Tuskegee Institute where certain faculty members were engaged in pro-integration activities. (The college received funds from the state for specified services rendered under a contractual arrangement.)

At the meeting, the speaker recounted the fruitless efforts of the committee to get a board appointed. After the petitions to Congress had circulated throughout the community for three weeks, the story had been retold many times. A large number of people had become familiar with the committee's efforts over the last six months. It was noted that several persons had offered to serve and that none of the TCA's requests for a conference nor any of the communications had been acknowledged. The fact that Representative Rogers had refused a letter from the TCA was good evidence of rejection by the state officials. It was not difficult to show that on the state and local levels the doors to the centers of policy-making were closed to the TCA. The speech cited an article which appeared in the *Montgomery Advertiser* on February 18, 1959 that stated that the Alabama Legislature had created a special committee "to recommend any legislation it thinks necessary to keep Negroes in Macon County from gaining political control." There was no choice but to turn to the federal government for relief.

On June 24, Representative Adam Clayton Powell introduced H.R. 7957 in the House of Representatives. The bill was almost a complete reproduction of the proposal the committee had sent to Powell and the other congressmen. It was referred to the Committee on House Administration. H.R. 7957 became a pass-word in Tuskegee. In about one month, the TCA had a bill in Congress, an occurrence which exceeded all expectations.

Some persons suggested that Powell's sponsorship was a political kiss of death. They felt that it would have been much better if a more "acceptable" political figure had introduced the bill. There was a great deal of speculation as to why Powell had "jumped the gun." The committee had hoped to confer with several congressmen in an effort to get joint sponsorship. Some people in the community indicated that this was another good issue for Powell to use as a personal sounding board. Most of the committee members concluded that they could not spend time bemoaning the fact that Powell had introduced the bill. There was some question whether the TCA's intentions were made entirely clear. The committee had sent copies of the proposal to the 35 congressmen without indicating to them the plan to have Douglas and Roosevelt introduce the bill. Under these circumstances, Powell's actions were understandable. In a sense, the committee felt that his sponsorship was an advantage, inasmuch as he might be prevailed upon to speak out frequently for it, and, at the same time, draw more attention to the situation in Macon County.

Mitchell wrote Senator Douglas, Representative Roosevelt, and several other congressmen advising them of the existence of H.R. 7957 and soliciting their support for the bill. On July 20, 1959, Senator Douglas wrote that he was "somewhat puzzled" as to what position he should take on H.R. 7957 in view of the fact that there were "numbers of other measures dealing with the same subject." Mitchell answered on August 8 that the TCA was unaware of a "bill in the Congress that would provide for the registration of persons in a given county once that county ceases to have a functioning board of registrars." Mitchell explained that H.R. 7957 "provides for a commission to proceed to register persons in a given county in the event that there is no functioning board of registrars in that county after a 60-day period."

Mitchell immediately realized that the chances for getting the bill considered depended in large measure on continuing efforts to pressure the state officials. The TCA could not hope to have H.R. 7957 reported during the 1959 congressional session, but it figured that by the time the second session opened in January, 1960, it would have had sufficient time to concentrate on "building a stronger case against the state appointing board while, at the same time, we were building a case for a Federal law." While the TCA would have welcomed any response from official Montgomery, some of the Negroes felt that Patterson's continued silence would begin to work in their behalf. This would help to show the absolute hopelessness of trying to deal with the Alabama officials.

APPOINTMENTS DECLINED

On July 16, 1959, the press announced that three appointments had been made to the Macon County Board of Registrars, a reflection, some thought, of the efforts to obtain a federal registration law. They believed that Patterson made the appointments to cut into whatever support the TCA might be able to build for a federal law. No one thought that the petitions and letters to the appointing board had brought this action. "There is one thing those people over in Montgomery fear and that's the Federal government," one Tuskegee faculty member stated. The mere appointment of a board was not sufficient. Mitchell decided that the petitions to the appointing board would continue until the new board actually began receiving applicants.

The *Montgomery Advertiser*, on July 17, 1959, contained the following article: "Macon Board is Undecided on New Posts:"

Those appointed to the board which has had difficulty keeping members in the racially tense county are Howard Lynn of Rt. 1, Notasulga, chairman, and J. H. Sadler and John Sullivan, both of Tuskegee.

Lynn said he hadn't yet received notice of his appointment and that it would take "several days to make up my mind" whether to accept. Sullivan declined comment and said it would also be a day or two before he would have anything to say about whether he would serve. The third man, Sadler, couldn't be reached for comment today but had previously said he would have to "look into the matter a little further" before making a decision.

Mitchell, the TCA secretary, said he was "very happy to have a board of registrars in the county again and hopes that it will function for all the citizens."

"However, we will continue to press for enactment of House Resolution 7957 now pending on Congress to set up a federal voter registration commission," he added.

Mitchell was a little skeptical about the sincerity of the appointments. He did not understand why Patterson had not received the consent of the persons or notified them before the release to the press. The committee also concluded that this could well have been an attempt to stop the continuous flow of petitions and letters to him. A few days later, the press announced that one of the appointees had refused the appointment. The Montgomery *Alabama Journal* ran the story on July 22 on page one:

J. H. Sadler of Tuskegee said he had decided against accepting the appointment because the small amount of pay involved wouldn't allow him to stay away from his service station on the first and third Mondays of each month that the board meets.

None showed up Monday for one of two monthly registration sessions, and an undetermined number of Negroes left the courthouse without registering.

One committee member had gone to the courthouse on that Monday morning and talked to and counted eleven Negroes who had come to register. He spent two hours at the courthouse. One Negro who waited about one hour stated: "They might as well come on down here, we'll be here when they get here." This man, who appeared to be in his late forties, was asked if he had tried to register before. He had not. When asked why he was doing so at that time, he simply shrugged and said, "It's about time, don't you think?"

Sadler's resignation did not mean that the board could not function. There were still two others. This possibility was erased two days later, however, when the following story appeared in the *Atlanta Constitution*: "Tuskegee Voter Bar Continues":

A seven-month breakdown of voter registration machinery continued in heavily Negro populated Macon County Thursday after three newly appointed white registrars declined to serve.

Governor John Patterson released copies of letters from Howard Lynn of near Notasulga, J. H. Sadler and John Sullivan of Tuskegee. They gave as reasons for declining to serve the pressure for Negro registration and federal intervention . . . the governor, a member of the state board which appoints registrars, said he and the other two members—State Auditor Mary Texas Hurt Garner, and Agriculture Commissioner R. C. Damberg "have tried and are trying to find competent citizens" to serve on the board. "Our job is difficult," Patterson added in a prepared statement, "because of the unwarranted harassment by the federal government and particularly the Civil Rights Commission. It is hard to ask a man to subject himself to such treatment as the previous boards of registrars have experienced in the past at the hands of the federal government."

This was the kind of public statement the committee had been awaiting from Patterson. Now he could be answered specifically by pointing out that there were Macon County citizens ready, willing, and able to serve. Mitchell decided to send Patterson a telegram in reply to his statement, and to release the telegram to the press. The hope was that the reporters would question Patterson on the contents of the wire. For a brief time, it appeared that a breakthrough had been made, and Patterson might be forced out of his silence. Because the record was so well documented, Mitchell felt that any reply Patterson made could be used against him. One very unfortunate mistake was made, however. The telegram was sent at a time when Patterson was out of the state. He could be approached when he returned, of course, but the matter of timing was very important, and the committee simply had slipped up.

The *Montgomery Advertiser* carried the story on August 2 entitled: "Macon Board Appointments Asked Again":

Another appeal for appointment of a voter registration board in Macon County was sent Saturday to Governor John Patterson by an official of the Tuskegee Civic Association.

William P. Mitchell, executive secretary of the TCA, a predominantly Negro organization, said he sent a telegram to the governor calling upon the state appointing board to provide the county with a board of registrars.

Patterson left Saturday to attend the governor's conference at San Juan, Puerto Rico, and was unavailable for comment.

The other two members of the state appointing board . . . were also unavailable. Mitchell's telegram referred to a news story of July 24, which quoted the governor as saying "we members of the appointing board have tried and are still trying to find competent citizens of Macon County to serve on the board of registrars."

"This will respectfully call your attention to requests made by eight competent citizens of Macon County to the appointing board to be appointed to membership on this board on March 14, May 21, and May 22," the telegram said.

"It appears that if a sincere effort was made to find three citizens to serve on the Macon County board that these citizens might have been considered."

The committee had missed its chance. There was no answer from Patterson to this news story when he returned to Montgomery. There was thought of having one of the white reporters ask him about the requests to serve, but this was never followed up. Mitchell did not want to give the impression that the TCA was trying to solicit the aid of the press. If the newspapers were objective in reporting the facts, this was all the TCA could ask.

MORE COMMUNICATIONS—UNANSWERED

After the unsuccessful attempt to engage Patterson in a public debate, the committee continued to publicize H.R. 7957, and Mitchell continued to communicate weekly with the state appointing board. All the letters were sent by certified mail with return receipts, and they followed the same general pattern.

September 7, 1959

This will again respectfully request you and your associates on the State Board of Appointment to provide Macon County with a publicly functioning board of registrars. You are aware that unregistered citizens in this county have not had an opportunity to register as voters for ten (10) months. Your attention to this very urgent matter would be appreciated.

September 18, 1959

Your failure to answer any of our many requests to you, Mr. Bamberg, and Mrs. Garner (the State Board of Appointment) seeking the appointment of a board of registrars for Macon County leaves us in a quandary. Surely, Mr. Patterson, your administration desires to serve the ends of democracy. The appointment of a functioning board of registrars here would make available to the thousands of unregistered citizens the most elementary of the rights inherent in our democratic process. We, therefore, call upon you and your associates again to appoint a board of registrars here, and repeat that many citizens are willing to assist you in finding qualified persons to serve as members on the Macon County Board of Registrars.

September 29, 1959

Our past requests to you to appoint a board of registrars have gone unanswered. We call upon you and your associates again to provide Macon County with a board of registrars in order that qualified citizens of this county might register as electors.

October 19, 1959

Representatives of the Tuskegee Civic Association respectfully request an audience with you and the other members of the State Board of Appointment at a time and date set by you for the purpose of trying to assist you in finding citizens in Macon County who would be willing to serve on the Macon County Board of Registrars.

APPROACHING OTHER GROUPS

During the late summer and early fall weeks, members of the committee spoke often before local social, fraternal, church, and student groups. The purpose, however, was to get these groups to write Congress in support of H.R. 7957, not to contact the Governor. The presentation always started with an account of the efforts of the committee to obtain relief from Alabama officials and then led into a discussion of the bill. Once, the suggestion was made to have these various groups contact the state appointing board in addition to writing Congress. The point was that this would tend to show wider representation. This was a valid point for consideration inasmuch as the committee had heard from a visiting group of white college students from Ohio several months before that some white officials in Tuskegee had told them that the TCA did not represent the interest of the majority of Negroes in Tuskegee, a common misrepresentation of Negro political action groups. There was a good opportunity to refute this claim in Tuskegee, because the TCA could get other groups to join its efforts to get a board appointed. The matter was discussed, but the decision was the same as that regarding asking the people at the mass meetings to write: the TCA would handle the business of approaching the state appointing board. The TCA would do nothing to discourage other groups from writing the Governor, but it would not suggest such action. The point was never raised by any member of the other groups. This was another example of the division of labor that prevailed in the community; civil rights was the exclusive province of the TCA.

In early August, the TCA invited several Negro leaders from other parts of Alabama to a one-day "strategy" conference on the best methods to build support for H.R. 7957. Leaders from Mobile, Birmingham, Montgomery, and several other areas attended. Again, the TCA gave the full account of its efforts to have a board appointed, and, again, Mitchell emphasized that this was not a "Tuskegee or Macon County bill," that H.R. 7957 would benefit many counties throughout the South. While the meeting was being planned, the point was raised whether these persons should be asked to write the Governor urging the appointment of a board for Macon County. The committee's response was almost unanimous: this was a "Macon County problem," and it would be handled by Macon County Negroes.

There were several reasons for this attitude. Many southern Negro political action groups took great pains to avoid the accusation that they had been influenced by "outsiders." The southern white politicians (and the press, to an extent) had used the label "outside agitators" to account for protest from Negroes and to discredit political movements among them. Normally, "outsiders" referred to northerners, but in the case of appointing a board for Macon County, some members of the committee felt it could refer to the next county. In addition, there was a strong inclination "to prove that we can solve our own problems." This was intended largely as a refutation of the idea of some southern white persons that southern Negroes needed "outside" help and guidance in their protest actions. This restriction of their activities disturbed some committee members, because they felt the committee was letting the white politicians determine its methods—to its detriment.

Another reason for looking upon the matter of appointing a board as within the exclusive jurisdiction of the TCA was the fact that there was some inter-group rivalry and jealousy that was difficult to overcome. This was due partly to mutual distrust of leadership, to differences in approach to various social issues and to the real problem of maintaining group identity. As could be expected, the new phenomenon of southern Negro protest created new problems among Negro leadership groups. The competition for headlines, the conflict of fund drives, and the desire for personal recognition were some of the factors injected into the struggle of a group of people intent on gaining status and benefits which a new day promised. Pronouncements such as "There's enough work for all of us to do" were made often, but one could easily detect, in many instances, an underlying jurisdictional dispute as to geographical area and subject matter.

The TCA had another opportunity to reach a wider audience with the combined story of efforts to get a board for the county and H.R. 7957 at the semi-annual meeting in Montgomery in October, 1959 of the Alabama State Coordinating Association for Registration and Voting. Negro leaders attended this meeting from a majority of the 67 counties in Alabama. The purpose was to work up effective ways to get Negro citizens registered throughout the state. Mitchell reviewed the work of the committee. H.R. 7957 was explained, and all groups were urged to conduct letter writing campaigns to Congress. No effort was made to bring statewide pressure on the Governor and the other members of the state appointing board.

TO SUE OR NOT TO SUE

By early October, the time had come to give serious consideration to an idea Mitchell had been nursing for some time; namely, a suit against the state appointing board to compel it to act. The committee was given authority by the executive cabinet to consult legal counsel to explore the possibilities of such a suit. It was understood that this would be a unique case, and there was no way of predicting the outcome. The committee was advised that the case was not hopeless, and that a court might be prevailed upon to rule in its favor, especially if it were taken high enough. (There was in 1959, understandably, a rather confident feeling among many Negro leaders about the liberality of the Federal Supreme Court, and the feeling that the time was ripe to argue for new interpretations of the Federal Constitution.)

Some persons questioned the wisdom of incurring the expense in view of the great uncertainty while others felt that the suit would definitely have nuisance value. Some were of the opinion that even if the TCA lost such a suit, this would help to define the law and to further point up the need for more effective federal legislation in the area of voter registration. There was concern that the Governor might appoint a board after a suit was filed and before a final determination. The fear was that a board might be appointed, serve for a short time to defeat the suit, and then resign. This could occur indefinitely, and the committee was not clear on the exact meaning of Judge Johnson's words that the court would "not sanction repeated resignations in bad faith. . . ." It was likewise understood that the TCA would have no right to ask for the appointment of persons of its choice. The lawyers with whom the committee consulted felt that the TCA could, under such circumstances, ask the court to hold the case on the docket; that once it was in court, it would not have to refile the suit.

Some preferred to have the legal aspects researched as thoroughly as possible before proceeding. One member of the executive cabinet was making a trip to Washington, D.C., in October, and she was to discuss the matter with several lawyers and law professors there. It was decided to defer a decision until her return, but it was the general feeling that such a suit would be worth the expense.

A few weeks later, the report from Washington was that the TCA could expect assistance in the form of advice based on legal research. The next decision was whether to file immediately or to wait for the preliminary research. Some members of the committee wanted to file suit immediately, but it was decided to discuss the matter fully with the executive cabinet before proceeding. As it turned out, the enthusiasm of the committee was not generally shared by the executive cabinet although the cabinet would have followed the recommendation of the committee. The prevailing attitude, even later shared by Mitchell, was that the TCA should forego any legal action for the time being in the hope that Congress would pass an effective law at the next session.

MORE APPOINTMENTS?

The terms of the members of the boards of registrars throughout the state expired in November, 1959. The committee waited to see what would be done for Macon County. As the days passed, the press announced several appointments for other counties. Mitchell wrote Patterson on November 9, 1959:

We note that you and your associates on the State Board of Appointment made assignments of personnel to boards of registrars in several counties last week, and the news story stated that others would be made this week.

We hope, Mr. Patterson, that a full publicly functioning board of registrars will be provided for Macon County in the near future.

Finally, on November 25, the *Montgomery Advertiser* ran the following article: "Macon Given New Board of Registrars:"

A new board of registrars has been appointed in Macon County but the identity of the members has not yet been made known. Governor John Patterson revealed Tuesday that the appointments in Macon had been made as well as in 18 other Alabama counties.
Patterson admitted that the state board had encountered "a lot of trouble getting people to serve."

"They don't get paid, and by serving they may be hauled into court by the FBI or the Civil Rights Commission," he said.

The committee did not understand the reference to pay, because the registrars were paid $10 per day.

The TCA awaited further announcement of the names and the acceptances. The July experience had shown that there was a definite difference between a board and a publicly functioning board, and the petitions and letters to Patterson continued. No further announcement was made, and, as far as was known, there was still no board for the county.

TO MARCH OR NOT TO MARCH

At a January, 1960, meeting, the executive cabinet discussed the program for the new year, including suggestions to the committee on possible next steps in efforts to get a board of registrars appointed. This was the time to present the idea of a march on the state capitol. There were a few who highly favored the idea as a means of further publicizing the registration stalemate. After a lengthy discussion, an agreement was reached to proceed with the march. Several things had to be decided: who would go? when? how? what would be done once the group assembled on the capitol steps?

At first, some felt the trip should be made only by those unregistered citizens who had signed petitions. This meant approximately 600 persons. Another member of the cabinet saw no reason why "we shouldn't get a thousand," that anybody who could get to Montgomery (forty miles from Tuskegee) should be asked to go. It was agreed not to limit the number. Mitchell counseled that all cars should park several blocks from the capitol building, and the persons should walk in small groups to the capitol, otherwise traffic problems might be encountered. Two executive cabinet members were designated to contact persons who had means of transportation and who could take the time off from their jobs.

There was general agreement that a good time to conduct the march (or motorcade) would be on or near February 15, 1960, the date the United States Senate was to begin debate on a civil rights bill. The suggestion was made to stage the march on a Monday so the TCA could take advantage of the event in order to attract a large audience to the mass meeting the following night. This might provide the stimulus for revived mass attendance. Another suggestion was made to plan the march at a time when Patterson was definitely in Montgomery. It was then decided to write Patterson requesting another conference, and if he refused, as he was sure to do, then the march could be publicized as an attempt on the part of citizens of Macon County to have an audience with their Governor. There was the belief that if Patterson had prior knowledge of the plan, he might arrange to be out of town, so no news releases were to be given to the press far in advance.

The executive cabinet never got around to discussing whether placards would be used or exactly what would be done once the group assembled on the capitol steps. The matter was left with the designation of two persons to develop specific details. The subject was never discussed formally again. February 15 came, and there was no march, and those who strongly favored the idea did not pursue it further.

Another factor intervened during the third week in February, 1960, that put an end to any possible plans of staging a mass protest march to Montgomery. This was the week that a group of Negro college students from Alabama State College in Montgomery attempted to integrate the lunch counter in the Montgomery County courthouse by "sitting in." This action led to a series of events, including a mass assembly on the capitol steps by hundreds of Negro students, the patrolling of the downtown Montgomery area by private white citizens carrying baseball bats, a motorcade through the downtown area by whites bearing anti-Negro placards, and a near race riot on March 8, 1960 when hundreds of Negroes attempted to hold another prayer service on the capitol steps. The city of Montgomery passed several ordinances, one of which forbade mass public demonstrations in the city without prior approval of the city officials. It was obvious that this meant the TCA would definitely not hold its mass march. Racial tension was very high in the capital city, and Montgomery officials announced that they would not sanction further mass demonstrations in the city by Negroes or whites. Some members of the committee, however, were never convinced that most of the officers of the TCA sincerely condoned the suggestion of a TCA-sponsored march, and the creation of a committee of two to formulate plans appeared to be one method of terminating the idea.

THE PRESS

The day-to-day operations of the TCA were not front page news items. In other places, perhaps, the silent treatment on the part of the Governor and other state officials toward a group of citizens would be of public interest, but not in Alabama—when that group was predominantly Negro. Weekly news releases were sent announcing the meetings and, occasionally, summarizing speeches, but these were never given prominent display by the white dailies in the state. A lengthy release was given reporting the June 16, 1959 mass meeting when the petitions and the proposed bill were sent to Congress. On that day, the *Montgomery Advertiser* ran a page one story of a pro-segregation Negro organization in Birmingham that had criticized "self-styled Negro ministers who substitute integregation and other social doctrines" for the gospel. The TCA story was carried on an inside page reserved for "Negro News Events."

A few of the larger Alabama dailies had editorialized in favor of fair registration and voting practices, but they never mentioned the efforts of the TCA to get a publicly functioning board of registrars for Macon County. Most of the editorials continued to insist that the matter of registration should be left to the several states. On February 8, 1960, the *Birmingham News* editorialized:

... this paper certainly has argued that there can be no arbitrary bar of the vote merely on the basis of color. We have so tried to influence our state officials toward a realistic policy on this matter. . . . Some qualified Negroes, we sincerely believe, have had difficulty registering in one place or another. But we do not believe they are in "large numbers.

It was not uncommon to read an editorial similar to the following which appeared in the *Talladega Home News* under the title: "The Feds Did It":

Certainly we are concerned over the plight of those citizens of Macon County otherwise qualified, who are unable to register as voters because no registration board exists. The blame for the distressing situation, of course, rests with the federal government and its program of harassment of southern registrars who do not permit Washington bureaucracy to dictate how they shall exercise their judicial functions. . . .

This is, of course, not the complete picture. Occasionally, an editorial would appear similar to the one in the *Lee County Bulletin* of February 2, 1960, on the proposal to provide federal registrars:

... it is simply a bill drawn by the attorney general and approved by the President which rescues thousands of colored voter applicants from a hopeless situation. Nothing is to be gained by crying foul. It is true that this matter ought to be handled by the states. But the states have failed to act fairly and honorably. Alabama, along with several others, has asked for what it is getting. At the time of the Civil Rights Commission hearings in Alabama last year this paper pleaded that Alabama officials ought to act in good faith in this matter of registering voter applicants regardless of race or color. . . .

Most TCA officials did not have great faith in the reporters from the southern white press. There was the feeling that "all they want is a story, preferably a sensational one." If the story would contradict another Negro leader or group, then this was even better. Mitchell explained his position at one of the mass meetings when he told the audience: "There are some reporters I don't talk to at all when they identify themselves."

There was a better reception from the Negro-owned weeklies in the state, but their circulation and their influence were not extensive. The TCA ran a short, weekly column in the local, *Tuskegee Southern Observer* (Negro owned) for about four months. The column, "From TCA Files," set forth the various efforts the TCA was making to get a functioning board, and it ran excerpts from letters received from governmental officials and others. While there was some disappointment that the *Observer* did not take a more militant editorial stand on the refusal of the Governor to appoint a board, the four-page paper did give considerable space to TCA meetings. It was recognized that, in addition to the small circulation, the Negro press suffered from the same lack of access to the state officials that plagued the TCA.

THINGS UNDONE

Over the year and a half there were some things the committee considered doing but on which it never followed up. The committee had thought of placing a full-page advertisement in the *Montgomery Advertiser* setting forth the complete story of its vain efforts, but the cost was prohibitive. The lack of money was due partly to the fact that on one occasion the TCA refused to accept an unsolicited, financial donation from a person outside Macon County. The reason was that the TCA did not wish to give the appearance of being a "money-grabbing organization." On several occasions, the pronouncement was made publicly that the Negroes of Macon County could finance their own battles. This appeared, again, to be part of the tendency to form no connections with "outsiders," and to give the impression that "we are willing and able to pay for our own rights with our own money."

Throughout the period, no attempt was made to reach the Governor or the other members of the state appointing board through private, influential white citizens. This was due largely to the fact that the committee simply did not know any such persons who would be so disposed. It felt that if a white citizen were friendly toward the TCA, then he would not be influential with Patterson, and vice versa.

The suggestion was made to contact a white newspaper reporter in the North to have him make inquiries of the Governor regarding the persons who had offered to serve. The committee also thought of asking a national Negro publication to come to Tuskegee and to do a feature story on the Macon County situation. It did not follow through on these ideas. Some of the inaction was due to the fact that most of the day-to-day work was handled by two or three persons. Time and energy were major factors, since no one could devote full-time to TCA business. Yet there was never a serious move to involve more people in the operation of the organization.

New ideas and new tactics were approached cautiously insofar as they involved dealing with the state officials. There was an overriding inclination to be "right and sound" that often gave the appearance to some of being too cautious and conservative. This was part of the hesitancy, in the final analysis, to proceed with the march to Montgomery. Some members of the executive cabinet voiced the opinion that "we are too conservative," and "the TCA is more an educational organization than an action group." Many ideas were brought up for discussion, but the basic pattern of protest had been set.

SHIFT IN FOCUS

After a year of petitions and unanswered letters, many Negroes were becoming convinced that Patterson would not appoint a board in the near future, and if a board were appointed, it would not function impartially. There were very few Negroes in Tuskegee who really believed that they would be given the franchise by state officials who would come to see the error of their ways and act justly. Very few Negroes believed, anymore, that the "Southern white man is our friend." There was disappointment and distrust. For decades, many Negroes believed that their problems stemmed from a handful of white politicians and that, when glaring injustices were exposed, all the "decent thinking white people" in the South would protest. Now, the Macon County situation convinced many Negroes that forces more powerful than they had imagined were arrayed against them. The most damaging realization was that most of those whites who were previously "friends" were nowhere to be found. They did not protest the inequitable treatment of Negro voter applicants; they did not offer to serve on the board of registrars. Many of these whites were in business, and they had solicited the Negroes' trade for years. The Negroes had given this trade, and now there was an intense feeling of betrayal. One member of the TCA's executive cabinet had served for 21 years as supply officer of the VA hospital. He had given many orders to white merchants in Tuskegee, and when he sought to register in 1957 and 1958, he "failed" the examination—three times.

There were several meetings with white ministers and a few other white citizens from nearby counties, but these were discussion sessions, aimed at "getting to know each other." One often heard that these persons could not afford to speak out forcefully in defense of the Negro's right to vote, that they were of greater service in their present roles. This seemed dubious to some Negroes in Tuskegee who felt that, although these persons had no influence with Patterson, the moral impact of a forthright stand would far outweigh the separate disadvantages that might accrue to some of them. This seemed to the Negroes to be an especially valid point in view of the comments often made by some of these white ministers that "you'd be surprised how many in my congregation really sympathize with you folks over here." Some Negroes felt that this subtle sympathy should have been turned into open organization to offset the organized racist groups. This was a frequently discussed subject among Negroes in the community, and there was by no means uniformity of opinion on it. One young Negro minister once commented: "I say the Southern white ministry is not to be congratulated or applauded if it speaks up on race matters favorably to the Negro. It is only doing what it should do if it believes in the gospel of Christ. First, a man must get conviction; if he has conviction, then courage is necessarily forthcoming. The Southern white 'liberal' must be willing to give up his job. If he has conviction, he will have the courage." In response to this another Negro minister stated: "A man must look out for his bread and butter first, and frankly, I can understand this. If my congregation told me to back away from this TCA business, you can bet I'd do it. This is only common sense. A person has to keep his body together. I have to watch that collection plate every Sunday. If I get up there and start talking things they don't want to hear, they'll stop giving and I'll feel it. Conviction is one thing, but pure reality is another. You,   , might not have that problem. Being   , your job is guaranteed. You're protected. But not me. I have to cater to that congregation if I know what's good for me. And I'm sure the very same thing is true of many southern white ministers. That's why I admire those who do finally speak out at great jeopardy to their jobs and families."

A combination of events throughout the 1950s had led the Negroes to feel that they no longer needed to rely solely on the goodness of the Southern white community. The Negroes of Macon County had seen the busses of Montgomery, Alabama, desegregated by a federal court order. They had seen a federal civil rights commission with a Negro member come into the South and require the local politicians to produce their records. They had seen federal troops escorting Negro children to a desegregated school in Little Rock, Arkansas. In August, 1959, they read the report of the Civil Rights Commission recommending federal regulation of registration and voting. In January and February, 1960, they read the new bills introduced into the United States Senate and the House of Representatives providing for some form of federal relief for voteless Negroes.

Many Negroes in Tuskegee came to realize that there was no need to submit to the system of accommodation of an earlier time. They could have economic security and political participation simultaneously, and they were beginning to believe that anything less was a denial of their dignity and self respect. There was, at times, sharp internal disagreement on approach, but this was the common attitude. This feeling was also aided by the national publicity focused on the South and the Negro. Many found personal satisfaction in telling friends in other sections of the country what "we" are doing in the "struggle down there." There was, to an extent, a feeling of competition among certain Negro communities —a kind of bid to "out civil rights" the others. This was evident in the speeches and actions at statewide and regional meetings and in private conversations. These factors cannot be overlooked in an attempt to understand why hundreds of Negroes in Macon County signed petitions and wrote congressmen, why some continued to attend the weekly meetings long after the TV cameras stopped coming, and why some offered to serve on the board of registrars. Others were inspired by the nationalistic struggles in Africa which were referred to often in speeches at the meetings.

Thus, while petitions and letters to Patterson and to the state appointing board continued, all eyes were on Congress.

In March, 1960, Mitchell sent an open letter to Patterson refuting the Governor's testimony of February 2, 1960 before the Senate Rules Committee. The letter was reported in the daily press, but there was, again, no answer from Patterson.

... You are quoted in the transcript of this hearing as having said that "usually there are only a few people complaining and usually they are already registered. ..." While you may have received "only a few" complaints from persons "already registered," we know it to be a fact, Mr. Patterson, that you have received 60 petitions during the 60 weeks that you have been in office as Governor, bearing 720 signatures of *unregistered* citizens of Macon County requesting you and your associates to appoint a publicly functioning board of registrars for this county. You have not acknowledged these communications.

In further argument before the Senate Rules Committee in opposition to the establishment of federal registrars, you stated, according to the record, that "the reason why we do not have it (boards of registrars for Macon and Dallas Counties) is because we are finding it difficult to get men and women who want to serve on these boards." Now, Mr. Patterson, to our knowledge, you have received communications from at least 15 civicly interested citizens indicating their interest in, and availability for serving as members of the Macon County Board of Registrars. In addition, you have received many offers to assist you in locating citizens who would perform this civic duty. Letters from these citizens have also gone unanswered or even acknowledged. . . .

Governor Patterson, we have been taught to expect a more accurate presentation of the facts from our public officials. To this end, we offer to assist you and other interested public servants in getting the facts pertaining to the activity, inactivity, record and public behavior of the Macon County Boards of Registrars over the past 20 years.

Copies of the letter were sent to several United States senators. Mitchell also had photostatic copies made of some letters and petitions to the Governor and sent them to several members of the United States Senate and the House of Representatives.

A NEW LAW, A NEW BOARD AND "14,000 . . . READY TO REGISTER . . ."

May 6, 1960 was an interesting day for those concerned with voter registration in Macon County. The new Civil Rights Act of 1960 was signed by President Eisenhower on that day. Attorney General William P. Rogers was reported to have said he hoped responsible state officials would act voluntarily to eliminate discrimination at the polls, but if they did not, the Justice Department would investigate complaints promptly and "proceed vigorously." The new law stated that there must be a "pattern or practice" of racial discrimination, and it provided for a court-appointed, local qualified voter (referee) to take testimony of registration denials. Several TCA officials looked upon the law as cumbersome, complex, obviously lacking in many respects, and much weaker than H.R. 7957.

On the same day, May 6, 1960, Patterson announced the appointment of two persons to the Macon County Board of Registrars. Although state law provided for three members, the board could proceed to operate with two appointees. The persons named were Wheeler Dyson of Tuskegee, who was designated as chairman, and Wayne Raney of Hardaway. Dyson, the press reported, had refused an appointment in November, 1959. The *Montgomery Advertiser* stated on May 7, 1960:

. . . with a functioning board of registrars in Macon County, Negroes may be delayed further in their efforts to register.

If there were no board, a federal referee would have grounds to begin an immediate investigation and take steps to set up registration machinery.

However, with a functioning board of registrars in the county, prospective voters would have facilities to seek the voting franchise. And they would have to show that they couldn't secure fair treatment by the state appointed registrars before going into federal court to seek appointment of a federal officer to consider their applications. . . .

On May 13, the *Advertiser* announced that Wayne Raney had declined the appointment and that Patterson had appointed another, Charles Donald Scott, of Tuskegee. Dyson qualified with the probate judge in Tuskegee on May 11. The *Advertiser* reported on May 13:

Racially troubled Macon County, where no new voter has been able to register for 17 months, expects soon to have a functioning board of registrars.

. . . Raney, in a letter to the governor, declined because "I am too old to be browbeaten by the various governmental agencies as well as private minority pressure groups."

. . . Scott's appointment was the ninth to the embattled Macon County board within a year. Others, like Raney, had said they turned down the job because of pressure from Negroes seeking to register as voters. . . .

A reporter telephoned Mitchell the evening of the signing of the civil rights law and asked if the TCA would use the new law to register Negroes. Mitchell replied: "No, the unregistered Negroes will use the law, not the TCA." The reporter than asked how many Negroes were unregistered in the county, and Mitchell indicated that the number was approximately 14,000. The next day, the news announced that William P. Mitchell stated that 14,000 Negroes were ready to register and to vote in Macon County under the provisions of the new law. Mitchell told the audience at the May 10 mass meeting that this was another example of misleading reporting and a gross misinterpretation of what he had said.

CONCLUSION

No one thought that the petitions and letters to Patterson led to the appointment of a board of registrars for Macon County. It was generally felt that mounting pressure from the federal government culminating in a law providing for federal referees was the major factor. Mitchell, however, pointed out that the detailed records and the continuous activity of the TCA probably contributed to the recommendations of the Civil Rights Commission which, in turn, "really started the Congress and the country thinking in terms of federal intervention." There was the general feeling that the utter hopelessness of the Negroes' condition in such counties as Macon was too much for the national government to continue to ignore. The appointment of a board, however, was viewed by many Negroes, ironically, as another delaying tactic to increased Negro registration as the *Advertiser* had indicated could be the case. Very few, if any, Negroes believed that any board appointed by Patterson would register persons without regard to race or color. Eventually, they believed, the Justice Department would be called upon to guarantee the vote to Negroes in Macon County.

To the extent that this is inevitable, it is, likewise, conceivable that Negro voters will eventually outnumber white voters in the county. What then? Gomillion stated in an interview with the press: "The idea that our people want to take over the government is simply not true. It's just poppycock." Mitchell has made similar statements to the press, to visiting groups and to members of the TCA. For years, when there seemed to be virtually no likelihood of extensive Negro participation in politics, such protestations were probably sincere, because few Negroes could conceive of the impossible. In 1960, however, the impossible had become, to a number of Negroes, the inevitable. One member of the executive cabinet spoke calmly and matter-of-factly about how "the whites are sure to move out when we elect a black sheriff and a black mayor." Several persons in the community looked upon a Negro-controlled county as an inevitable occurrence. They frankly asserted that "we will build a machine, promise to pave streets, pave them and enjoy some of that power the other people have had all the time. Why shouldn't we?"

If they are unsuccessful, it will not be because they did not try. Possibly, new leaders will emerge in this Negro community, more mass oriented than the TCA, less concerned to be "right and sound," and more anxious to be "powerful and victorious." They may, at first, use the race issue, but they will say they are justified in doing so. In the light of past action (and inaction) and attitudes, they will challenge the sincerity of any local white citizen running for public office. The feeling of betrayal will not be easily erased. They do not foresee any major opposition from the top leadership of the TCA, because that leadership has shown no inclination to enlist a mass following so necessary to building a political party organization and to winning elections. The deliberate, "letter-writing" approach of the TCA no longer appeals to many of the more aggressive Negroes. It was "too slow, too gradual, and too polite." The methods of the committee were described by one Negro as "almost apologetic. What was really done for a year and a half? Just letters and petitions."

Other Negroes were disturbed by the obvious political ambitions of some of their fellow black citizens. They saw a black oligarchy being substituted for a white one, and they feared the Negroes would be just as despotic as some of the whites had been. One group of Negroes talked "morality and brotherhood," the other talked "reality and politics." The latter were quick to point out that there will be a major difference from the present white-dominated government: "The whites can vote if they want to; we'll just out-vote them."

This is what the southern white community fears. It does not believe Gomillion's statement, and it knows that the Negroes will vote in Macon County for Negro candidates. The following editorial appeared in the *Montgomery Advertiser* for May 17, 1960, entitled: "Macon Government Functions Again":

In regarding the social and political problems of Macon County, *The Advertiser* never permits itself to be doctrinaire and theoretical. The whites of this splendid old county are, in the words of Grover Cleveland, "confronted with a condition, not a theory." Citizens of Montgomery are remote from Macon and they do not know how they would feel or how they would react if, like Macon, Montgomery's Negro population was more than 80% and led by a concentration of advanced, aggressive college faculty members.

But after a two-year lapse, there is now a functioning board of registrars and citizens, white and colored, can presumably undertake again to qualify to vote. The fact that it was possible to recruit Macon citizens to serve on the board indicates that the whites had come to see that the present suspension of government could not be maintained.

As it was, neither white nor colored could qualify to vote. That meant that a son of Sam Engelhardt turning 21 could not become a voter any more than a Negro doctor at Tuskegee Institute. Such a governmental shutdown obviously was too radical and sacrificial to endure.

Negro voting and Negroes butting their way into white schools where they are not wanted are organically different matters. It's not a federal dispensation, but the *law of Alabama enacted by Alabamians* that qualified Negroes are entitled to vote. Qualified Negroes are entitled legally and morally to vote.

Qualified Negroes are going to vote in Alabama and the south in growing numbers. Some unhappy consequences undoubtedly will attend this condition; they will surely vote in blocs for an indeterminate period, though finally the bloc will fragment like any other group vote.

Counties such as Macon are few. If in time an unbearable domination threatens, it will be up to other counties to make possible the rescue abolition and absorption. (sic) Apparently, in view of the revival of voter registration in Macon, something of the kind represents the thinking of local citizens.

The idea of abolishing Macon County and dividing it among the five adjoining counties to split the Negro vote has been considered by the state Legislature in previous years. A Macon County Abolition Committee was established in 1958 by the Alabama Legislature to investigate the possibility of such action. (The committee made a "wait and see" report.) This did not cause the politically ambitious Negroes of the county great concern, although they were not sure of the legalities and the possibilities involved. They looked upon abolition, if it happened, as just another obstacle to overcome, and they had begun to look upon themselves as being fairly adept at overcoming obstacles.

NOTES

1. In *Gomillion* v. *Lightfoot*, 81 S. Ct. 125 (1961), the United States Supreme Court unanimously ruled that a state may not gerrymander municipal boundaries on the basis of race. It decided that the Negroes of Tuskegee must be given the opportunity to prove their claim that the Alabama stature was motivated by race.

2. Applicants for voter certificates must complete a detailed questionnaire as to their residence, personal history, and items such as: "Name some of the duties and obligations of citizenship."

3. On April 19, 1948, a fair complexioned Negro (who could have been mistaken for a white citizen) had to locate the meeting place of the board after several Negroes were refused the information. The board did not function again publicly until January 17, 1949.

7

The Crisis of the Republic: Reflections on Race and Politics

Matthew Holden, Jr.

AUTHOR'S NOTE: *When this lecture was first delivered (during the election campaign of 1964) there was a certain pessimism associated with the idea of backlash. When it was being revised for publication during the winter of 1965, there was a certain tendency toward optimism. Both these seemed slightly out of focus. The purpose of the essay, then, was to call attention to the very process of shifting moods and symbols in the discussion of racial politics, and to suggest some of the fixed realities which might make it legitimate to speak of "two nations entangled in a single republic."*

THE EBB AND FLOW OF MOODS AND SYMBOLS

AS THE CIVIL RIGHTS issues have arisen in this generation, the most striking element has been the rapid fluctuation of moods and symbols. After *Brown v. Board of Education* there was an upsurge of optimism and even whites thought it only a matter of time, although how much time depended on whom you heard, before the decision would permeate the culture through "natural processes."

It was in this context that the mood of moral disbelief emerged from the Little Rock crisis. Above all, it emerged from the dramatic use of the coercive power against Dr. King's followers in the Birmingham crisis of 1963. Police dogs appeared a particularly repellent symbol—even to people who did not account themselves "integrationists."

From Washington one could pick up some of the feed-back. Senators from the Missouri Basin, whose normal goal would be to preserve their alliances with Southern senators, felt obliged to give their Southern colleagues the following message: "We hope that you will not promote the filibuster at the moment because if you do we are not sure we can stay with you. The reason is that we are getting an awful lot of letters from Methodist preachers, who we normally don't hear from, about what an awful thing it is to set dogs upon school children."

Reproduced from *Forum of Public Affairs* by permission of Wisconsin State University, Platteville, Wisconsin, and the author.

The March-to-Washington in August of 1963 evoked for many white persons amazement at its orchestration: "A quarter of a million people into Washington and out with nothing happening!" The March evoked a mood of wariness as well as one of awe: "Civil rights is *not* just a Negro elite goal. It is not just a goal of the professional agitators. The mass of ordinary Negroes take this goal seriously." For Negroes it evoked manifest destiny: "We Shall Overcome!" Mr. Roy Wilkins said it from the podium when he told the assembled marchers: "After seeing all of you here, I shall never be afraid again." In the history at the Negro American that probably represents the most significant of all themes: *never to be afraid again.*

Before the end of that year, the undercurrents of another mood were felt: the mood of white resistance—"backlash"—as it quickly came to be called. It was the voice of the ordinary white American. Ambivalent at best, the ordinary man might even have thought he favored "giving the Negroes an even break" but did not truly understand his own preference for the racial hierarchy. Now what he began to say was: "the Negroes have gone too far"; "they have been given an inch and are taking the mile"; "the government is surrendering white men's rights to Negroes' demands."

Governor Wallace's performance in Wisconsin, Indiana, and Maryland catalyzed the mood and brought it sharply to the consciousness of the rest of the country. Scholars and scribes were forced to the recognition that they had overestimated the depth of the change of attitude in the country as a whole, and, so in due course most observers switched rapidly from a denial of the "backlash" to an overemphasis of the "backlash." The defeat of Senator Goldwater gave rise to still another mood: that "backlash" was not relevant at all. And, indeed, when the Episcopal Church chooses a Negro suffragan bishop in Massachusetts, when a university of which Robert E. Lee had been president announces its intention to admit Negroes, when the Democrats in Senator Byrd's Virginia invite Negroes to their fund-raising dinner and the subsequent parties, when the Attorney-General of Mississippi urges the sheriffs' association to comply with the Civil Rights Act, the grounds for optimism about the future of American race relations would appear very substantial. Yet, I come with a more conservative, more skeptical argument. The optimism is superficial and, even, dangerous, to the extent that it encourages belief in easy answers or obscures the gravity of the crisis in the republic.

THE FINAL TEST: INTEGRATION IN THE NORTH

The civil rights conflict cannot be understood chiefly as a moral issue —as urgent as the moral dimension may be—nor can it be understood chiefly as a failure of the American Republic to deliver on promises implicit in the Declaration or the Constitution. These views of the issues are mythology—noble mythology perhaps, but mythology still—and the effective resolution of hard problems is more often aided by a clear comprehension of essentials and realities. Without such comprehension, men too often engage in meaningless ritual.

The persistent disparities between Negro and white, whether indicated by economic benefits or cultural symbols or legal rights or actual political opportunity, and the sudden mushrooming of articulate and massive protest against those disparities evoke a sense of analogy to Chartism in Britain, and suggest to me the pertinence of Disraeli's image of "the two nations." The civil rights conflict can better be understood if one recognizes that, by design rather than by accident or oversight, the position of the Negro population has been that of a second nation—bound by the legal obligations of the American order, but regularly relegated to a secondary place in the rank of ordering of esteem, benefits, and power —a secondary place maintained by symbolism where possible and by coercion where necessary.

Until this very generation, the common American expectation was that governmental activity would sustain an order in which racial hierarchy constituted an essential principle or, as is expressed in the cynical Negro aphorism "if you're white, you're right; if you're black, stay back." It is from this perspective that one may justify the somewhat melodramatic caption: "the Negro revolution." This peculiar revolution, so dependent on prayers and petitions, is nonetheless a kind of internal "war" between the two nations which inhabit the one republic. Like most sizeable wars, it has more than one theater, and as often occurs, the theater in which the most dramatic battles occur is not entirely the most crucial if seen in a grand strategy.

So it is here. The ultimate resolution of the civil rights issues must come not from the Southern theater, but from the Northern. (I am, of course, using "North" as verbal shorthand to cite the area outside the Old Confederacy and Kentucky.) To be more rashly exact, I assert that the future of the United States lies in sixty-four Northern cities.

The problem of the South is ultimately military. *In the absence of external coercion and pressure, internal coercion and pressure are dominant.*[1] In Birmingham or Neshoba County, Negro resistance is indispensable to shake the existing order but external support (which means coercion of the dominant white elite) is indispensable for a constructive definition of a new order. Federal policies are the major instrumentality of external coercion. These policies will be brought to bear, and will induce the related support of private institutions, e.g. industry, *to the extent permitted by Northern politics*.[2] The relevance of civil rights to Northern politics will be formed and tested by the volume, intensity and management of ethnic conflicts inherent in sixty-four cities which have more than 100,000 people and which have five per cent or more Negro populations.[3] These are also the cities in which, due to economic history, the late nineteenth century migration produced a complex, multi-national, multi-religious structure in which ethnicity becomes crucial for political choice. The critical importance of ethnicity in urban politics means that civil rights issues will become increasingly controversial *in the North* and thus generate Northern resistance to active Federal policies in either region.

The nature of the controversy in Northern cities will be set, first, by the claims made by Negroes upon the political economy of the region in which they are to be found. These claims are likely to involve both *the politics of respect* and *the politics of benefit*. By the politics of respect I refer to those political behaviors and strategies which are activated by a sense of humiliation and insult. From this sense of humiliation and insult comes a need to *assert* oneself in such a way as to enforce demonstrations of respect from other parties in the political system. Nothing is more essential to the reduction of underlying tensions than the evaporation of those elements of law and policy which to a subordinate group, stand as testimonials to the contempt in which they are held. Such issues run through the American social order. And the ugliest of them all is that of marriage. It would be the merest nonsense to suppose that actual marriage patterns are, one way or another, significantly likely to change at any time which living man can foresee. (One of the simplest tests is that marriage between persons of different races is quite trivial in its extent in the United States—except, possibly, Hawaii—where it is clearly legal.)

Alteration of the actual pattern of marriage relations is not a policy objective. Yet this issue, which neither Negroes nor white are free to discuss with candor, hangs over the political community like a blanket of emotional smog, and now has come to the Supreme Court of the United States, exactly because the limitations, where they exist, represent a clear and unmistakable judgment by the community that Negroes are "naturally" inferior to other peoples. There is no doubt something dark, obscure, fundamental about it, but a political scientist is well advised to leave the etiology of this syndrome to the dual doctorate of human distress—psychiatry and religion.

Yet there is one hard-core political problem which it raises. As Norton

Long has suggested, the key may come from Roman Law's approach to inside and outside peoples. Some possessed the *commercium*, the right to be treated as equals in the economy (and Long treats FEPC as the beginning of *commercium* for the Negro), while most favored possessed the *conubium* or the right to enter what the State would regard as a fully valid marriage. Such a distinction implies a public distinction as to respect. It is difficult to see where such an issue may lead, but it would be dishonest to deny its presence.

For the time, and probably for a very long time, the most important issues will be articulated in terms of the politics of benefit, although the politics of respect will seldom be far beneath the surface. The politics of benefit refers to behaviors and strategies calculated to achieve tangible results, changes in large-scale conditions of life and protections from what may be regarded as realistic threats. The claims will increasingly be pressed forward in domains where people do not normally think of Negroes as having a racial interest (or any interest), but the central problems will lie in economics, education, housing, and public order.

Let us briefly sketch some of the major dimensions which have already arisen in education and in public order.

Nothing weaves together the politics of respect and the politics of benefit so much as educational policy, nor is any issue more likely to magnify ethnic tensions in the Northern cities. Educational policy involves three distinct problems: (1) curriculum policy and evaluation. (2) *de facto* segregation, and (3) the utilization of Negro personnel in public school systems. Although de *facto* segregation or "racial imbalance" constitutes the cutting edge, the disputes are actually disputes about curriculum policy and evaluation.[4]

Any large-city school system which has "too large" a proportion of its Negro students in predominantly Negro schools will continue to be under pressure to change that fact. However, most white parents would prefer their children to remain in all-white schools (or, at the most, to have no more than token integration), because they believe the "cultural deprivation" of Negro children depresses academic standards, because they simply prefer to keep them away from Negroes of any type, or because they fear that, eventually, a school will "tip" so that their children will be in the minority—with all its purported psychic consequences.

The Negroes' objective seems determined in part by a conviction that any concentration of Negro students, however arrived at, leads to an inadequate educational performance. In part, this is an argument from social psychology which demands further exploration. In part, however, it is quite a pragmatic judgment that whenever such concentration occurs the services and facilities provided by educational decision-makers lead to situations in which inadequate educational performance is inevitable. There is some considerable merit to the claim.

On balance, the actual investment of resources in the schools which serve Negroes is inferior to that in schools which serve white students.[5] This much is a problem of simple discrimination. The second, and more complex, problem is that the educational program is designed on the assumption of possession of those cultural qualities which characterize the white, middle-class population. John Brewer, a thoughtful principal whose work has earned national repute, has said: "What happens is that a youngster goes to school and he goes to school with what amounts to an academic mortgage on him when he arrives. By the eighth grade, we foreclose him and flunk him out." The actual objective of educational policy is, assuming a particular end-product as desirable, to develop practices which will take account of cultural diversity leading to academic proficiency in a common culture.

The consequence of such an objective is that the educational decision-makers must be brought to face the strategic use of money, time, and professional skills which are most important of all. School administrators are, prudently, unlikely to offend the more sophisticated, and historically more favored, parents unless and until the demands from the less-favored (which will include the Negroes) is overwhelming. Yet until allocation decisions change, the actual educational offerings for Negro students will not change significantly.

Finally we come to personnel policy. To what extent does the school system undertake to facilitate the rapid promotion of Negroes into major administrative and staff positions? How can it do this without violence to existing promotional criteria and the vested interests of teachers' unions, principals' clubs, etc.? To what extent does the school system undertake to assign teaching, adjunct professional personnel (e.g., school social workers), and adjunct service personnel (e.g., clerks) in contravention of the prior racial patterns in the community. How can this be reconciled with principals' concern for their authority, with the ethnic cleavages which exist within the personnel system, etc.?

Governmental action to secure order in the community has a plethora of ethnic aspects. The most immediate are related to the "first line of defense" function performed chiefly by police departments. Negro claimants argue that police in the normal administration of the criminal law are abusive[6] of the rights of Negroes (as per the Fourth Amendment), exceed proper discretion in the suppression of activity associated with civil rights, provide distinctly lower quality protection and service to Negro areas, and discriminate against Negroes within the force.

Let us consider only the first claim. It is in connection with the abuse of discretion against Negroes that civil rights organizations have in recent years developed the highly controversial proposals for "police review boards" to adjudicate complaints which they make. But the standard police force operates in a professional culture, military in structure, which all existent research seems to indicate is more distinctly averse to "outside interference" than most professional cultures. It is therefore inevitable that police administrators, backed by the Fraternal Order of Police and the various policemen's associations, should desperately resist the effort of outside groups to determine internal procedures. Because the police department tends to form part of the basis of political influence, it is politically essential for city administrators to let the police department manage itself by its own criteria as far as possible.

How far "possible" is, depends on the alignment of political support. The NAACP can be counted as a constant on one side. But what are the constants, and what are the likely supporters, on the opposing side? At least the following become relevant: (a) groups that normally are allied with the police, including homeowners' associations, and which have a vested interest in maintaining the overall structure of ethnic relations, (b) such groups as major commerical interests in downtown areas which may or may not conceive of themselves as opposing racial change, but which do require a stable working relationship with what they conceive to be an effective force, (c) those illicit commercial enterprises which require favorable discretionary action by the police administrators,[7] and (d) the white mass audience which may, more often than not, look to the police to control what it regards as "the Negro crime problem."

It is not alone the police agencies which are involved in these matters from a Negro viewpoint. The growth of civil rights pressure brings new attention to the public prosecutors who perform the critical role of intervening between the police and the courts. No office has more important discretionary powers in state and local government—and much conflict arises over the exercise of discretion. The more precisely such problems are defined in ethnic or civil rights terms, the more difficult they become. If the political atmosphere of the community is hostile to civil rights action, then the prosecutor may move fairly quickly to use his office when civil rights organizations appear to be engaged in equivocal behavior. Does he move equally quickly in initiating enforcement of the state civil rights legislation? There are now, for instance, twenty-six states in which racial discrimination in public accommodations is a statutory offense punishable by fine and/or imprisonment.[8] Eleven of these states have no administrative agency except the public prosecutor and in many others the prosecutor may play a key role. And it must be obvious that so "political" an officer is precisely in the middle on such controversial issues.

These issues of education and public order are but the beginning of a bewildering array of complicated, practical, policy problems which have to be dealt with if racial tensions are permanently to be reduced.

STRUCTURAL BARRIERS IN URBAN DECISION-MAKING

I expect that federal action will be withheld even in the South except for those situations where state and local decision-makers are *patently obstructive* and, *a fortiori*, this must be even more so in the North. Attorney General Katzenbach, whose personal commitment to civil rights seems indubitable, suggested the approach just after the 1964 election that we had "crossed the bridge and left behind us the use of state facilities to frustrate the civil rights movement." Increasingly, he foresaw reliance on state and local governments for reasonable settlements.[9] While fully consistent with the Johnson Administration's optimistic approach to consensus and to "creative federalism"—manifested equally well in the Appalachian program and the "War on Poverty"—such reliance is wholly inadequate because urban political leaders increasingly are losing any capability to manage racial conflict.[10] In virtually all the sixty-four cities which have a rather complicated ethnic system, political decision-makers are recruited from the various groups which comprise the system (Italian, Polish, Irish, etc.) most of which have very high resistance to changes which, to some considerable degree, improve the position of Negroes relative to themselves or, as they see it, at their expense.

Effective resolution of the developing urban conflicts demands not merely the avoidance of public action to frustrate the civil rights movement,[11] but actual and positive governmental action to facilitate civil rights. The ethnic conflicts which have always been latent in the cities now demand policy settlements rather than the management of patronage and ritualistic "recognition" which has been the stock-in-trade of the politicians in the cities.

Politics in the normal sense obstructs such policy-making because those who have access to policy-making positions must save themselves by sacrificing the interests of Negroes to the interests of competing ethnic clienteles. This raises a new dimension in our discussion—the conflict over "Negro representation" as well as the conflict over what is to be done by whoever holds the policy-making position.

There is no doubt that "Negro representation at the policy-making level" will increase. But because of the division of interests between the

Negro politicians and the civil rights leaders, the changes in the actual results for Negro communities are likely to lag behind such formal changes in representation very considerably. If Negro politicians are *Negro*, they also are *politicians* interested in the same specific short-run, and somewhat personalized gains which interest their white colleagues. Vigorous pursuit of civil rights goals threaten their interests because it threatens the interests of their white colleagues, and thus forces them to support their white colleagues lest they be penalized for not doing so.

They can only make a serious break, which is what civil rights action demands, if they can fall back upon the Negro communities for *material support as well as moral support* and thus escape the penalties which white colleagues will tend to impose upon them. It will require extraordinarily strong "motivation" for the Negro politicians as a group to exchange the material rewards derived from their white liaisons for the psychic and symbolic rewards which Negro populations might choose to bestow on "strong race men." In larger cities at least a few Negro politicians can earn their incomes from the Negro community alone. Such leaders will be more "independent" and by the "example" of their independence they will embarrass their colleagues into seeking a somewhat closer identification with civil rights. This will be more difficult in the smaller cities, those under half a million, where the Negro population is simply too small and too poor to support them, nor will it be easy in those larger communities where economic controls tend to be fairly well centralized.

Nonetheless, one may expect the pressures for civil rights to build up in all urban Negro communities. Even Negro politicians who are not going to take serious risks will engage in the ritual of supporting "civil rights" as a symbol, while saving themselves from "downtown" penalties by opting out on the more dramatic strategies.

Such pressure will also change some of the ritualistic behaviors of white politicians. But it is one thing for a Mayor to appear unannounced, with becoming modesty and apparent sincerity, at a COFO rally. It is still another (and less likely) for him to ask the Democratic congressman (whom he helped to nominate) to support COFO's demand that Mississippi congressmen be excluded from the United States House of Representatives. And it is still quite another (and far less likely) for him to intervene with the apartment owners association (for whom he often does favors), quite unofficially, to see if they cannot find practical means to end lily-white tenancy policies.

This all means that the key initiators of civil rights action must continue to be those organizations which have already been committed in this domain—or their replacements. In the absence of other allies (or other forces working independently to the same set of problems), they must emphasize *racial* goals. In the immediate future, it seems most likely that they will seek to utilize racial goals as a key to *electoral* political action,[12] yet they are subject to important constraints in this process. The basic constraint arises out of the nature of their clientele. These are essentially three: (1) the educated and middle-class or upper-class Negroes who are doctrinal militants, (2) the lower-class Negro adults, and (3) the lower-class Negro youth. These distinctions must be somewhat fluid, and so must any efforts to generalize them. On balance, however, it is undoubtedly true that the most important support for civil rights action, prior to 1960 (when the student sit-ins began) came from the educated middle-class and upper-middle class Negroes. It is not true that all, or even most, of this class was deeply committed to the civil rights objective—nor that lower-class support was wholly lacking. But the center-of-gravity was midde-class, which probably explains why, until quite recently, the objectives of civil rights organizations—as well as their tactics—were those with which such people could be comfortable.

While the lower-income adults share the resentments which activate the educated and the well-to-do, they are, like most lower-class populations, much more apathetic and cynical. I remember being told by an elderly lady up in the middle of one Negro slum in Pittsburgh last August, "we all just have to remember that we're colored." She was not a militant advocating racial unity. She was rather, a realist—indeed a fatalist—arguing that only undesirable results can come from trying to change the racial hierarchy. Such people have heard all this talk about "equal rights" before and they have judged it to be no more than talk. They have practical problems trying to get along. You know one must make this week's rent, somehow; one must meet today's problems, everyone must do this. And the millennium—well that's another story.

The lower-class youth have a different form of cynicism which leads not so much toward apathy as toward rebellion against organization and control. These were, please remember, the people who most actively participated in the physical disturbances in 1964 and their actions directly expressed their frustrations. And it is extremely difficult to give them, as Burke would put it, "a stake in society." Moreover, like all young people —as Erikson seems to me to have shown[13]—they make demands on the world in "all or nothing" terms. They have not discovered the gray wisdom of the world.

The strategic problem of urban Negro leadership is to find the clearest and simplest terms in which to articulate the expectations of all three groups in such a way as to achieve mass support. This must mean goals which seem achievable in the short run. "Beat Barry!" was such a goal in 1964, but there are few such goals in the real world. Most such goals demand a racial emphasis which threatens to evoke polarization. The potentialities of such polarization are foreshadowed by the presidential election of 1964 in which we estimate that more than 95% of the Negro voters supported the Democratic ticket. Such Negro behavior was rational in the sense that there was no option left by the tone of the 1964 Republican campaign, but it makes the Negro population captive to the Democratic party—will the obvious result that the Democratic need to consider the interests of the Negro population automatically diminishes. Yet interest bloc voting is most effective when the competitors for the vote think there is both need to compete and that whether one competes makes some difference. Bloc voting is effective, moreover, only if potential opponents have other interests which take such high priority that they cannot afford to spare the effort for organization into counter-blocs.

This is precisely what is no longer true in the cities. Ethnic polarization is a serious risk precisely because so many of the other groups have a strong interest in "stopping the Negroes!" Observe the experience of Detroit, 1964. In the City Council—nine members elected at large—the one Negro member resigned. In the consequent by-election the two top candidates were a Negro candidate and a white candidate—best known as the spokesman for certain white home-owners' associations—who outdistanced his Negro competitor by 2-1. In the run-off the white candidate, predictably, won the seat.

At the very same time, the electorate adopted a "Homeowners' Rights Ordinance" which specified that anyone had an absolute right to sell his property under any circumstances or to refrain from doing so. From the lawyer's viewpoint, such an ordinance was of dubious validity, but its psychological-political meaning was far more relevant. It represented one more expression of white property holders' opposition to open occupancy legislation—an expression coming on top of similar rejections in Berkeley, Seattle, Tacoma, and the State of California.

Polarization in the urban centers has consequences for both State and Federal politics. The disparity between central city (the seat of urban racial conflict) and suburban areas, and the evident fact that one major element in suburbanization has been the desire of white families to separate themselves from Negro families, is one focus. Since the consequence of *Baker* v. *Carr* is that the suburban areas must increasingly become politically influential at the State level through the legislatures, one would expect an increased state legislative intervention into the internal affairs of the central cities for the purpose of protecting the suburbs.

Moreover, the respectable re-entry of racism into politics could not but have its effects on congressional politics in urban centers. In those districts where the Negro population is truly dominant, congressmen would naturally find it prudent to join the Negro side. But in most other districts, they would find it prudent to oppose Negro claims, and their intervention at the Federal level further must inhibit the discretion of Federal administrators.

Our discussion of the polarity of voting which seems possible elecits a more basic observation. *Every tactic is adaptable for opposing ends and by opposing sides.* This political version of the doctrine that "the Devil may quote Scripture for his own purposes" must be understood in relation to the massive moral protest, the commonest form of direct action, which is almost surely to be revived in due course exactly because of the likely failure of "normal" politics.

The Negro boycott may be a highly effective weapon if the school administration can be induced to take the basic decisions required *before counter-boycotts emerge*. However, if the Parents-and-Taxpayers' model in New York City should be emulated at an earlier stage, in those cities where integration programs are still at the lowest level of discussion or not being discussed at all, then the school administrations are unlikely to be moved to integration by this method. They will be so moved only if they have independent incentives (such as their own preferences) or if a Negro direct-action campaign is regarded by them as far more punitive than a white counter-campaign.

This raises a fundamental problem which is well known to students of international politics. The ability to impose penalties upon the opposite party is an essential condition of political success. It is not sufficient, but it is essential. Strategic problems begin to arise when one calculates the various resources which one may use to impose penalties.[14]

Urban civil rights leaders, lacking the resources to use any other unitive strategies, must often have recourse to those mass-action strategies which may be of dubious legality or, even, on the face of it illegal.[15] If such measures are effective, there is no problem. But mass action soon reaches limits where a deliberate decision to escalate, which may be required if one is to be sufficiently punitive to be received seriously by the other party, involves the risk of violence. Despite, or perhaps because of, the great role of violence in American development, the national culture embodies a mystique according to which violence is always "bad." Violence is not merely one man's behavior, or one group's behavior, but the interpretation which another man or another group puts on that behavior. In the American mystique of peaceful settlement, violence is always bad, but *it is worse if the perpetrators are Negro and the victims white than if the perpetrators white and the victims Negro.*

I discussed some of these matters in 1963 with a big-city schools superintendent. At the time the superintendent—whose personal lack of "prejudice" seemed to me greater than most people's—observed that he would be opposed to any "violent" action to change *de facto* segregation. "I would," he volunteered, "include a boycott as violent." If he actually faced a boycott, and made a TV speech calling it "violent," many white viewers would accept and respond to this symbol, *regardless what the boycotters actually did.*

Consider the meaning of the word "riot." In ordinary American experience, a "race riot" has been an organized white marauding expedition into Negro communities, an expedition which sometimes leads to white deaths and almost always leads to more Negro deaths. *In the summer of 1964 no white person was deliberately killed by any Negro in the context of any of the controversies.* Instead, the crowds inflicted substantial damage upon property and, while this is entirely objectionable to the public order, it is not the same as murder. Yet the outburst of sporadic, unorganized violence in the summer of 1964 was received as if it were some latter-day Nat Turner's rebellion, or Revolt of Denmark Vesey. In the simplest terms, the common reaction was "the Negroes have gone too far!"

Yet more outbursts would seem predictable, exactly because of the oscillation between hope and despair. There is persistent unemployment and a much-advertised job market in which employers are prepared to take Negroes, but the jobs require skills which the unemployed do not have and *cannot learn in short order.* College admissions are increasingly open but high schools remain so bad that Negro students who think they are prepared experience high academic mortalities in the freshman year. Mayors pay symbolic deference to civil rights but police continue to "shove around" Negro youngsters who are "out of bounds." Urban renewal and open occupancy laws promise a freer housing situation, but actual housing for most urban Negroes continues as bad as ever. The "cause of civil rights" is talked in a large sense and petty reality retains its old, sharp, bitter taste. All these are tensions which mass action catalyzes and sometimes controls. If present leadership cannot produce, for those who are not yet rewarded, then present leadership has little alternative except to escalate or to be replaced. To discredit organized leadership would only turn loose feeling which is expressive, but hardly instrumental. This is the etiology of the Harlem-Rochester-Philadelphia experience in which the purported leadership is completely unable to "turn off the explosive fury"[16] which it had never really controlled, intended, or desired.

Finally, we must note a third level of the problem. The concept of "self-help" has recently come into vogue among Negro leaders. It is surprising that it has not done so before, for it represents a deep and inarticulate desire to be autonomous or in common language, "to be rid of that white man." If white Americans are approving of these efforts, particularly when they take the form of community development projects and small business ventures, they must also be realistic enough to recognize that any population which adopts the "self-help" concept sooner or later adopts its physical dimension whenever the likelihood of physical protection from the public authorities seems remote.

Self-defense forces comparable to those which have arisen in parts of the South are much less likely. What we cannot exclude, however, is the adaptation of the citizens' patrol.[17]

One of the harsh experiences of Negro urban life is the omnipresence of violence and the lack of police protection. In New York, in 1964, the first "citizens' patrol" was formed in a Jewish area, as protection against marauders—many presumably Negro. After some initial complaints of vigilantism, the idea was adapted by Negroes for much the same purpose, to the consternation of the Police Commissioner. The prospect is indeed grim if one considers the likely step in the event of racial trouble. It is almost unthinkable that such patrols could avoid the next step of arming —they are not presently armed—and of using their arms in delicate circumstances.

These lines of thought bring us, then, once more to the question of what happens when results are not achieved and conflicts are escalated. The experience of race relations in American provides, I should think, no reason to assume that each tactic used by white or by Negro will not be met by a similar use on the other side. However, since it is the threat of "Negro violence" which is most feared by the white majority, the latent hostilities could easily call for actions leading to a more important police role than one has ever seen in American experience.

Although this is not a jeremiad, let us examine some practical situations. In Philadelphia, the riots cost the city several million dollars in damage claims—apart from extra police costs—and it is reasonable to suppose that many white Philadelphians emotionally charged the cost to "the Negroes." When the Rochester riots were over, a reporter asked the Mayor why it had happened and what should now be done. The Mayor had nothing but puzzlement at the event, and his idea of a future solution was that "some of the responsible ones" (Negroes) should get up a fund to indemnify the property-owners who had been damaged. Shades of the Boxer Rebellion!

THE PRICE OF DOMESTIC PEACE

The price of domestic peace is the price of all successful statecraft: realism. Realism demands, to begin, an explicit understanding that the conflicts between white and black are real and not imaginary. All politics involves conflict over the distribution of advantages and disadvantages.[18] Any group which is unable to assure that its vital interests are usually considered and sometimes given preference over, or at least reconciled to, the interests of other groups when policies are being made may be said to be an "outside" group. The most excluded or "outside" groups are those which are not merely denied favorable policies all or most of the time, but which are also in such a weak position that their most significant symbols are held in disesteem—or even proscribed. Realism also demands a recognition that neither can "triumph" at the expense of the other. We need not consider whether the position of the Negro civil rights issues spring from some peculiar moral flaw in the American character. The core of the problem is that these issues involve the element of a *struggle* in which each side seeks to force its objectives upon the other. The civil rights crisis in the United States is fundamentally similar to that between English and Irish ending with the breakup of 1922, or to that which now strains the bonds of Canadian politics. Such a struggle constitutes a grave threat to the republic. *Salvation of the republic itself demands the conversion of this struggle into a bargaining problem where the parties may increasingly find mutual terms consistent with their interests and their self-respect.*

In the end, "integration" must mean the existence of a common nationhood within the republic, a state of affairs in which the exercise of rights, the achievement of power, the pursuit of benefits and the conferral of respect does not take account of race at all. But such a state is difficult to achieve and requires serious effort. The actions which men may take today and tomorrow *are not themselves* "integration." A city is not "integrated" simply because white leaders finally agree to the appointment of a Negro in the mayor's cabinet. Those who think that it is delude themselves. A city is not "integrated" simply because formal segregation of the schools ceases and every classroom is a picture of racial diversity. Those who think that it is delude themselves. These are only techniques which have meaning within a deeper understanding of "integration" as essentially a four-fold process for the resolution of conflict amongst groups.

(1) The indispensable step is *bargaining* and bargaining depends on an effective structure within which the leaders of various sides can accept each other as "authoritative." It would be impossible to make effective economic policies but for the fact that the farm organizations and the committee system establish procedures which give authentic farmer spokesmen. It would be impossible to make effective economic policies but for the fact that there are authoritative spokesmen for "big business."[19] It would be impossible to make effective labor policy without the procedure which allows systematic choice of a bargaining agent, or some reasonable substitute for it.

The problem of bargaining over civil rights is far more complex. It is not merely that Negroes resist *bargaining* (which means compromise) *over rights* (which are deemed absolute). It is rather that ethnic disputes allow much room for determining who or what is an "authoritative" spokesman because the issues are so diffuse and because white leadership prefers not to bargain at all. They are, so it will be judged, the "losers" in the sense that bargaining also implies a change in the *status quo* with which they are already satisfied. As Lewis Coser so persuasively argues, the termination of conflict lies in the hands of the "loser." It is he, who, depending on his judgment of the issues and their meaning, must call a halt or insist upon indefinite prolongation.[20]

Hence, the public officials and others against whom pressures are brought play a major discretionary role in choosing Negro leaders by deciding to whom they will or will not grant audiences—with whom they will and will not bargain. In the short run, this may be a reasonable strategy for the Mayor or school board which faces Negro pressures. In the long run, it is harmful to the interests of the community because it simply forces such claimants to leadership to organize the massive demonstrations which are their only real power.

This leads back to a politics in which the explicit emphasis is on symbols and a politics of symbols makes us all demand that out opposite numbers behave consistently in ways which satisfy all the symbols we prefer. Thus, symbolic politics lends itself to indefinite expansion with no satisfactory settlement. Neither white nor Negro populations, nor any other human groups, can be free from profound irrationalities. Effective resolution does not demand dissolving the irrationalities but on establishing practical conditions which lead to mutual existence. This means that a strategic problem of both white and Negro leadership is, as far as possible, to avoid those symbolic demands which require the psychological political equivalent of total and unconditional surrender.

(2) Integration as a process also depends upon pragmatic accommodation by leaders on each side to the results which they create by bargaining. Thus, one can get a bargaining situation merely for the purpose of stopping a street dispute, but that by itself settles nothing and, indeed, may create the conditions under which leaders will repudiate the whole arrangement if they are disappointed in themselves and embarrassed in front of their followers. Leaders across the bargaining lines must be able to take the position that there is more to gain than to be lost by continued bargaining. In due course, if the integrative process is to be effective, they must also come to internalize the values of the new situation which they are helping to create. The founders of the nation, if I may illustrate the point by some examples which no longer carry heat, engaged initially in

a political deal. And some, e.g. Messrs. Hamilton and Jefferson, accepted the deal and stayed with it in the first decade chiefly because there was more to gain than to lose in not staying with it. In due course, they developed an orientation toward it which meant that they actually preferred the new institution to be maintained—even if they sometimes lost immediate objectives within it.

(3) In the current racial issues, an indispensable element in moving from the merest mechanical bargaining to a stable institutional pattern is in the developments of policies which will convey important benefits to the Negro population at large. *Such an approach calls for a specific extension of the historic pattern of American public policy.* Policy-makers make specific and strategic decisions about the ends which they wish to serve and allocate resources accordingly. Thus, Senator Goldwater could strongly defend the specific investment of public resources in the Central Arizona Project. In tax policy it is characteristic that decisions are made with a fairly good understanding of those whom they will give preference and those from whom they will withhold preference.[21] Similarly, all agricultural policy is a policy of preferential support. When Canadian farmers begin to outsell American farmers, in the world wheat market, the United States immediately increases its export subsidy in order to permit the American farmers to hold their position.[22] At a certain point, when political support for unionism is rising, the Congress enacts the Wagner Act which gives the unions legal support and preference in their efforts to establish themselves as collective bargaining agents—and the power of the United States Government is mobilized in their favor and against the recalcitrant companies. At another point, the policy is shifted in the favor of the companies by the passage of the Taft-Hartley Act.

The concepts of preferential policies can reasonably be defended on its main basis: that disparities of the magnitude which now separate white and Negro are a standing provocation to tension and strife, inconsistent with the public interest in domestic tranquility. Since it has historically been observed that, in the integrative process, "down payments" by stronger to weaker sides have much effect in stabilization,[23] it becomes urgent to conceive policies which direct special attention to those problems which significantly affect Negroes. It is not essential, or even helpful, to construct such policies upon some mystical doctrine of historical debt[24] or to carry them out in such a way as to impose arbitrary penalties upon persons who are white.

(4) The final stage in the process of integration is the development of values which are common to both Negro and white populations at large, and which are meaningful in the sense that they govern the action which each takes toward the other in common-sense, every-day, garden-variety

matters. It is therefore incumbent upon leadership to take those actions which will reduce the burden of governmental decision. This imposes particular demands upon white leadership for *it is through the mechanisms of white leadership that the actions which subordinate Negroes take place.* Precisely because symbolic actions are important in the minds of people, it is important not to impose symbolic deprivations and to relieve them where they exist. The failure to do so, and the knowledge that there is a specific purpose *not to do so,* is precisely what provokes recourse to governmental machinery. Domestic peace requires, therefore, that issues in conflict be decided at private levels to the utmost extent possible, reserving governmental decision to those few strategic cases where such decisions can significantly affect the main flow of events.

There are many private bodies with some capability to act. The trade unions have a vital interest, and the continuing rift between labor and civil rights organizations ought to be warning enough. The warning appears to have been understood at the top level of the AFL-CIO. And it appears to have been understood at the top of some of the major internationals.

Whether it has been understood at the level of the central city bodies remains to be seen. To take the homely barbershop example, it ought to be a relatively simple matter for the barber's union to agree—without compulsion or pressure—most customers will be accepted without arbitrary racial distinctions.

The crucial institutions, which have barely begun to notice the problem, let alone assume a role, are the nation's major industrial and financial entities. These constitute the one group whose resources give them access to all parts of the community. Moreover, they have a high strategic incentive. No institutions could be more seriously injured by failure than those which have a vital interest in continued economic development of the major urban regions. Hitherto, they have had little reason to consider these matters. But if resources for action are exhausted and civil disorder should mount, the effort which they have put into other aspects of urban development—industrial relocation, urban renewal, etc.—would diminish with breathtaking rapidity.

First, the major corporations control, in alliance with the unions, the employment system and it lies within the ability of the corporation to establish and to enforce employment policies which will assure (a) that a favorable atmosphere exists for Negro applicants, (b) that the organization actually searches—within and without—for hireable (or promotable) Negroes, and (c) that production and work requirements are rationally examined to see whether Negroes are excluded because more formal schooling is demanded by personnel administrators than the jobs actually require.[25] Regardless of what some public agency may do, the aggressive impact of the firms is far greater, and very few firms have yet set about enforcing such policies with the same seriousness that they would seek to avoid anti-trust prosecutions, stockholder revolts, or the theft of secrets about their key processes.

Second, major corporations may re-examine their licensing and franchising policies to consider the practical means of facilitating the growth of Negro-owned or Negro-operated business enterprises which serve some realistic function within the major industrial system. This is of major importance precisely because it may contribute to the process of capital development within Negro life sufficient to reduce the dependency of Negro communities upon mere beneficence and this is an indispensable element of the autonomous strength which leads to integration.

Third, the major corporation may make a major impact on housing policies by relatively simple measures. Apart from mere prejudice, one of the major reasons for middle-class resistance to integration of the housing market is a status fear which, ultimately, is translated into fears about consequences for careers. If one recalls the upsurge of political interest, half a dozen years ago, at the behest of corporate political education directors, the same key may be presented. There is no reason in the world why the corporate elite should not make it very clear that no stigma attaches to a junior executive because his wife has joined a "fair housing committee." Moreover, this would reduce the inhibitions not merely on whites but on those Negroes who have, by virtue of corporate employment, acquired the financial support necessary for fairly free entry into the market. Such Negro personnel are on occasion subtly discouraged from leaving areas they do not prefer, and going into other areas, by the hint that "if this becomes a controversial matter, it would be bad for company public relations."

The major financial institutions have a similarly strategic role in regard to the housing market. One of the critical barriers to achieving a fluid housing market, in which race is not a significant criterion, is an element of restriction in lending policies. Such restrictions may well have the effect of vitiating the housing orders issued by the late President Kennedy by shifting financing to the conventional market. In Cleveland, in 1964, the major banks of the city, subsequently joined by about half the savings and loan associations, adopted a common statement of policy that, thenceforth, normal credit-worthiness would be the sole test applied to applicants for housing financing. Such an action, assuming its effective implementation, is far more significant than any of the devices specifically meant to create "model" integrated communities, or other similar actions.

Finally, there is another dimension of private activity which offers possibilities. In every major city, the fact of life is that the Negro population is remarkably dependent on the services of the health and welfare cluster—both public and private. In the final analysis, these agencies depend upon private industry, upon labor in lesser measure, and upon state and local government—directly or indirectly. They do not yet seem to have comprehended the problem. They do not yet seem to have understood that the provision of services in Negro communities, apart from consultation with leadership in such communities, increasingly is likely to be regarded as "social work 'colonialism.'"[26]

Whether a fundamental reorientation is possible depends chiefly on: (a) whether the professional specialists who set the tone of thought and discussion in such agencies can comprehend the pressure of the civil rights agencies—or continue to regard them as "mere agitators," and (b) whether the vital interests of those upon whom the professionals rely for support will permit redirection of policies.

THE CONFLICT OF TWO NATIONS

The conception which I have been presenting, resting upon the premise of "conflict between 'two nations,'" leads me to the argument that the present mood of satisfaction is sentimental and ultimately dangerous *precisely because it ignores the firm foundation on which ethnocentrism stands in American culture and may seriously underestimate the potentiality of a drastic reaction against civil rights as Negro claims pass the borders of sentimental allegiance to "the American dream" and into the rough terrain of real and pragmatic interests.*

In sum, I have been suggesting . . . that the integrative process demands two major approaches. (1) It demands a complete repudiation of the notion that diminution of Federal interest and pressure, limited though Federal resources may be, will in any way assist the resolution of ethnic ontroversy in the urban North. On the contrary, this can only foster such controversy by increasing the resistance of those whose preference is for the *status quo*. It becomes essential to find means to move civil rights issues from the domain of struggle to the domain of bargaining, and this implies the adoption and effective execution of the realistically-conceived packet of preferential policies designed to reduce disparities between white and Negro so that bargaining (which means compromise) becomes legitimate and feasible. (2) The integrative process cannot stop at mere bargaining, but demands the strengthening of core values, consequent to the development of common interests, between white and Negro and in this the essential role must be played increasingly by private groups, for private groups alone have the effective power to create those situations which lead to an evaporation of the politics of respect.

Let me conclude this analysis by reversing the normal order of argumentation to emphasize that I am now adding a historical dimension which may provide perspective. The concept of two "nations"—some might prefer two "cultures"—is not merely figurative, although it has that element in it. First, it is hardly necessary these days to demonstrate the wide economic disparities which persistently show up if one examines data referring to Negroes and to whites. If one needed a single, suggestive key one might go to the *Economic Report of the President*, 1963. Chapter 5 of that *Report* presents the now-famous $3,000-a-year family-income test of poverty, and calculated that about one-fifth of the population fell between the "poverty line." But it would immediately appear, from the same source, that about one-half of the Negro families fell beneath that "line." To go on would be tedious in this place.

But there is a different kind of test. One of the boundaries between peoples is the culture-hero boundary. What symbolic figures do they esteem? This is a simple test of respect. Ask the question: prior to the emergence of Ralph Bunche (who *may* be an exception) what major Negro figure—also excepting athletes and entertainers—simultaneously stood as a culture hero for black Americans and for white? Booker T. Washington would, I think, be regarded by Negroes as having been too willing and convenient an instrumentality for the white majority. (Personally, I think this is unfair to Mr. Washington, who was a very sophisticated realist playing a very difficult and perhaps an impossible role.) Frederick Douglass is a culture hero for some Negro intellectuals, but the white audiences have never heard of him—although their great-grandfathers did. Marcus Garvey was, for some, a sort of lower-class hero, but his memory too is cold. Paul Robeson even, despite his unfortunate politics, is well regarded because Negroes—even conservative, Republican, middle-class, affluent Negroes—regard him as having sacrificed a remunerative career out of racial anguish.

Is he not anathema to whites?

To most Negroes the racial culture-hero stands as a symbol of hope —of the unrealized potentialities of the race, but to the dominant element of white Americans, he is simply the "exceptional" figure who stands in the same relationship to the white American as the talking dog did to Dr. Johnson. But the talking dog was not a figure Dr. Johnson would incorporate into his own pantheon.

The Negro culture-hero becomes more highly esteemed, by Negroes, when he actively identifies himself with them, even if his style and his aspirations must sometimes pull him into another realm. The more militant the figure (Douglass, Garvey, Robeson) the less likely he is to be accorded respect from white Americans. After all, the brothers Maccabeus were not accorded respect by the Romans. Flavius Josephus was.

Because the political system is surely regarded as the common tie, I find the image of the "two nations" is ultimately sustained by much more than demarcations between two domains of culture-heroes. It can be summarized in the broad course of American public policy since the foundation of the Republic. Whatever we may say for his legal reasoning or his political wisdom, Mr. Chief Justice Taney's reading of the social psychology of the American Constitution was correct. From the foundation of the Republic until the Civil War, the specific policy of the Federal Government—and of most of the States, North and South—was one of racial hierarchy. The three-fifths formula and the attendant constitutional recognition of Negro slavery was part of the bargain essential to the success of the Constitutional Convention and one of the very earliest major pieces of legislation—the Fugitive Slave Act of 1793—placed the support of Congress behind slavery. Northern state legislation forbidding the residence of Negroes, requiring them to have licenses in order to maintain residences, and constitutional provisions denying Negroes access to the franchise (such a provision, a dead letter now, still remains in the actual wording of the Ohio State Constitution), all expressed the dominant conception that the American order was a hierarchy in which white dominance over black—with or without the economic structure of slavery—was to be preserved.

The obvious fact is that the Civil War is the single most important experience for Negroes because it eventuated in the Emancipation, yet that war constituted no more than an interregnum—a holding period between the active legal support of racial hierarchy before the War and the tacit (but equally effective) support of racial hierarchy after the War. The Reconstruction is significant as the one period before Little Rock when the authority of the Federal Government, as manifested by Presidential and Congressional politics, was cast actively on the side of diminishing the barriers between the two nations and of integrating them into one. From the Southern viewpoint the Reconstruction was not to be resisted because of its purported "corruption." C. Vann Woodward, Howard K. Beale and others have demonstrated that Reconstruction governments were no more corrupt than other aspects of American politics at the same time, nor, for that matter, no more corrupt than antebellum governments. Nor, for that matter, were these governments Negro-dominated.[27] It simply was that *any significant influence by Negroes was to be resisted as a form of insurrection against a social order of white dominance.*

The Hayes-Tilden election settlement meant, in racial terms, a Federal commitment to take no action which would challenge the re-established racial hierarchy, and Southern white leadership was once more free to utilize whatever resources—legal, illegal, or extra-legal, symbolic or violent—deemed necessary and proper to maintain the racial hierarchy. Moreover, succeeding Federal Administrations actually moved to reinforce that hierarchy, particularly in the re-introduction of racialist influences during the Wilson Administration.

New Deal politics represented the first cracks in active Federal support of racial hierarchy. In view of the importance of Presidential leadership on basic policies, I find direct demonstration of the potent national commitment to racial hierarchy in the course of President Franklin D. Roosevelt. The President's broad personal sympathies seemed fairly clear to interested observers,[28] but the President himself prudently remained disengaged from any racial policy issues which might have challenged the national consensus. The New Deal strategy may be called "benign racism" in contrast to the "malignant racism" of those who specifically sought to keep the Negro population in the most deprived position. The strategy assumed, correctly, that the economic problems of Negroes were so severe that Negroes simply would not pursue any racial challenges to a point at which the coalition on which economic benefits depended might be threatened.

Like President Lincoln, President Roosevelt first faced the problem of a significant change in race relations consequent to the exigencies of war.[29] And, under the circumstances the Presidential action was forced by the threat of a "March-on-Washington,"[30] and the action itself was a proclamation justified chiefly in terms of a more efficient utilization of manpower. Nonetheless, it introduced into the political economy of the United States, the concept of *governmental action* to support "fair" employment practices.

The active pursuit of "integration" as a national policy demanding a major Federal role and a significant investment of Presidential time—emanates from the Report of the President's Committee on Civil Rights (1947) and with President Truman's absorption of these issues into his 1948 campaign.[31] The implicit challenge of Executive Order 8802 then became a major item of government.

There is a very simple way to put it. The problem of melding two nations into one republic indivisible *was first becoming* a major issue of policy when the college freshmen of 1965 were being born. If we consider the gravity of the issues, the deep feelings involved, the natural resistance of whites to losing a position of unqualified dominance and the natural hostility of Negroes that dominance should so long have gone unchallenged, then we are forced to consider that principles are easier to declare than policies are to adopt, that policies are easier to adopt than they are to administer, that the burdens upon government and society are extraordinary.

Moreover, it is the North which is just becoming the testing-ground for large-scale racial change and the lessons of conflict are remarkably clear. Nowhere does a social structure adapt easily. In Calvin's terms, "will" is more important than "reason," and it is far from clear, as the hard issues are presented to the urban Northern decision-makers, whether or not "will" may accommodate to "reason" without much deep and bitter struggle.

NOTES

1. One of my academic colleagues from a Southern, white, state university—who must perforce remain nameless—put it to me thusly: "you in the North have the obligation to help us modernize our society in the South so as to bring it up to the national level."

2. A similar view is presented by my colleague, George D. Blackwood of Boston University in his paper, "Civil Rights and Direct Attention in the Urban North," read at the American Political Science Association meeting, September 1964. It may be important to specify that Professor Blackwood's analysis partakes more of the "liberal" approach to American politics than this present paper does.

3. This group of cities contains about one-third of all American Negroes. On the basis of the 1960 data, more than 5,000,000 Negroes are to be found in the seventeen Northern cities of 500,000 or over. About one and one-half million are to be found in cities from 100,000 to 500,000. I make these calculations for the data presented in, U.S. Housing and Home Finance Agency. Office of the Administrator. *Our Non-White Population and Its Housing, The Changes from 1950 to 1960*, (Washington: HHFA, 1963), particularly Tables 7 and 9.

4. I may not stop to elaborate now, but curriculum increasingly comes to be a controversial item in terms of the politics of respect. As an ideological point, Negro claimants (and other claimants) sometimes criticize the curriculum because it uses material which either ignores them altogether (as they see it) or which constructs adverse images in the minds of children. This explains the disputation about such things as the Joel Chandler Harris stories.

5. Some of the relevant evidence is cited in Charles Silberman. *Crisis in Black and White*, (New York: Random House, 1964).

6. See the experience of the so-called "dragnet" which was regarded by Detroit Negroes (of all classes, occupations, and levels of education) in 1961 as a virtual military occupation. The Detroit newspapers for the first few months of 1961 will record the story, as will the dramatic defeat of the incumbent Mayor that fall, partly by virtue of an overwhelming Negro vote for his opponent (a political unknown) in the subsequent campaign.

7. Here one should note Congressman Powell's claims of ethnic discrimination in these favorable discretionary ameliorations of the formal legal requirements.

8. *Background Report on State Activity to Foster Non-Discrimination in Education, Employment, Housing and Public Accommodations*, Governors' Conference, 56th Annual Meeting, Report of the Executive Committee based on Replies from the Governors, Cleveland, Ohio: June 6–10, 1964, p. 21, Table 3.

9. This is reported in a dispatch by Jack Vandenberg of UPI in *The Pittsburgh Press*, November 18, 1964, p. 32.

10. The logic of this is further developed in, Matthew Holden, Jr., "Limitations on the Integrative Function of Party: Recruitment and Socialization in Urban Politics," (in preparation).

11. We cannot even assume the absence of obstructionism in the urban North. The author is aware of one Community Action Program under the Economic Opportunity Act which was long delayed because the school board president vetoed all potential appointees to the governing body of the proposed CAP agency who had any record of civil rights action.

12. The re-emphasis on electoral tactics rather than mass-actior tactics is clearly conveyed in reports of the February 1964 "summit" conference of Negro leaders in New York. See *New York Times*, Sunday, January 31, 1965, p. 64; and Monday, February 1, 1965, p. 30.

13. Erik H. Erikson, *Young Man Luther: A Study in Psychoanalysis and History*, (New York: W. W. Norton and Co., Inc., 1962).

14. The steel companies were able to impose a painful, but purely symbolic penalty, upon the late President Kennedy after his intervention in 1962 price decision. They were easily able to stigmatize him as "anti-business."

15. They must do this in the hope that, in due course, the final court will say that the action *was* legal, thus overruling earlier administrative or judicial rulings. See the discussion of "accidents of litigation" and their impact on what "is" or "is not" legal, in, C. K. Allen, *Law in the Making*, (New York: Oxford University Press [Oxford Paperbacks No. 29], 1961), pp. 298–299.

They may sometimes also hope that the community-at-large will be more impressed with moral claim and dismiss the technical violation as of little import. Witness, here, the long controversy between Mr. James B. Donovan and the various school boycott leaders in New York City, notably the Rev. Milton Galamison.

16. The phrase is used by, Arthur L. Whitaker, "The Anatomy of a Riot," *The Crisis*, Vol. 72, No. 1 (January 1965), pp. 20–25.

17. See, for instance, the story on the "Deacons for Defense and Justice," *New York Times* Sunday, February 21, 1965.

18. In this formulation, I follow Lewis A. Froman, Jr., *People and Politics*, (Englewood Cliffs, New Jersey: Prentice-Hall, Inc., 1963).

19. Bernard D. Nossiter, *The Mythmakers: An Essay on Power and Wealth* (Boston: Houghton Mifflin Company, 1964), pp. 2–6, describes the successful effort of big business to resist Secretary Hodges' pressure for reorganization of the Business Advisory Council.

20. Lewis Coser, "The Termination of Conflict," *Journal of Conflict Resolution*, Vol. 5, No. 4 (December 1961) pp. 347–353.

21. Bernard D. Nossiter, *The Mythmakers: An Essay on Power and Wealth*, (Boston: Houghton Mifflin Company, 1964) discusses this in a particularly illuminating way, when considering the fiscal policies of the late President Kennedy.

22. *New York Times*, Wednesday, January 27, 1965, p. 45.

23. Karl W. Deutsch, et al., *Political Community and the North Atlantic Area: International Organization in the Light of Historical Experience*, (Princeton: Princeton University Press, 1957), pp. 186–187.

24. The emergence of the "doctrine of debt" is briefly noted by Charles Silberman, *Crisis in Black and White*, pp. 237–238.

25. I acknowledge the adaptation of this idea from a speech written by Marion Folsom, who had in mind certain practical attacks on the current poverty problem, as presented at *Conference on Poverty in America*, University of California, Berkeley, California, February 27, 1965.

26. Harlem Youth Opportunities, Inc., *Youth in the Ghetto: A Study of the Consequences of*

Powerlessness and a Blueprint for Change. (New York: HARYOU, 1964), pp. 23–27.

27. An essay demonstrating the limits of Negro influence is presented in, C. Vann Woodward, *Civil War and Reconstruction*, (Baton Rouge: Louisiana State University Press, 1960), ("The Political Legacy of Reconstruction"), pp. 98–107.

28. Walter F. White, *A Man Called White: The Autobiography of Walter White.* (New York: The Viking Press, 1948).

29. A good, brief summary of President Lincoln's path to the Emancipation Proclamation will be found in, Benjamin Quarles, *Lincoln and the Negro*, (New York: Oxford University Press, 1962), pp. 125–130.

30. Herbert Garfinkel, *When Negroes March: The March on Washington Movement in the Organization Politics for FEPC*, (Glencoe: Free Press, 1959), also White, *op. cit.*

31. It should be recalled, in perspective, that the President's absorption of the issue into his campaign followed a floor fight at the 1948 Philadelphia Democratic Convention. The "strong" civil rights plank was pushed through, over the objections of Truman Democrats, by a "liberal" coalition. Vice-President Humphrey's career as a national figure dates from his successful floor leadership of that coalition.

PART THREE

Problems and Aspects of Black Politics

8

The Negro Vote: Ceteris Paribus

Chuck Stone

> *Many wise men hold that the white vote of the South should divide, the color line be beaten down, and the southern states ranged on economic or moral questions as interest or belief demands.*
> *I am compelled to dissent from this view. The worst thing that could happen, in my opinion, is that the white people of the South should stand in opposing factions, with the vast mass of ignorant or purchasable negro votes between.*
> *Consider such a status. If the negroes were skillfully led—and leaders would not be lacking—it would give them the balance of power.*
>
> HENRY WOODFIN GRADY,
> prominent southern journalist and orator, 1886

THE HISTORICAL PARANOIA of southern whites about a black voting bloc rising like a Phoenix from the ashes of white oppression to become the decisive balance in all elections was a subconscious recognition that white brutality might one day ignite black retaliation.

The only reason blacks would be compelled to act or vote as an ethnic bloc would be to respond to a corresponding pattern of white behavior. It had never occurred to most whites—although a few did peer beneath the hypocrisy of their self-declared supremacy—that negroes would lose their sense of ethnocentricity only as they moved out of the maelstrom of slavery into the mainstream of democracy.

Instead the South, tormented by the constant threat of a black electoral juggernaut lurking in white backyards ready to crush white supremacy, chose to build a caste wall between the two races. The great irony of southern history is that the black vote as a balance of power—with the one or two exceptions already noted—never became a serious threat to white unity and its attendant ethic of white supremacy. It was in the North that the black vote was to gain strength in electoral power politics.

While white southern politicians fretted over the threat of the black

---

From *Black Political Power in America*, copyright © 1968, by C. Sumner Stone, reprinted by permission of the publishers, The Bobbs-Merrill Company, Inc.

vote as the difference between victory and defeat, northern politicians joyfully realized it could be controlled. To the northern political machines, the black vote was purchasable as a reliable and dependable guarantee of victory. It was to be bought after, cherished, and coddled. If treated properly, it would return its electoral affections with unthinking devotion. If carefully trained, it would not desert its masters in some whimsical exercise of political independence, but would allow itself to be trotted out on election day like a dog on a leash, vote as it was paid to vote, and then be hustled back to its comfortably furnished outhouse to await the next election. And the black vote followed this course with astonishing predictability.

Because of its controlled habits, the black vote can expect to be nothing more than an occasional and minimal influence in national, state, and local elections. For the negro vote to become a true balance of power, perpetually to be reckoned with, the element of *ceteris paribus*—all other things being equal—must be a precondition.

All other things being equal contains three factors:

1) Black political cohesion—a bloc vote.

2) A two-way split of the white vote—obviously, a preponderantly unified white vote will always defeat a preponderantly black vote, unless blacks are in the majority.

3) The political oscillation of fragile loyalties—the negro vote has to swing back and forth periodically between the two parties, shifting its loyalties with the same frequency as the white vote.

The third factor is the most important because once the negro vote is taken for granted—as it has been nationally since the New Deal—it loses its bargaining power. In politics, the predictable votes are never rewarded as abundantly as the uncontrollable groups who are ready to change their affiliation.

As I shall discuss in this chapter, owing to the absence of all three factors, *ceteris paribus*, in national, state, and local elections of the last twenty years, the negro vote has been considered more a loyal ally than a neutral balance of power by white party bosses. This is the principal reason that negro political power has not been accorded its share of the political spoils. The fact that blacks have not been able to translate their vaunted balance of power at the polls into jobs after an election seriously calls into question the loyal-ally concept.

Power is power only when it is exercised. Power does not exist in a vacuum, nor can it remain unrelated to political needs and aspirations. In world affairs, a nation that holds the balance of power is rewarded concretely with the protection of one or both of its neighboring enemies or with some form of technical, financial, economic, or military assistance.

Power can be measured, and the effects of its application can be quantified.

Consequently, when the concept of the balance of power is applied to the black vote, an ancillary question must thus be raised: what have negroes gotten in political rewards for holding the balance of power? The answer is: virtually nothing, considering their proportion in the population and the crucial proportion their votes made between victory and defeat. It is, therefore, not completely accurate to conceptualize the negro vote as holding the balance of power—at least not in today's world of negro political weakness.

Black politicians and writers have understandably sought to aggrandize black electoral power.[1] Writers and politicians reasoned that if they could convince the white political bosses of the vote's size, its fragile political loyalties, and its capacity for retribution, the black community would be awarded more patronage and assigned a larger percentage of policy-making and job-dispensing positions.

Instead, just the opposite has been true of the black vote. It has always been: (1) smaller than the comparable proportion of the negro population as well as of the total vote; (2) unerringly loyal to one party; and (3) too unsophisticated to punish or defeat prechosen white carry-overs who have long ceased to serve black interests. Only when these political misfits were openly antagonistic to the black community has the vote addressed itself to their retirement.

The black vote as a national balance of power was first comprehensively described by Henry Lee Moon, in his book *Balance of Power: The Negro Vote*, published in 1948, just before that year's presidential election.[2] In this penetrating and scholarly analysis of the negro vote as a newly matured political force, Moon traces the vote's emergence from its chained nonexistence in the post-Reconstruction period to its curried omnipresence in the 1948 presidential election. Because Moon was the first political writer to set down with precision the historical and political factors responsible for the negro vote as a balance of power in national elections, both his theory and its supporting array of facts deserve a separate critique.

According to Moon, the "maximum negro voting strength" as of 1948 was 7,250,000 negroes—all negroes over twenty-one years of age as counted by the U.S. Census. With a total U.S. population of 91,600,000 citizens over twenty-one years of age, negroes comprised a maximum potential of only 7 percent of a projected national vote.

The number of potential voters, however, is usually smaller than the number of registered voters or of those who finally vote on election day. In 1940, as Moon indicates, there was a total vote turnout of only 49,-

815,000, or 54 percent of Americans eligible to vote. In 1942, an off year, the percentage dropped to 32 percent, or 29,441,000 votes. In 1944, a presidential-election year, the size rose sharply to 52 percent, then dropped again in 1946 to 38 percent, or 35,000,000 votes.

As of 1948, two-thirds of the potential negro voters still lived in the South. By Moon's count, there were 750,000 qualified negro voters in the southern states. He anticipated that more than one million negroes would be qualified to vote, indicating a possible total of 3,500,000 negro voters in 1948.

In contrast to their southern brothers, black people were able to register in the major northern cities with little difficulty. They slowly became serious repositories of political strength in the states of New York, Pennsylvania, New Jersey, Ohio, Indiana, Michigan, Illinois, and Missouri. This apparently explains why Moon hailed the importance of the negro vote in the 1944 elections:

... without it, Franklin D. Roosevelt could hardly have been elected—it can, with wise and independent leadership, be even more important in the 1948 elections.
... This vote is more decisive in presidential elections than that of the Solid South. In sixteen states with a total of 278 votes in the electoral college, the Negro, in a close election, may hold the balance of power; *that is, in an election in which the non-Negro vote is about evenly divided.*[3]

Moon then explains why he believes Roosevelt's 1944 victory was primarily the result of the negro's balance-of-power vote:

In the 1944 elections there were twenty-eight states in which a shift of 5 percent of less of the popular vote would have reversed the electoral votes cast by these states. In twelve of these, with a total of 228 electoral college votes, the potential Negro vote exceeds the number required to shift the states from one column to the other. Two of these marginal states—Ohio with 25 votes and Indiana with 13—went Republican. The ten remaining states—New York, New Jersey, Pennsylvania, Illinois, Michigan, Missouri, Delaware, Maryland, West Virginia and Kentucky—gave to Mr. Roosevelt 190 electoral college votes essential to his victory. The closeness of the popular vote in the marginal states accented the decisive potential of the Negro's ballot.[4]

Concerning the role of the black vote in congressional elections, Moon believed that "an alert, well-organized Negro electorate can be an effective factor in at least seventy-five congressional districts in eighteen northern and border states."

Although there is a paucity of specific examples supported by actual voting statistics in negro precincts to fully authenticate the balance-of-power theory, Moon nevertheless is on solid ground in his contention, if for no other reason than that both Roosevelt and his closest political advisers were convinced the negro vote would be a key factor in his re-election. Accordingly, the black political community was wooed and caressed in 1944. The CIO-PAC which played a leading role in organizing the labor, negro, and urban vote devoted special attention to negro precincts.

According to Moon, their efforts were rewarded by a loyal Democratic negro vote. Although the statistics Moon uses are not so conclusive as some that he uses to validate his balance-of-power theory in other elections, his analysis does merit consideration:

> A post-election analysis by Herbert Brownell, Jr., chairman of the Republican National Committee, claimed that "a shift of 303,414 votes in fifteen states outside of the South would have enabled Governor Thomas E. Dewey to capture 175 additional electoral votes and to win the presidency with an eight electoral-vote margin." In at least eight of the fifteen states listed by Brownell, the Negro vote exceeded the number needed to shift in order to place them in the Republican column. In Maryland the 50,000 votes which Negro citizens in Baltimore alone cast for F.D.R. were more than double his 22,500 state plurality. Negro voters of five New Jersey cities gave the President a total of 28,780 votes to assure him a winning margin of 26,540. Michigan, which Roosevelt lost in 1940 by the narrow margin of 6,926, was carried by 22,500 with the colored citizens of Detroit casting 41,740 votes for him. Negro voters in Kansas City and St. Louis accounted for 34,900 of the President's margin of 46,180 in Missouri. In Chicago, 121,650 voters in predominantly Negro districts contributed to the 140,165 margin by which the President carried the state of Illinois. The black belts of New York City and Buffalo accounted for 188,760 Roosevelt votes or more than half of his state plurality of 316,000. The combined American Labor and Liberal party tickets for which many Negroes voted gave the President a total of 825,640, enough to overcome the Republican lead over the Democratic slate and hold New York's 47 electoral votes. The President carried Pennsylvania by 105,425 votes, to which Negro votes in Pittsburgh and Philadelphia contributed no less than 52,000. These seven states account for 168 votes in the electoral college and were essential to the Roosevelt victory. In addition, Negro votes contributed substantially to the Roosevelt lead in West Virginia, Kentucky and Delaware.[5]

It should be noted that Moon uses the word "contributed" in discussing the role of the black vote in this analysis. To be an effective balance of power in any election, a vote does not contribute to the outcome, it *decides* the outcome. This, Moon is unable to substantiate by use of the above figures.

The one critical omission Moon makes in this analysis of the negro vote as the balance of power in Roosevelt's 1944 victory is the failure to compare the proportion of the white vote with that of the negro vote that went to Roosevelt. For example, unless the white vote was split almost evenly and the negro vote was fairly solid (70 to 80 percent) for Roosevelt, the negro vote cannot be viewed as a balance of power. It does little good to cite the number of negro votes in a city or state for Roosevelt unless the total number of negro votes is also cited, determining what percentage of the negro vote Roosevelt won to guarantee him victory. Thus, if the figures cited by Moon represent a heavy majority of the negro vote, then that vote can indeed be accorded a significant share of credit for Roosevelt's victory.

It must always be remembered, however, that the white vote must *first* split if the negro vote is to be considered a balance of power. This did not happen in 1948. It did in 1960. Truman defeated Dewey, 24,179,345 to 21,991,291, while J. Strom Thurmond, the States Rights candidate, polled 1,176,125 votes and Henry A. Wallace, the Progressive party candidate, polled 1,157,326 votes. But in 1960, Kennedy, as will be shown later in this chapter, defeated Nixon by only 112,827 votes. The white vote was split almost equally in 1960. It was not in 1948.

Republicans can count just as well as Democrats. It is significant that Brownell did not attribute Dewey's loss to the Republicans' failure to win the negro vote in 1948, but Thruston Morton, the Republican National Committee Chairman in 1960, did.

Moon does cite one off-year congressional election in which the negro vote was measurably decisive. In 1946, the Kansas City Pendergast machine decided to retire Fifth Congressional District Representative Roger C. Slaughter for his unshakable conservatism and opposition to President Truman's liberal legislation. As a key member of the House Rules Committee, the "traffic cop" of House legislation, Slaughter had arrogantly boasted: "I sure as hell opposed the bill for a Fair Employment Practices Commission, and I'm proud of the fact that my vote [in the Rules Committee] was what killed it."[6]

Although black people comprised 15 percent of the potential total electorate in Slaughter's district, he apparently did not believe that they were in any way responsible for his 5193-vote margin in the 1944 elections. Moon describes what happened in the 1946 Democratic primary:

> In the next election he was defeated by a margin of 2783, with 7000 Negro votes cast against him. His vote in the thirty predominantly Negro precincts was negligible. In two of these precincts he received not a single vote, and the highest was 35. This solid Negro vote was the decisive factor in the defeat of Slaughter.[7]

A similar classic example of the negro vote as a balance of power in a local election occurred in Atlanta's 1961 mayoralty race. A racial moderate, businessman Ivan Allen, Jr., defeated staunch segregationist Lester Maddox by a vote of 64,000 to 36,000. The white vote divided almost equally, with segregationist Maddox garnering a slight majority of Atlanta's white votes. An estimated 36,000 white votes were won by Maddox compared to Allen's estimated 33,000 white votes.

The black vote proved to be decisive for Allen's victory. Of the estimated 31,000 votes cast by negroes, according to an analysis of the negro weekly newspaper, *The Atlanta Inquirer*, only 179 negro votes were cast for Maddox.

Ceteris paribus, the negro vote in Atlanta in 1961 was the balance of power in deciding the outcome in favor of Mr. Allen—a passionately united negro vote and a schizophrenically divided white vote.

THE 1960 AND 1964 PRESIDENTIAL ELECTIONS

Just as it was possible to measure fairly accurately the black vote's major role in defeating Kansas City Congressman Slaughter in 1946 and Atlanta's apostle of apartheid, Maddox, in 1961, the 1960 presidential election offered the first unchallengeable evidence of the black vote's decisive effectiveness as the balance of power in a national election. On the other hand, the 1964 presidential election proved how totally ineffective the black vote as a balance of power could be when the element of *ceteris paribus* is missing.

In 1960, after John Fitzgerald Kennedy announced his candidacy for the presidency, there were some uneasy feelings in the negro community. For one thing, the young Massachusetts Senator was an unknown quantity with regard to civil rights. He was no bigot, but he was no advertised friend of racial equality. For another, he had breakfasted with Alabama Governor Patterson in what appeared to be open courtship of the white southern vote.

As a result, the Kennedy campaign failed to excite any real enthusiasm among black people. Furthermore, negro voters had begun to augment a political shift that took place in 1952. In that year, when 57 percent of the white electorate voted for the Republican, Eisenhower, only 21 percent of the black electorate did.

But by 1956 the negro electorate, unquestionably influenced by the U.S. Supreme Court's unanimous 1954 decision outlawing racial segregation in public schools and by the belief that the Eisenhower-appointed Chief Justice, Earl Warren, had played a decisive role in the decision, deepened its affection for the Republican party. The estimated 1956 negro vote for the Republicans was 39 percent, the highest for a Republican presidential candidate in twenty years.

In 1960, there was no reason for black people to be suspicious of Nixon as an anti-civil-rights candidate. In fact, Nixon's backers spread the word that he had been one of the civil-rights proponents in the Eisenhower administration. If the country seemed unable to make up its mind as the campaign progressed, negroes were equally irresolute until Kennedy made one of the most famous and critically decisive telephone calls in political history. On Wednesday, October 26, 1960, he called Mrs. Martin Luther King, Jr., to express his deep concern about a four-month prison sentence meted out to her husband in Georgia on a technical charge of not possessing a driver's license. No other important political figure had publicly expressed any dismay at this latest miscarriage of white southern justice, and Kennedy's call to Mrs. King electrified the black community.

Word of the telephone call swept the Negro community. King's father, the Reverend Martin Luther King, Sr., who had earlier endorsed Nixon —some suspected because of an entrenched Southern Baptist lack of affection for Catholicism—quickly changed political horses. "Because this man was willing to wipe the tears from my daughter's eye, I've got a suitcase of votes and I'm going to take them to Mr. Kennedy and dump them in his lap," he declared. Kennedy's phone call broke the ice. He was now the negro's friend. Other Baptist ministers followed the Reverend King's endorsement, and the negro vote was no longer in doubt.

While Kennedy's wafer-thin margin of victory over Nixon was attributed to many factors, few political observers could disagree that the 112,827-vote margin out of a total 68,770,294 votes was due to the negro vote.

Estimates of Kennedy's share of the national negro vote range from the Gallup Poll's estimated 68 percent to this author's estimated 77 percent to that of several political experts whose calculations went as high as 80 percent.

Because of this wide discrepancy, it might be instructive to re-examine the negro vote in several of the nation's largest cities. According to a more detailed analysis of specific negro precincts reported in a November 21, 1960, issue of *U.S. News & World Report*, this is a cross-section of the Negro vote for Kennedy:

City	Base	Percent of Vote
Chicago	4 wards	77.7
Cleveland	10 wards	77.5
Detroit	4 wards	89.9
Gary	36 precincts	81.9
Los Angeles	5 precincts	86.6
New York City	4 districts	76.3
Philadelphia	20 divisions	77.1

Using those very same figures in conjunction with a more comprehensive analysis, the *New York Times* concluded that "Nationwide . . . close to 80 per cent of the Negro voters cast their ballots for [Kennedy]."

When one remembers that New York City, Los Angeles, Chicago, Philadelphia, Detroit, and Cleveland are respectively the country's first, second, third, fourth, fifth, and eleventh largest cities and that they had a total 1960 black population of 3,671,500, or one-fifth of the nation's negroes, then the voting percentages for Kennedy in those cities are far more persuasive than Mr. Gallup's ubiquitous polls.

Whatever the exact percentage of the negro vote for Kennedy in 1960, it was his insurance of victory. Rarely mentioned by any of the postelection analysts was the fact that Nixon actually won the white vote while Kennedy won the black vote and the presidency of the United States. Theodore H. White, in his comprehensive *The Making of the President 1960*, assigned significant credit to the relationship between the Kennedy telephone call to Mrs. King and the negro vote's responsibility for Kennedy's victory.

One cannot identify in the narrowness of American voting in 1960 any one particular episode or decision as being more important than any other in the final tallies: yet when one reflects that Illinois was carried by only 9,000 votes and that 250,000 Negroes are estimated to have voted for Kennedy; that Michigan was carried by 67,000 votes and that an estimated 250,000 Negroes voted for Kennedy, that South Carolina was carried by 10,000 votes and that an estimated 40,000 Negroes there voted for Kennedy, the candidate's instinctive decision must be ranked among the crucial of the last few weeks.[8]

The electoral college votes of those three states—Illinois, twenty-seven; Michigan, twenty; and South Carolina, eight—totaled fifty-five. Subtracting those fifty-five votes from Kennedy's electoral-college vote total of 303 and adding them to Nixon's 219 reverses the outcome in favor of Nixon, 274 to 248. A small shift in the negro vote to Nixon in those three states alone would have given Nixon the presidency with five more than the required 269 electoral-college votes. What White does not point out, however, is that the negro vote was larger than the total Democratic majority not only in those three states, but also in the four states of Mississippi (eight electoral-college votes), New Jersey (sixteen), Pennsylvania (thirty-two), and Texas (twenty-four). For example, Kennedy won Texas, where an estimated 100,000 black people voted for him, by only 46,233 votes.

The day after the 1960 election, Thruston Morton, Republican Senator from Kentucky and Chairman of the Republican National Committee at that time, said in a television interview that it was obvious that the Republicans' loss of the negro vote played a major role in Nixon's defeat.

In 1960, the element of *ceteris paribus* was operative in the negro vote's decisive role as the balance of power. Black political cohesion was reflected by the more than 70 percent of the national negro vote for Kennedy. The equal split of the white vote was indicated by the difference between the winning and losing percentages of 49.7 and 49.5. The possibility that the negro vote might complete its defection to the Republican party, already underway in the 1956 presidential election, was neutralized by Kennedy's accelerated aggressive campaigning for negro votes and Nixon's failure to do so. The political oscillation of fragile loyalties oscillated no longer after the Kennedy call to Mrs. King.

In the 1964 presidential election, the political situation was completely reversed. Openly expressing opposition to the 1964 Civil Rights Act, the Republican presidential candidate, Senator Barry Goldwater, frightened the black community with his campaign's latent racial hostility. His speeches were directed solely to the white community, and neither Goldwater nor his aides made any attempt to mask their contempt for the negro vote. But if negroes were dismayed by his lack of compassion for the Civil Rights Act, the white electorate was stunned by his Charge-of-the-Light-Brigade foreign-policy proposals. Whether he intended to or not, Goldwater gave the impression that his election as President would mean a quick escalation of the war in Vietnam. His conservative pronouncements on domestic affairs offended many prominent Republican businessmen who would ordinarily be expected to support the Republican candidate.

It was soon evident that a massive swing to the Democratic incumbent, Lyndon B. Johnson, was in the making. Equally obvious was the fact that Johnson would receive an overwhelming majority of the white vote, and that he would not have to rely on the black vote for his victory. He conducted his campaign accordingly. Preaching his peculiar brand of consensus politics, Johnson egomaniacally pursued the broadest spectrum of electorate support. He had been reared in the tradition of southern politics that was founded on an old axiom: "If you get the white folks on your side, you don't need the niggers."

Besides, the black vote had nowhere else to go. The Republican candidate did not seek it, and Johnson became for many negroes the lesser evil. Whereas Kennedy had several black people in key campaign positions in various cities and as members of his personal campaign team, Johnson had none. Johnson even kept his favorite "house negro," loyal and devoted Hobart Taylor of Detroit, under wraps after he realized he had secured the negro vote.

On November 3, 1964, Johnson had racked up an electoral-college total of 486 to Goldwater's fifty-two. Out of a total popular vote of 70,643,526, Johnson's plurality was 15,951,083—the highest ever. His winning percentage of 61.1 over Goldwater's 38.5 also broke an election record, exceeding the former record of 60.8 held by Roosevelt in the 1936 election. Negroes had given Johnson 94 percent of their vote.[9]

His victory was so overpowering that he could have lost all five northern states whose black votes gave Kennedy his margin of victory—and still have won. Furthermore, Johnson could have conceded the four southern states whose black vote totals were greater than his margin of victory—and still have defeated Goldwater.

Of the seven states—Illinois, Michigan, Mississippi, New Jersey, Pennsylvania, South Carolina, and Texas—whose 1960 black vote totals were greater than Kennedy's margin of victory in those states, two—Mississippi and South Carolina—shifted their fifteen electoral-college votes to Goldwater in 1964.

If the 119 electoral-college votes of the other five states are also subtracted from Johnson's winning total of 486 and shifted to Goldwater, Johnson would have still defeated Goldwater, 367 to 171. In those five states, Johnson's percentage of the total vote rendered the black vote harmless as a balance of power:

State	Johnson	Goldwater	Electoral Vote
Illinois	59.5	40.5	27
Michigan	66.7	33.1	20
New Jersey	65.6	33.9	16
Pennsylvania	64.9	34.7	32
Texas	63.3	36.5	24
			119

Because of the 1964 Civil Rights Act, political observers carefully scrutinized the 1964 election results to determine whether the act's passage had any substantial impact on the ability of southern negroes to register as voters and thereby contributed to Johnson's victory.

Perhaps their overzealous analyses led them to their effusive conclusions about the southern black vote. Expert after expert seemed to discover some hidden meaning in these facts: (1) Arkansas, Florida, Tennessee, and Virginia would not have gone Democratic without the black vote; and (2) the five southern states that did swing their electoral-college votes to Goldwater—Alabama, Georgia, Louisiana, Mississippi, and South Carolina—might have gone Democratic if black voters had been permitted to register in numbers approximating their proportion of the population. Neither fact was significant for Johnson's 1964 election. If the forty-three electoral-college votes represented by the four southern states of

Arkansas, Florida, Tennessee, and Virginia are added to the 119 electoral-college votes represented by the seven states of Illinois, Michigan, Mississippi, New Jersey, Pennsylvania, South Carolina, and Texas (states whose N. gro votes gave Kennedy victory in 1960) and then subtracted from Johnson's final electoral-college tally of 486, he *still* would have defeated Goldwater, 324 to 214.[10] Only one salient fact emerges from this analysis: Johnson simply did not need black people to win in 1964.

As for the five southern states that went Republican because of official resistance within these states to increased black voter registration, Johnson had already lost them. The probable fact that an increased black registration in those five southern states would have switched those states to Johnson would have resulted in his gaining what the late E. E. Schattsneider, distinguished professor of political science at Wesleyan University, once labeled "the unearned increment of politics"—unnecessary additional votes for victory.[11]

If there is one political fact a candidate for public office knows as well as he knows his name, it is who was responsible for his election. In 1960, Kennedy, his advisers, and most political observers knew the black vote had been responsible for his election to the presidency. The immediate civil-rights thrust of his administration, with its historic negro appointments, established this fact. In 1964, Johnson likewise knew that the black vote had played no significant part in his election. Furthermore, the Republicans had written off the black vote by their nomination of Goldwater, who, in the words of one Democratic leader, had "shot Lincoln in the head as surely as John Wilkes Booth."[12]

That Johnson introduced and supported less legislation and fewer programs favorable to negroes than Kennedy is a result of their electoral base as well as their personal and political attitudes toward civil rights. Kennedy's victory in 1960 proved that the black vote could be a balance of power in deciding election outcomes if—and only if—the condition of *ceteris paribus*—all other things being equal—is controlling. Similarly, as 1964 proved, the black vote as a balance of power is inconsequential and politically impotent where the condition of *ceteris paribus* is inoperative.

THE 1932, 1936, 1952, AND 1956 PRESIDENTIAL ELECTIONS

Like situations also occurred in the 1932, 1936, 1952, and 1956 presidential elections. In all four elections, negroes exerted no influence on the final outcome because of their emotional attachment to the political party which the rest of the country was retiring.

The firm devotion of negroes to the Republican party for their manumission was highlighted in 1932, when the Democratic candidate, Roosevelt, swept forty-two of forty-eight states for 472 electoral-college votes to Herbert Hoover's fifty-nine. While white voters were displaying a massive disenchantment with Hoover's "Mr. Magoo" ineptitude, black voters nestled snugly in the Republicans' bed as visions of emancipated slaves danced in their heads. The Democrats did manage to crack through this stubborn fidelity in New York City, Kansas City, Detroit, and Pittsburgh. But in New York City and Kansas City, two of the country's most efficient and corrupt political machines, Tammany Hall and the Pendergast machine, were responsible for the negro shift to the Democrats. In Chicago, where, in 1967, the negro vote is the exclusive property of the Democratic party, Roosevelt received a paltry 23 percent of the negro vote. In Cleveland's negro wards, only 24 percent of the vote went Republican. This pattern was repeated in Baltimore, Columbus, and Philadelphia.

By 1936, negroes, economically benefited by the employment and welfare policies of the New Deal, began to shift their votes to the Democrats, but still at a slower pace than the rest of the country. This time, the negro vote came as close to splitting as it ever has in a presidential election. This split rendered it ineffective. Furthermore, Roosevelt's percentage increase of the white vote negated any potential impact of the negro vote on his re-election.

Gunnar Myrdal's analysis in *An American Dilemma* of fifteen negro wards in nine cities indicates that the Republicans were still able to hold the negro vote in six of those fifteen wards.[13] Not until 1940 was the negro vote to complete its spiritual transformation as a unified Democratic ally.

In the 1952 and 1956 presidential elections, the national negro vote, already welded together as a bloc vote by big-city Democratic machines, was estimated by the Gallup Poll as 79 percent Democratic in 1952 and 61 percent Democratic in 1956. In those two elections, the white vote was estimated by the Gallup Poll to be 57 percent Republican in 1952 and 59 percent Republican in 1956. Because the Republicans were able to win both presidential elections without the support of the black voters, it was politically understandable why there was no sense of urgency within the party for a more aggressive posture on civil rights. Had there been a greater shift of the negro vote in 1956 to the Republican party, there likewise might have been a more rapid liberalization in the national Republican policy on civil rights.[14]

MOON REVISITED

Political hindsight always enables the critic to look better than the exponent, for at least the critic has not made predictions that were struck down by unforeseen events. Moon, in an otherwise excellent political analysis of the negro vote and its growth to a power of national significance, has nonetheless occasionally permitted his ideological bent to shape his final conclusions and value judgments. For example, he writes that "unlike the southern vote, the negro vote is tied to no political power. It cannot be counted in advance."[15]

By 1948, when his book was published and when Truman unexpectedly beat Dewey, the negro vote had matured so much into a bloc vote for the Democratic party that it was unable to shake its unthinking loyalty and join the country's political shift in 1952. If, as Moon indicated, the negro vote could not be counted in advance, somebody forgot to inform the Democratic machine bosses of all the major cities in 1952 and 1956.[16]

Naturally, a party does not reward loyalists in its hip pocket with the same amount of political patronage as it does its uncertain or more casual supporters. Once married, the husband is not the ardent wooer of the housewife as he was the capricious maiden. It would, therefore, be to the political advantage of the negro politician or writer to merchandise the impression that the negro electorate is more than a dancing puppet in order to entice both parties to compete in the expenditure of political attention and favors. This possibility explains Moon's judgment that "the vote of negro citizens in 1948 will certainly not be a bloc vote. It will probably not go overwhelmingly to either party unless one of the parties chooses completely unacceptable candidates."[17]

The 1948 Republican presidential nominee, New York Governor Thomas E. Dewey, was certainly not an "unacceptable candidate" to negroes, in view of his record as the first state governor to get a Fair Employment Practices Commission passed. Yet negroes voted as a bloc for Truman in 1948, giving him an estimated 69 percent of their votes. Truman's margin of victory over Dewey in three crucial states—Illinois, 33,612; California, 17,865; and Ohio, 7107—was due to the negro bloc vote. Moon's conclusions must be seriously challenged when he states: "The negro vote is in the vest pocket of no party. It is certainly as independent as the vote of any considerable segment of the American electorate."[18]

Were it not for Moon's respectable credentials as both a civil-rights and political analyst, such a statement would be ridiculed by the very facts he has assembled to reach his conclusion. The negro vote was held by the Democratic party in 1944 and has remained there snugly oblivious to the world.

To be an enduring "balance of power" in elections, any interest group must enjoy a certain amount of independence and capacity for political oscillation. Above all, it must receive its proportionate share of public offices and appointments. This the negro has not been able to do as of 1967. Until black people operate as do other ethnic groups, with the same critical appreciation of the element of *ceteris paribus* in national elections and the demand that they get their 10, 20, or 30 percent of the jobs and elective offices, their political power as a major factor in future presidential races will be circumscribed by their shortsighted single-party loyalty.

Until the black vote learns that the political oscillation of fragile loyalties is the only ultimate insurance of secured participation in the policymaking councils of both parties, Democrats will continue to treat it like a stepchild and Republicans will deny it was ever a member of the family.

Finally, and of greatest importance, the black vote cannot be accurately classified as a true balance of power until the decisive role it has played in specific elections results in a proportionate acquisition of top-level jobs and appointments, just as in the cases of the Irish, the Italians, the Jews, and the Poles. These four ethnic groups . . . have been a true balance of power in many elections. They, in turn, have managed to garner their proportionate share of the political spoils.

Power is power only when it is applied. The black vote did this in two elections in 1967–the election of mayors in Cleveland and Gary. In both elections, the overwhelming solidity of black voters was necessary for victory. If anything, the white vote in both cities was the balance of power, and both newly elected black mayors recognized this fact by appointing whites to key jobs in their administrations.

Eventually, the black vote will become a true balance of power by securing a proportionate share of the elective offices and top-level appointments that the black percentage in the population deserves. Until that day comes, the black vote as a balance of power resembles a conceptual toy for political scientists and writers.

NOTES

1. During his editorship of negro newspapers in Chicago, New York City, and Washington, D.C., this author was equally guilty.
2. Garden City, N.Y.: Doubleday & Co.
3. Moon, p. 10.
4. Moon, p. 198.
5. Moon, pp. 35–36.
6. Moon, p. 51.
6. Moon, p. 51.
8. Theodore H. White, *The Making of the President 1960* (New York: Atheneum, 1961), p. 323.
9. In Harlem's four assembly districts, the Eleventh, Twelfth, Thirteenth, and Four-

148   PART THREE. PROBLEMS AND ASPECTS OF BLACK POLITICS

teenth, Johnson received 122,194 votes to Goldwater's 7928, or 94 percent. In Chicago's predominantly Negro Second, Third, Fourth, Sixth, Seventeenth, Twentieth, and Twenty-Fourth Wards, Goldwater only squeezed out 7,372 votes from a total of 217,438, or 3 percent. In the Twenty-Fourth Ward, there were 296 Goldwater votes, or 1 percent of the total of 22,194. Asked to explain Goldwater's ability to win so many votes in Harlem despite his anti-civil-rights stand, Adam Clayton Powell replied: "We got our kooks in Harlem, too."

10. The four Southern states whose 1964 negro votes exceeded the Democratic margin of victory were:

STATE	NEGRO VOTE	MARGIN OF VICTORY
Arkansas	67,600	65,400
Florida	211,800	37,800
Tennessee	165,200	126,000
Virginia	166,600	76,704

11. As of 1964, the percentage of eligible negro voters registered in these five states was as follows: Alabama, 19.2 percent; Georgia, 27.4 percent; Louisiana, 32 percent; Mississippi, 6.7 percent; and South Carolina, 37.3 percent. (These figures were compiled by the U.S. Civil Rights Commission and published in March 1965. The commission noted that official southern registration data "vary widely in accuracy," and that unofficial figures "are subject to even greater inaccuracies."

12. Quoted by Paul Duke in his article "Southern Politics and the Negroes," *The Reporter*, December 17, 1964.

13. PERCENT OF MAJOR PARTY VOTE FOR ROOSEVELT, 1932, 1936, 1940, IN EACH WARD HAVING MORE THAN HALF ITS POPULATION NEGRO, SELECTED CITIES

	BALTIMORE			CHICAGO		COLUMBUS	
WARD	5	14	17	2	3	6	7
1932	46.4	49.2	43.0	25.4	20.7	27.9	23.2
1936	64.2	54.6	46.9	47.9	50.1	47.7	46.6
1940	72.1	60.7	59.6	51.2	54.2	50.7	57.1

	DETROIT			KANSAS CITY, KANSAS	KANSAS CITY, MISSOURI	NEW HAVEN	PITTS-BURGH	WILMINGTON
WARD	3	5	7	2	4	19	5	6
1932	46.0	50.2	53.9	41.5	70.8	38.9	53.3	28.3
1936	71.4	75.0	79.0	61.3	79.4	61.0	76.6	40.1
1940	75.3	79.2	80.0	59.6	66.5	58.7	77.1	41.5

The cities selected are all those with over 100,000 population, containing wards having 50 percent or more of their population Negro, where Negroes were allowed to vote unhampered or almost unhampered, and where ward lines were not changed over the period 1932–1940. The only exception is Philadelphia, which refused to supply information. The data in this table were collected for this study by Shirley Star.

14. President Eisenhower, in a moment of exasperation while discussing the negro community's failure to support him or the Republican party more heavily in 1956, is reported to have remarked: "What does it take to get these people to support you?"
15. Moon, p. 11.
16. When Harlem Congressman Adam Clayton Powell unexpectedly switched his public support from Stevenson to Eisenhower in 1956, his charisma, which had made him one of the most powerful and nationally beloved negro politicians, did not shake the devotion of Harlem voters for the Democratic party. They still gave Stevenson over 70 percent of their vote.
17. Moon, p. 213.
18. Moon, p. 213.

9

The Negro Elected Official in the Changing American Scene

Kenneth B. Clark

IN ADDITION TO its other ingredients, effective politics must be realistic. Realism and racial problems are not often, if ever, compatible.

Nonetheless, the first challenge of the Negro elected official is that if he is to be effective, he must be realistic. He, more than others, cannot afford to be taken in by illusion—either his own or the illusion of others. A political official is a broker in the commodity of power. The problem of power is a particularly complex and difficult one for the Negro political official because he must come to grips with the paramount reality that the racial problem in America—like all other problems of justice and equity—is a problem of the discrepancy between the power of whites and the traditional lack of power of Negroes. The demands of Negroes for equality and democracy in America is essentially a demand that whites share their power with Negroes. The resistance of whites to meeting this demand reflects the unwillingness of any group with power or status to share these with lower status and powerless groups—lest in so doing they lose that critical amount of power which makes it possible for them to control, determine the destiny and exploit those without power.

Probably at no previous time in American history has the rate of change been greater than it has been since May 17, 1954 up to the present. In handing down the *Brown* decision, the United States Supreme Court precipitated a series of crises in the Negro-white relations. In reversing the "separate-but-equal" mockery which had dominated race relations in America since the latter part of the 19th century, the Supreme

---

Kenneth Clark's article was first delivered as a speech for the Conference of Negro Elected Officials, 1967. © Center on Urban and Minority Affairs, 955 South Western Avenue, Los Angeles, California. Reprinted from *The Black Politician* (Fall 1969) by permission of the publisher and the Center.

Court disturbed irrevocably the racial status quo.

While the *Brown* decision demanded major social changes, it is not now clear in what direction America will move. At times it seemed as if America were moving irresistably toward racial progress and would eventually include the Negro in the educational, economic and political life of the nation. This was a period of hope and high morale for Negro Americans.

Among the signs of high morale and positive movement on the part of Negroes stimulated by the 1954 Supreme Court decision were:

The refusal of southern Negroes to continue to cooperate with traditional forms of racial segregation and humiliation.

The magnificent and successful Montgomery Bus Boycott led by Martin Luther King.

The non-violent sit-in movement led by Negro college students throughout the south.

The ability of Negroes to resist the brutality of the Bull Connors, the dogs and the cattle prods, the murders and the church bombings as they insisted upon their rights as free men and as they demanded for their children that human dignity which American racism sought to deny all Negroes.

The late 1950's period of hope, faith and the belief in the inevitability of racial progress which provided the American Negro with the psychological basis to endure what he believed to be the final spasms of cruelty and barbarity of white segregationists, culminated in the dramatic "March on Washington" of 1963 with its optimistic "I have a dream" keynote.

It seemed that soon after this mass emotional expression of America's rededication to racial democracy and good will the early clues of a period of racial retrogression became first insidiously and later flagrantly clear.

The bombings of Negro churches in the South increased in tempo.

Four Negro children were killed in an explosion set by racists while attending Sunday school in Birmingham, Alabama.

Negro and white civil rights workers were intimidated and killed while seeking to implement the promises of racial justice for the southern Negro.

Negro and white students, once partners in the quest for racial justice, became disenchanted with each other and decided to go their separate ways as the drama and the fervor of the interracial justice honeymoon waned.

Further evidence that we were entering a period of racial retrogression was found in the fact that there was no rational revulsion against the intensified barbarity of the segregationists and there was no national committee appointed to look into the problem of the pervasive violence being perpetrated upon the Negro throughout the Deep South. But probably the full negative meaning of these early signs of racial retrogression was obscured by the following facts:

—tokenism in public school desegregation,
—southern Negroes did win the right to sit anywhere in a bus and to be served in places of public accommodation,
—fairly strong civil rights and voting rights laws were passed in 1964 and 1965,
—the Federal Government did become more active in attempting to secure the rights of southern Negroes to register and to vote,
—President Lyndon Johnson did make strong civil rights statements.

But the fact persisted that there remained a discrepancy between promises and fulfillment and a resulting increase in the frustrations, cynicism, hostility and aggressions of the masses of Negroes. Specifically:

Aside from mocking tokenism, the walls of racial segregation in all levels of American education remain massive and invulnerable.

Millions of Negro children remain doomed to criminally inferior segregated schools and resulting lives of stagnation and futility.

While northern Negroes were being told by their leaders, by white liberals and by public officials that they were the beneficiaries of great legal and legislative victories, they were still confined involuntarily to bleak ghettoes, and they need only experience for themselves the stark oppressive realities of being required to live in houses unfit for human habitation; the unsanitary, if not filthy streets which dominated their racial compounds; the quiet but persistent educational and economic discrimination which doomed them to status of a menial and a hopeless poverty of things and the spirit.

Under these conditions too many Negro males could not realistically hope to earn the respect of their wives and children as they remained powerless to assume the masculine role of protecting them from indignities and inhumanities.

During the past few years it became excruciatingly clear for the Negro that the more things changed the more they remained the same—or worsened. The promises and hope for progress became a relentless quagmire of words.

The drama of direct action, non-violent confrontation of the more obvious signs of southern racial injustice became trite and not particularly relevant or effective in dealing with the persistent, pervasive and subtle problems of racism which afflicted the northern Negro. More appropriate and effective methods have not yet been found to deal with northern racism.

The guilt and indignation of some northern whites against southern forms of racism turned into white blacklash or mutism when the northern Negro began to take seriously the claims of civil rights progress and sought some observable sign of them in northern cities.

The anguish and desperation of the northern Negro have been expressed in the latest series of ghetto eruptions which started in the Harlem riot of the summer of 1964, reached a crescendo in the Watts Riot of 1965 and continued through the current series of riots in Newark and Detroit. Another significant expression of the northern Negroes "no-win" fatalism is found in the rise of the "Black Power" slogan and momentum which skyrocketed at the time of the Meredith shooting in Mississippi in June of 1966 and continue as an obligato to the sounds of ghetto violence and futility.

It is important to keep in mind the date (June 1966) when the "Black Power" slogan became nationally advertised—in order not to be confused about the cause and effect relationship between "Black Power" and "white backlash."

Whatever may be its tactical, strategic, and rational shortcomings and its ambiguity, "Black Power" did not cause "white backlash" . . . The existence of white backlash, the unwillingness of whites to be serious in meeting the demands of Negroes for the same rights and responsibilities granted as a matter of course to all other Americans—including the newest refugee from European, Latin American or Asiatic oppression—caused the outbursts of hysterical bitterness and random hostility inherent in the cry of "Black Power."

"Black Power" emerged as a response to the following facts:

—a recognition of the fact that the center of gravity of the civil rights movement had moved to the northern urban racial ghettoes where it was now immobilized by ambiguity, intensified white resistance to any meaningful change in the predicament of Negroes;

—the recognition of the fact that successful litigation, strong legislation, free access to public accommodations, open housing laws; strong pronouncements on the part of the President, governors or mayors; and even the right to vote or to hold office were not relevant to the overriding fact that the masses of Negroes were still confined to poverty and the dehumanizing conditions of the ghetto;

—and that in spite of the promises of a great society and the activity of the war on poverty, his children were still doomed to criminally inferior schools and his youth and males the victims of unemployment, underemployment and stagnation.

"Black Power" is the cry of defiance of what its advocates have come to see as the hoax of racial progress—of the cynicism of the appeals to the Negro to be patient and to be lawful as his needs are continually subordinated to more important national and international issues and to the needs, desires and conveniences of more privileged groups.

How is this relevant to the Negro elected official?

Whites, by virtue of their numerical, military and economic superiority, reinforced by historical American racism which grants higher status to whites by virtue of skin color alone, do have the power to decide whether the future of Negroes—the Negro masses, the Negro middle classes, or the Negro elected official—will be positive, negative or stagnant.

This core reality of the dynamics of power is not likely to be influenced by sentimental and idealistic appeals for justice, by smiles or promises or by emotional sloganeering.

Another reality which the Negro public official must take into account is the contemporary reality of the mood of the Negro. The Negro of today is clearly less hopeful than he was five years ago. He is more frustrated, more cynical, more overtly bitter, hostile and prone to random and at times self-destructive mass aggressiveness.

"Black Power," in spite of its ambiguity, its "no win" premise, its programmatic emptiness and its pragmatic futility does have tremendous psychological appeal for the masses of Negroes who have "nothing to lose" and some middle-class Negroes who are revolted by the empty promises and the moral dry-rot of affluent America.

"Black Power" is a bitter retreat from the possibility of the attainment of the goals of any serious racial integration in America . . .

It is an attempt to make a verbal virtue of involuntary racial segregation . . .

It is the sour-grapes phenomenon of the American racial scene . . .

"Black Power" is the contemporary form of the Booker T. Washington accommodation to white America's resistance to making democracy real for Negro Americans. While Booker T. made his adjustment to and acceptance of white racism under the guise of conservatism, many if not all of the "Black Power" advocates are seeking to sell the same shoddy moral product disguised in the gaudy package of racial militance.

Nonetheless, today "Black Power" is a reality in the Negro ghettoes of America—increasing in emotional intensity, if not in rational clarity. And the Negro political official, if he is realistic, cannot afford to pretend that it does not exist. Even in its most irrational and illusory formulations— and particularly when it is presented as a vague and incoherent basis upon which the deprived Negro can project his own pathetic wishes for a pride and an assertiveness which white America continues mockingly or piously to deny him—"Black Power" is a powerful political reality which cannot be ignored by realistic Negro or white political officials.

It might be true that one of the inconsistencies of some "Black Power" advocates makes them argue that Negroes should refuse to register to vote at the same time that they ask that "Black Power" be mobilized. But it is also possible, in this nonrational world and racist country of which we are a part, that many of those who do vote may vote their "Black Power" emotions rather than reason.

It is all too clear that among the casualties in the present phase of American race relations are reason, clarity, consistency and realism. Some "Black Power" spokesmen, like their white segregationist counterparts, demand the subjugation of rational and realistic thought and planning to dogmaticism and fanaticism. By their threats and name calling, they seek to intimidate others into silence or a mindless mouthing of their slogans. And the Negro elected official is not immune—in fact, he is exposed.

Some "Black Power" advocates in their pursuit of political and general nihilism confront Negro political candidates and officials with racially polarized formulations of issues which, if accepted or rejected as such by the Negro politician, destroys his base of political maneuverability or erodes political effectiveness. The tendency of some of the more extreme "Black Power" advocates to engage in undisciplined name calling of those who differ in any way from them in tactics, techniques or style; the tendency toward oversimplification of all issues; and the tendency toward rigidity, dogmatism and bombastic demagoguery—are all inimical to the solid study, preparation and hard work necessary for effective political strategy and action. This type of "Black Power" advocate is unquestionably a liability for the serious Negro political official. But, it must be repeated, he cannot be ignored. He does wield a curious type of emotional power in Negro communities. He strikes a responsive chord in an undetermined number of Negroes—particularly among Negro youth. Ways must be found to deal with him—and above all the oppressive realities which make him possible and which provide the base of his apparent appeal.

Some of these individuals give every evidence of being racial racketeers and can be bought off. They sell themselves to the highest bidder and they are not bound by ideals, ideological or racial loyalties.

Others are sincere, dogmatic, if not fanatical individuals who pride themselves on the fact that they have "the truth" and "the answers." These individuals are unwilling to engage in any discussion of facts or strategy unless it can be established before such discussions that their view, their methods and their goals will prevail.

There are, fortunately, some advocates of "Black Power" who are reasonable men and with whom rational communication is not only possible but could be fruitful. The late Malcolm X was moving rapidly toward a rational integration of his role in the overall struggle for racial integration in America at the time of his murder.

One must believe that it is possible for the Negro elected official to find some formula whereby there can be a reasonable working relationship with some elements of Negro nationalism . . . Such a formula, when it emerges, must be one in which the Negro elected official is not intimidated by the emotional appeals of these men, nor is he required to subordinate his practical political knowledge of power and how it operates in our present imperfect democracy; nor can the Negro elected official be passive and succumb totally to the advocates of "Black Power." Rather, the Negro elected official, if he is to interact constructively with Negro nationalists, must learn as much as possible from them and, while keeping the lines of communication as open as possible, seek to discipline the constructive emotional and practical potentials of this movement.

Another problem, not unrelated to the problem of "Black Power," for the Negro elected official is the fact that in the present doldrums of the civil rights movement the cleavages between the masses of Negroes and middle-class Negroes have become more clear and exacerbating. The masses of Negroes are now starkly aware of the fact that recent civil rights victories benefited, primarily, a very small percentage of middle-class Negroes while their predicament remained the same or worsened. Added to Ralph Bunche and our traditional civil rights leaders who are invited to Washington, we now have Thurgood Marshall, Robert Weaver, Walter Washington as the appointed Mayor of Washington, D.C., a few vice presidents in private industry, a few more Negroes in New England prep schools and Ivy League colleges; and more white colleges and universities are looking for one or two "qualified Negroes" for their faculties. These and other tokens of "racial progress" are not only rejected by the masses of Negroes but seem to have resulted in their increased and more openly expressed hostility toward middle-class Negroes. They see the advances of the middle-class Negroes as being at their expense, at worst, or obscuring their plight or, at best, not being in any way relevant to their being condemned indefinitely to their dehumanizing predicament. There are some clues which suggest that the recent ghetto implosions were not only anti-white, but also involved vague stirrings of anti-Negro-middle-class sentiment among the rioters.

Negro political officials are seen as and are, in fact, middle class. The fact that they hold office may be cited as an example of racial progress. Most, if not all Negro elected officials, are in office through the votes of a substantial proportion of Negro voters. Ordinarily one would expect Negroes to be proud of Negro elected officials and to derive the same type of vicarious satisfaction from Negroes in important political office which other ethnic groups, e.g. Irish, Polish, Jewish, Italian, seem to have when a member of their group is elected or appointed to high public office. Before the present conflict, ambivalence and cynical despair which seem to dominate the present climate of the civil rights movement and the feelings of Negroes, this expressed satisfaction in the political achievements of one of their group was also true for Negroes. It may be one of the casualties of the present confusion in the changing American racial scene that Negro elected public officials are not now viewed as unalloyed racial heroes by the masses of Negroes—but rather are viewed with suspicion, distrust or considered cynically irreverant. Probably the last of the mass political heroes was Adam Clayton Powell. His inability to resolve his present difficulties in ways which would maintain his flamboyant defiance of the white society—its morals and its hypocrisy—at the same time that he maintained his power; the demonstration that he was as vulnerable to the vindictiveness and racial double standards of the white power system as any other Negro, and his abandonment of his constituents as he remained in protective exile all contributed to his loss of status as a hero for the Negro masses and reduced the chances of other Negro political personalities attaining a similar status in the near future.

To remove himself from the suspect status reserved for almost all middle-class Negroes, the Negro public official must produce observable positive results for his Negro constituents. He will not escape the castigation, strident or covert, of being considered a tool, handyman, messenger or co-conspirator of the white establishment by militant words and promises at election time and silence when in office: Nor is he helped much merely by sponsoring legislation which meets the usual fate of nonenforcement of most civil rights legislation.

To be effective and to increase his chances against the name-calling verbal racial militants, the Negro elected official must demonstrate that he is concerned and can bring about some positive changes in the following intolerable areas of ghetto life:

1. criminally inefficient and racially segregated public schools;
2. dehumanizingly poor housing;
3. pervasive job discrimination and joblessness;
4. shoddy quality of goods and high prices in local stores;
5. the dirt, filth and stultifying drabness of ghetto streets and neighborhoods;
6. the adversary relationship between police and the residents of the ghettoes.

The problems of the Negro elected official are compounded by the fact that he usually does not have the power to change the conditions of the masses of Negroes merely because he is in office—in spite of the fact that he might have been elected initially because Negroes expected him to do so. *Politics is generally considered a realistic basis for social change.* Negroes are exhorted to register and vote in order to better their circumstances. A crisis in confidence and credibility among the Negro masses will reach serious proportions paradoxically as more Negroes vote and as more Negroes hold public office and as the living conditions of the Negro masses do not change or continue to deteriorate. One could speculate that under such conditions the frequency and intensity of urban ghetto eruptions will increase and the Negro political official could be an additional and specific target.

In this regard it is a fact that Negro public officials do not have the power ordinarily to change the living conditions of the average Negro. Even those elected to high and powerful office find that their power tends to be restricted compared to the power held and used by their white predecessors or successors. Negroes in politics can exert power only through the usual processes of exerting political power—making deals and arrangements, patronage and other forms of quid pro quo. These traditional and generally acceptable forms of the transmission and the exercise of political power seem all too often curtailed or restricted for Negro public officials. Their actions are more severely scrutinized by the press and others unless they act as messengers or intermediaries for the white dominated political machine. The recent experiences of J. Raymond Jones as county leader in New York suggest that if a Negro political official seeks to function as a dominant or primary source of political power he is likely to be blocked not only by overt racists but by the pious and hypocritical denunciations of northern white liberals. In the exercise of even the vestiges of the political power which he believed inherent in his office, the Negro public official is required—indeed constrained—to be more virtuous than Caesar's wife. In fact, in seeking to impose upon the Negro public official these devices of constraints, the white-controlled system seeks to reduce him to the status of a political power eunuch. If this succeeds, the Negro public official is caught between the demands of the masses of Negroes that he exercise his power for their benefit and the fact that those with power in the white world effectively prevent his doing so. He has the symbol of power without the fact. In this tenuous position he can either be ridiculed or rejected—or join, and exploit, the cynicism of the larger society or succumb to the futility of random verbal racial militance.

Or he may resign. Or he may insist upon exercising the power inherent in his office, assuming the risks and preparing himself to meet the consequences of his unwillingness to curtail his functions in terms of race. In accepting this latter option, the Negro politician might contribute significantly not only to *racial democracy but also to political integrity.*

The problems of those Negro public officials whose constituents comprise as many or more whites than Negroes are even more complex and demanding. Political reality demands that they appeal for votes primarily in terms of general, rather than specific racial issues. Particularly if they are opposed by a white candidate in the primary or general election, they cannot permit their campaign to become polarized on racial terms. Negro candidates in these circumstances must somehow manage the difficult task of running a campaign and projecting an image as if America had in fact reached that stage of racial maturity where race and color are irrelevant and where a candidate would be judged and selected by the electorate in terms of his intelligence, competence, experience and integrity. He must do this in order not to alienate his white voters and because if he fails to do this the racism inherent in America will defeat him. But if he runs a campaign in which racial issues are in fact subordinated, he runs the risk of alienating a substantial proportion of his Negro constituents. For the Negro, race is a salient political reality. If a Negro candidate subordinates race he is not only suspect as a latent or deliberate "Uncle Tom," but he may be considered a traitor who is willing to sell his own race down the river in order to enhance his own chances of personal advancement. As more Negroes seek public office outside of the confines of the ghettoes, some formula must be found whereby they can campaign with dignity and integrity and deal with the larger issues and with relevant racial issues. They must do so without either pandering to the latent racism of whites or being intimidated by impractical racial emotionalism of Negroes, thereby contributing to the general education and increasing maturity of the American people.

The Negro public official is the cutting edge of American racial democracy. Although his role cannot be effective and pragmatic and at the same time emotional, dramatic and flamboyant, his fate will determine the fate of the masses of Negroes. If he is relegated to the role of the powerless supplicant and can find no way of breaking out of this role into one of genuine power and responsible decision making; if he accepts the status of messenger or pacifier of justified Negro indignation, he will remain irrelevant for Negroes and whites. And if he is deluded in believing that mere majorities of Negro voters in our cities will bring genuine power to Negro politicians, he has learned nothing from the blood and bullets of Newark, New Jersey, and therefore does not deserve power.

To be a serious agent of desired social change, the Negro public official cannot define the realism of his politics in terms of expediency. The Negro political official must assume the additional burdens inherent in defining politics as requiring a tough-minded and realistic appraisal of the power available to him, a determination to obtain and use effectively the power necessary to effect desired and observable changes, and balance this by a stable, deep and broad sense of human values. With this clarity of goals and stability of values, the effective Negro public official must have also the flexibility of tactics and the sense of strategy which differentiate him from the dogmatists and fanatics.

The predicament of the Negro in America and the destiny of our nation are much too critical in these times for the Negro public official to confuse histrionics with the hard thinking and work necessary for effectiveness. If the Negro in America is to survive—and if he does not survive America cannot survive—then the cold, calculating realism of the Negro elected public official must be combined with the values and concern for humanity necessary to make survival possible.

10

Negro Interest Group Strategies

Harry A. Bailey, Jr.

NEGROES ARE ORGANIZED around their communality, and have developed strategies to change the distribution of social and economic values consistent with their needs and aspirations. This paper attempts to make plain the strategies of some of the major Negro interest groups which pursue race goals, and to explain why some strategies are used by some participants in the struggle and other strategies by others. Throughout, we hope to show something of the impact of the various strategies on the political system. In this way, we hope to elucidate a significant area of our common political life.

ORGANIZATION AND POWER

Political organization and political power are inextricably intertwined. An unorganized mass of people can have little impact on the governmental allocation of social and economic values. However, power has bases other than political organization. Votes, money, prestige, and knowledge constitute additional significant resources which can be translated into political power.[1] Any cursory survey of the Negro's environment will reveal that Negroes have all these resources in varying amounts; but relatively speaking, their greatest assets are political organization and the ballot.

Negroes in the North can use the political parties to further race goals. But even in the North this option is limited. The existence of other

---

"Negro Interest Group Strategies" by Harry A. Bailey is reprinted from *Urban Affairs Quarterly*, Volume IV, Number 1 (September 1968) pp. 27–38, by permission of the author and the publisher, Sage Publications, Inc.

interests to be considered makes it difficult for either of the parties to move directly on Negro demands. In the South, Negroes can rarely use existing political organizations to promote their own interests.[2] The political parties in the South, at both the state and local levels, are controlled by whites who are primarily concerned with winning elections in a region where to be identified as pro-Negro is to court political defeat. The result, in both North and South, has been the necessity for Negroes to create their own political organizations.

Two sorts of political action groups have grown to primacy in the Negro sub-community:[3] those relying on the middle-class politics strategy[4] and those relying on the nonviolent direct action strategy. The middle-class politics model assumes the pursuance of goals within the framework of traditional processes such as lobbying, electioneering, and litigation. The nonviolent direct action strategy assumes the pursuance of goals through peaceful public protests and confrontations with the political establishment or with the obstacles to one's goals. Each of these will be discussed in turn.

The Middle-Class Politics Strategy

The best example of a Negro interest group which has utilized the middle-class politics strategy is the National Association for the Advancement of Colored People. The NAACP, the largest and oldest of the Negro political interest groups, emphasizes the legal approach, lobbying, and education. The organization operates on the assumption that the traditional channels of judicial appeals, of legislative and executive lobbying, and of informing the public are the means through which desired social change can come about.

The NAACP has utilized litigation in the federal courts to achieve race policy, in the absence of action by legislative bodies. It has made the test case the foundation of its legal strategy to bring issues to the courts "at the appropriate time and under the most propitious circumstances."[5] Moreover, the NAACP has relied upon the use of class action rather than individual action to achieve race goals. Its strategy is designed "to secure decisions, rulings, and public opinion on the broad principle instead of being devoted to merely miscellaneous cases."[6]

In recent years, the NAACP has won almost every Supreme Court case in which it has been involved.[7] Since 1941, NAACP lawyers have successfully argued at least 43 of the 47 cases in which they have appeared before the Supreme Court.[8] Among the cases they have won were those outlawing the white primary in the South, the abolition of judicial enforcement of racially restrictive covenants in housing,[9] and the barring of racial discrimination in the public schools.

At the legislative level, NAACP lobbyists have been instrumental in the enactment of fair employment practices acts in at least fifteen states and twenty-six cities,[10] the passage of the Civil Rights Acts of 1957, 1960, and 1964,[11] the Voting Rights Act of 1965, and the Civil Rights Act of 1968.

The NAACP, through its program of education and information, also claims to have brought about a greater recognition of Negro achievement, though this claim is less easy to assess.

A fourth, but usually little-noted tactic of the NAACP has been the use of pressure on the Chief Executive.[12] President Truman's Executive Order of July 26, 1948, banning racial discrimination in the armed forces, is said to have come about as a result of pressure from the NAACP and other groups.[13] The NAACP was also instrumental in getting President Kennedy to issue an Executive Order in 1961 establishing a Presidential Committee on Equal Employment Opportunity,[14] and an Executive Order in 1962 requiring equal opportunity in federally supported housing.[15]

Finally, it should be noted that implicit in the NAACP's efforts to remove obstacles from Negro voting is the belief that the ballot can pave the way for all other political and social rights. Such, at least, seems to have been the reasoning behind the Civil Rights Acts of 1957 and 1960 and the Voting Rights Act of 1965. All three of these deal primarily with the right to vote. While historically identified with judicial attacks on segregation, the NAACP is also committed to a "battle of the ballots."[16]

Whether or not the successes of the NAACP alone is increased the expectations of Negroes is difficult to determine. There is considerable belief, though, that the Supreme Court's decision of 1954 (in which the NAACP participated), outlawing racial segregation in the public schools, broadened the margin of Negro freedom and aspirations and thus led to increasing demands for "freedom now" in all areas of American life.[17] In response to those unhappy with the slow pace of change came individuals and groups devoted to the use of strategies designed to redistribute values more quickly. The doctrine of change through the use of the middle-class politics strategy had reached its zenith.

The Nonviolent Direct Action Strategy

Those groups utilizing the nonviolent direct action strategy are represented by the Southern Christian Leadership Conference, the Congress of Racial Equality, and the Student Nonviolent Coordinating Committee.

The nonviolent direct action strategy assumes a variety of open protests and confrontations with the obstacles to integration and full citizenship, in order "to create a situation so crisis-packed that it will inevitably lead to negotiation."[19]

The first spectacular success of nonviolent direct action came in the boycott of the public transportation system in Montgomery, Alabama, under the leadership of Dr. Martin Luther King. The organization formed to coordinate the boycott was the Montgomery Improvement Association. Since Negroes constituted a majority of the regular bus users, the economic impact was effective, although the city of Montgomery steadfastly refused to change its policy of discrimination. However, on November 13, 1956, almost a year after the boycott had started, the United States Supreme Court affirmed a lower federal court's decision declaring Alabama's state and local bus segregation laws unconstitutional.[19] The strategy of direct action combined with litigation had won an important victory.

Out of the Montgomery Improvement Association grew Martin Luther King's Southern Christian Leadership Conference. Founded in 1957, the organization of Negro clergymen set as its goals the immediate achievement of full citizenship rights for Negroes and the integration of the Negro into all areas of American life. Its methods were those set out initially by Dr. King in the Montgomery bus boycott. In addition, voter registration drives were to be made to get additional Negro voting power, to augment the direct action strategy.

The general strategy of direct action, utilizing a wide variety of tactics, was taken up in a number of situations with increasingly greater results. Important impetus to the strategy was provided by a group of Negro high school and college students who, in February, 1960, inaugurated the "sit-in" tactic at lunch counters in the stores of Greensboro, North Carolina. A significant element of the strategy was the selection of stores —usually parts of nationwide corporations, thus enabling demonstrators to bring to bear important economic sanctions through sympathizers in other cities, including Northern ones. By the end of 1960, the "sit-inners" were dizzy with success; 126 cities had desegregated facilities at their lunch counters. In January, 1962, the number of "success cities" was in the neighborhood of 200.[20] The 1964 Civil Rights Bill has since opened up all public accommodations.

Interestingly enough, as Louis Lomax has said: "Greensboro happened by itself; nobody planned it, nobody pulled any strings. Negro students simply got tired and sat down."[21] However, once the sit-ins began, southern white opposition mounted and national civil rights organizations joined the fray. One of the first was the Congress of Racial Equality.

Although founded in 1943, the Congress of Racial Equality was a relatively little-known organization until the 1960 sit-ins. However, CORE has from its inception advocated the strategy of nonviolent direct action. It assumes that legalism is not a sufficient means to win race goals. After entry into the sit-in efforts, CORE played an important role in organizing, coordinating, and advising protest demonstrators. Since the sit-ins, CORE has used the tactic of "freedom rides" to achieve desegregation of interstate transportation terminal facilities. The freedom rides initiated by CORE began in the spring of 1961 and continued through the summer, after which the Interstate Commerce Commission issued a nondiscrimination order to bus companies and terminals throughout the country. The order went into effect November 1, 1961.[22] The important difference in strategy between the sit-ins and the freedom rides was that the former depended largely on the effort of *local* Negro students, whereas the latter relied mainly on "outside" help.

Despite the fact that CORE and a number of other civil rights organizations came in to assist the sit-inners, the students decided to form an organization of their own. It was their feeling that they could accomplish more if students on each college campus set up their own nonviolent protest movement under the guidance of a South-wide group. Thus, in April, 1960, the Student Non-Violent Coordinating Committee was formed.

Like CORE, SNCC feels that legalism is insufficient for the accomplishment of race goals.[23] SNCC argues that "They who would be free themselves must strike the first blow."[24] Since its beginning as a *coordinator* of protest work of student groups, SNCC has moved to *initiating* protests and has carried out voter registration projects in Mississippi. SNCC's efforts in Mississippi are seen as having brought considerably stronger federal action to protect prospective Negro voters,[25] and increasing the number of registered Negro voters.

As legal barriers to Negro participation in the South have fallen, the direct action groups have moved from a position of dealing primarily with Negro problems in the South to that of dramatizing the economic and social difficulties of Negroes everywhere in the United States. As this is written, the Southern Christian Leadership Conference is preparing a "poor folks" march on Washington, with the ambitious goal of "camping in" near the Capitol until Congress passes legislation to meet the needs of the poor, both black and white, in the country. In the case of some direct action groups, notably SNCC, the strategy of nonviolence is espoused no longer, at least by its leadership. Moreover, the use of violence to achieve race goals has been openly advocated by Stokely Carmichael, the former head of the Student Nonviolent Coordinating Committee, and H. Rap Brown, the present head of the organization. What this new turn of events may mean is yet to be decided.

The Significance of the Strategies

We began this paper by asserting that Negroes have developed interest groups and strategies to help win race goals. It is now important for us to show why the need for different strategies: why the middle-class politics strategy in some cases and the nonviolent direct action strategy in others. It seems appropriate, however, before we do this, to make a brief statement of how policy outcomes are achieved in the American political system.[26]

In the American scheme, powers and opportunities to act effectively on public policy, at any level of government, are parceled out to the chief executive, to the legislature, to the courts, to independent regulatory agencies, to various of the administrative bureaucracies, to the political parties, and to interest groups. In the major areas of public policy determination, they share powers.[27] Because this is so, they can achieve their ends only by cooperating with other participants in the system. To get something, participants must be able to give something. In addition, the actual ability of participants to influence policy outcomes depends not only on their resources, but the skill to use these resources as well. Values are thus allocated to those individuals and groups who are skilled in using their resources to best advantage.

Racial inequalities in political resources have long been documented.[28] The vote, however, is perhaps the largest political resource that Negroes have. The importance of this resource for Negro politics, however, assumes the viability of the middle-class politics model for the achievement of race goals.

Many observers of the American political system, most of whom accept the middle-class model of politics, have assumed that the vote will automatically give Negroes influence over public policy commensurate with their numbers in the population. Once Negroes vote in substantial numbers, they say, public officials will either respond to Negro demands or suffer at the polls. But as the plight of Northern Negroes who have long had the vote attests, the vote alone can hardly achieve race goals. The linkages between votes cast in elections and public policy outcomes are exceedingly complex, precisely because of the pluralistic nature of power and decision-making discussed above. As William R. Keech has said, "Candidates for public office will have reasons other than their own values to be reluctant to concede to Negro demands. Negroes are not the only important group of voters in the electoral environment. Candidates for office are no freer to ignore the demands and concerns of these non-Negro voters than they are to ignore those of Negroes. . . ."[29] Thus Negroes will have less influence over policy than their proportionate share of the electorate would indicate.

This is not to argue that the vote is of little or no value to Negroes. It is to say that the vote is not a guarantee *per se* for any policy output. Negro voting does increase the probability that certain race goals will be realized, without being a sufficient condition for this to occur.

An important consideration for Negro voting strategy is how evenly divided white voters are. Where white voters are almost evenly divided, as they were in the presidential elections of 1948[30] and 1960,[31] Negroes can hold the balance of power. To the extent that the election of candidates constitutes some sort of influence over public policy, Negro voting can be meaningful in these instances.

Another important consideration for Negro voting strategy is the formal electoral system and the residential configuration of the Negro population. Are elections at-large or by wards? Are Negroes residentially concentrated or dispersed? The former is usually an important question; the latter is not. Negro voters will have the greatest chance of influencing a candidate's election if elections are by ward. Where this is the case, Negroes are likely to slate and elect their own to public office. This is so because where there has been a poverty of Negro representation in the political system, as has been the case almost everywhere in the United States, the presence of an "ethnically relevant" candidate does not suffice;[32] only an ethnic candidate of one's own group satisfies.[33]

The election to public office of whites who are sympathetic to Negro needs, as a result of Negroes holding a balance of power, or the election of Negroes to public office as a result of Negroes having a majority in a given constituency, is only part of the vote goal. A more important question for Negro voting strategy is: Are votes translatable into public policy once elections are over? Are the elected officials and parties able devices for the redistribution of values?

Obviously, in a government of shared powers, the allocation of values according to the absolute needs of any one group is very near impossible. This is not to say that no race goals can be achieved. It is to say that goals on which there is a modicum of consensus by both whites and Negroes have a greater prospect for success than those that do not.

To be sure, the election of Negroes to the federal Congress, to state legislatures, to city councils, and, more recently, to the mayor's post in several northern and midwestern cities, is a significant development for the obvious reason that it places the Negro representative in the formal political framework where he can maneuver, report, and press for action. But however important formal penetration into the strategic political decision centers may be, the Negro politician's relative success in attaining race goals depends in part upon the extent of party strength among the general electorate and the amount of party control in the legislature. When the party is extremely strong in either or both cases, the Negro politician is less able to use his influence to effect civil rights policies; where the party is relatively weak, the Negro politician has a better chance. In Chicago, for example, where the Democratic party is strong and there is little interparty competition, Negro politicians have relatively little success in the pursuance of race goals; whereas in New York, where the party is weak and a great deal of interparty competition exists, Negroes have a relatively greater amount of success.[34]

While strong interparty competition is critical for Negro achievement of race goals, so is the existence of party discipline. Duane Lockard has shown that state legislation furthering Negro goals is affected by party alignments.[35] When the roll is called on key issues, such as civil rights, state legislators tend to line up by party. The extent to which party members will line up behind civil rights legislation will depend upon the degree of party discipline and accepted party position on key issues. Where there is tight party discipline, Negro politicians have only to persuade the key party leaders and the battle is almost won. In states with relatively less party discipline, party membership continues to be significant, although the lack of party discipline precludes leadership control over votes. However, party control over legislative offices and legislative schedules, plus a similarity of attitudes among party members around key issues, tends to influence policy outcomes.

Another major question for Negro voting strategy is which of the major parties serves the Negro interest best. Are both parties equally responsive to Negro aspirations? The record clearly shows that Negroes "feel" the Democratic party best serves their interest.[36] With the exception of minor defections to the Republican party in the presidential elections of 1952 and 1956, Negroes have been solidly in the Democratic camp since 1932. Moreover, there is ample evidence to show that the Democratic party best serves the Negro interest. Duane Lockard, in a review of 30 roll calls of partisan differences in voting for civil rights legislation in eight northern states between 1944 and 1963, "found that Democratic delegations voted 90% or more for the bills most of the time, whereas Republicans infrequently achieved high unity even where they favored the issue."[37]

A final question for Negro voting strategy is: Should Negroes place all their voting eggs in one basket or should they keep their vote "free-floating"? For the present, the answer is to be found more in the behavior of the political parties and less in the Negro voting strategy. So long as the Republican party policy offers less in the way of race needs, symbolic and material and social and economic, the "free-floating" vote strategy could not work anyway. Thus the bloc vote. On the other hand, although the Negro vote has not shown any great flexibility to date, there does seem to be some indication that it is growing more sophisticated and is prepared to move to whichever parties and candidates offer the best policies and programs commensurate with Negro needs.[38]

Precisely because the Negro vote remains largely a one-party vote and because Negroes are registered in proportionately smaller numbers than whites, due mainly to socioeconomic conditions, and because Negroes are without a considerable number of additional political resources necessary to make the voting strategy pay off, they will have a better chance of achieving some types of racial objectives by modes of attack than the ballot box.

At present, the legal status of the Negro in the United States is almost equal to that of whites.[39] After almost a century of litigation, the Supreme Court has struck down virtually every state action segregating Negroes or discriminating against them. The actions of the United States Congress between 1957 and 1968 have legitimized and extended the governmental judgment of Negro equality. But the formal status of equality can be empty if opportunity is not fully equalized. Social inclusion of the Negro is the more difficult task remaining.

The Negro in America continues to suffer considerable cumulative disadvantage. The first problem is mainly financial. For an individual to be able to take advantage of available opportunities, he must have not only the capacity but also the financial means to do so. With about 43% of America's Negro population living in poverty, and a considerable additional number living only slightly above that level, it goes without saying that many opportunities available to Negroes will go untaken. Nothing short of a radical new economic policy can alter this fact.

The second problem concerns the underlying capacity of people, especially families, to function effectively in the environment in which they are placed. The Moynihan report of the Negro family in the ghetto makes it clear that the fabric of family relationships there has all but disintegrated, and that without family stability a large proportion of Negro youth can never learn even the basic human interaction skills necessary to cope with the environment. This problem is related to the first, in that without a radical redistribution of wealth the basis for family unity can hardly be achieved.

The third problem concerns the social exclusion of the Negro on the basis of alleged inherent inferiority. The extension of full membership to the Negro in the American community still awaits considerably more evaporation of the notion that Negroes are inherently inferior and that the American community will deteriorate if Negroes are admitted under the standards of full citizenship.

The resolution of these problems is likely to be less responsive to the middle-class politics strategy than to the nonviolent direct action strategy. Quite clearly, the middle-class politics model assumes a matrix of competing pressures, all of which must receive relatively equal recognition. It appears at this time that only the nonviolent direct action strategy can have the power to override those pressures which stand in the way of the achievement of future race goals. As James Q. Wilson has said in a comparable context, "This is not a counsel of despair but only a sobering reminder that political activity can only produce political gains and that other—and far more difficult—remedies must be sought for most problems of race relations in America."[40]

NOTES

1. For a detailed list and discussion of resources which can be translated into political power, see Robert A. Dahl, *Who Governs?: Democracy and Power in an American City* (New Haven: Yale Univ. Press, 1961), p. 226.

2. Donald R. Matthews and James W. Prothro, *Negroes and the New Southern Politics* (N. Y.: Harcourt, Brace and World, 1966), p. 203.

3. The use of the term *sub-community* to refer to the Negro community is spelled out in Harry A. Bailey, Jr. ed., *Negro Politics in America* (Columbus, Ohio: Charles E. Merrill, 1967), p. 1.

4. See Everett C. Ladd, Jr., *Negro Political Leadership in the South* (Ithaca, N. Y.: Cornell Univ. Press, 1966), pp. 164–165. The middle-class politics model is implicit in any textbook on American politics which describes how competition for scarce values goes on.

5. Abraham Haltzman, *Interest Groups and Lobbying* (N. Y.: Macmillan, 1966), p. 137.

6. Herbert Hill and Jack Greenberg, *Citizen's Guide to Desegregation* (Boston: Beacon Press, 1955), pp. 56–57.

7. W. Haywood Burns, *The Voices of Negro Protest in America* (N. Y.: Oxford Univ. Press, 1963), p. 23.

8. *Ibid.*

9. For an interesting account of NAACP strategy in this effort, see Clement E. Vose, "NAACP Strategy in the Covenant Cases," *Western Reserve Law Review*, VI (Winter, 1955), pp. 101–145.

10. R. Joseph Monsen, Jr., and Mark W. Cannon, *The Makers of Public Policy* (N. Y.: McGraw-Hill, 1965), p. 142.

11. For a list of backers of the 1964 Civil Rights Act, see *Legislators and the Lobbyists* (Washington: Congressional Quarterly Service, undated), p. 65.

12. See, however, Clement E. Vose, "Presidential Activism and Restraint in Orders and Proclamations on Race," paper delivered at the 52nd Annual Meeting of the Association for the Study of Negro Life and History, Greensboro, N. C., October 13, 1967. For an earlier study of pressure on the Chief Executive by a Negro political organization, see Herbert Garfinkel, *When Negroes March: The March on Washington Movement in the Organizational Politics of the FEPC* (Glencoe, Ill.: Free Press, 1959).

13. Burns, *The Voices*, note 7, p. 25.

14. Executive Order No. 10925. 26 *Fed. Reg.* 1977 (1961).

15. Executive Order No. 11063. 27 *Fed. Reg.* 11527 (1962).

16. Donald R. Matthews and James W. Prothro, "Negro Registration in the South," in Allan P. Sindler ed., *Change in the Contemporary South* (Durham, N. C.: Duke Univ. Press, 1963), p. 121.

17. See Harmon Ziegler, *Interest Groups in American Society* (Englewood Cliffs, N. J.: Prentice-Hall, 1964), p. 224.

18. Martin Luther King, Jr., "Letter From Birmingham Jail," *Christian Century* (June 12, 1963), 768.

19. *Gayle v. Browder*, 142 F. Supp. 707 (M. D. Ala. 1956), affirmed, 352 U. S. 903 (1956).

20. Burns, *The Voices*, note 7, p. 43.

21. Louis E. Lomax, *The Negro Revolt* (N. Y.: New American Library, Signet, 1963), p. 134.

22. Constance Baker Motley, "The Legal Status of the Negro in the United States," in John P. Davis, ed., *The American Negro Reference Book* (Englewood Cliffs, N. J.: Prentice-Hall, 1966), p. 500.

23. Monsen and Cannon, *The Makers*, note 10, p. 145.

24. Burns, *The Voices*, note 7, p. 46.

25. *Ibid.*, pp. 58–59.

26. Our discussion of policy outcomes follows Nelson W. Polsby and Aaron B. Wildavsky, *Presidential Elections: Strategies of American Electoral Politics* (N. Y.: Scribner, 1964), pp. 189–190.

27. Richard E. Neustadt, *Presidential Power: The Politics of Leadership* (N. Y.: Wiley, 1960), pp. 33–34, remains the best statement on this point.

28. Perhaps the best and most recent documentation is that of Matthews and Prothro, *Change*, note 2, esp. p. 478.

29. William R. Keech, "Some Conditions of Negro Influence Over Voting Policy Through Voting," paper delivered at the 1966 Annual Meeting of the American Political Science Association, New York City, Sept. 6–10, 1966, p. 16.

30. See R. H. Brisbane, "The Negro's Growing Political Power," *Nation* (Sept. 27, 1952), pp. 248–249; and Oscar Glantz, "The Negro Voter in Northern Industrial Cities," in Bailey, *Negro Politics*, note 3, pp. 338–352.

31. See Theodore H. White, *The Making of the President 1960* (N. Y.: Pocket Books, 1961), p. 283.

32. An "ethnically relevant" candidate is a member of another ethnic group sympathetic to the aspirations of the Negro, or a white liberal who is seen not as one of his own, but in opposition to his own. See Harry Holloway and David Olson, "Electoral Participation by White and Negro in a Southern City," *Midwest J. Polit. Sci.*, X (Feb., 1966), p. 115.

33. James Q. Wilson, "How the Northern Negro Uses His Vote," *The Reporter*, March 31, 1960, p. 20.

34. See James W. Wilson, "Two Negro Politicians: An Interpretation," in Bailey, *Negro Politics*, note 3, pp. 144–162.

35. Our discussion of the place of party in the achievement of race goals relies heavily

on Duane Lockard, *Toward Equal Opportunity: A Study of State and Local Antidiscrimination Laws* (N. Y.: Macmillan, 1968), pp. 46–49.

36. For a summary of some of the evidence, see Glantz in Bailey, *Negro Politics*, note 30, pp. 338–352. The only qualification to this argument is that southern Negroes are not as firmly committed as are northern Negroes to the Democratic party. See James Q. Wilson, "The Negro in American Politics: The Present," in Davis, *The American Negro*, note 22, p. 441.

37. Lockard, *Toward Equal*, note 35, p. 47. The "Northern" states are California, Connecticut, Massachusetts, Minnesota, New York, Ohio, Pennsylvania, and Rhode Island.

38. A case in point is Henry Lee Moon's analysis of the Negro vote in the 1956 presidential election. See his "The Negro Vote in Presidential Election of 1956," in Bailey, *Negro Politics*, note 3, pp. 353–365.

39. For a review of the evidence, see Motley, "The Legal Status," note 22, pp. 484–521.

40. James Q. Wilson, "The Negro," note 36, p. 457. To be sure, Wilson limits "political activity" to what we have called the middle-class politics model. For the evidence, see his "The Negro in Politics" in *Daedalus*, XLIV (Fall 1965), p. 949. We, however, place the direct action model within the pale of politics, since politics is, for us, any activity by which conflict over goals is carried on. The "far more difficult remedy" is, for us, then, the nonviolent direct action model.

11

The American Crucible: Black Identity and the Search for National Autonomy

J. Don Granville Davis

THERE IS A standing and time-honored assumption that citizenship and nationality in any given country are naturally and automatically accrued by virtue of being born within its territorial boundaries. At the level of rhetoric, this assumption is logically irrefutable. One born in the United States should be an American. But this same assumption taken to the level of fact and experience assumes the uncertain character of what it is —an assumption. An American is something more than one born within the territorial boundaries of America. He is the product of a total historical, psychological (emotional), and physical experience, an experience that is in no way guaranteed to everyone born in the right place to have it. Further still, one may actually share an experience with others physically but, because of—or in spite of—the circumstances under which the experience is shared, fail to share its meaning. We may cite, for example, the recent experience of the American moon-landing, an experience that was indirectly shared by millions of Americans. The fact of the matter, nevertheless, is that millions of us, for reasons alike and unalike, did not share what was generally accepted as the national meaning of this experience. And this, some of us would argue, was a matter of no small difference. It was instead, we think, a manifestation of a major difference which divides and distinguishes us not only in terms of our priorities and objectives, but also in terms of our national character and collective psyche. In other words, this raises the question of who we are as a people—one, two, or several?

It is not possible to overemphasize the urgent need for black people who are called Americans to come to grips with this question. The question of group (national) identity is a most important one, as it is profoundly involved with major aspects of the group's life, such as its culture, politics, and ultimate destiny. When a group's identity is confused and in question, it is only logical that its culture, politics, and ultimate destiny will be confused and in question. Such is now the case with black people who are called Americans. The American experience thoroughly pervades our lives, but we are rarely a part of it. If we are, the involvement is one-dimensional. We are physically involved (as in war), but not psychologically or emotionally. We are psychologically and emotionally involved (as in a presidential election), but not physically. We are rarely part of the total experience. And this is our strongest and most persistent common experience: mutual exclusion, our inability to experience totally and completely that which is known as "the American experience." Certainly, there are black people who will protest this contention. And if they are true to their denial, then they are simply not a part of us (black people) and may, in fact, constitute a separate group in and of themselves, as it is unlikely that Americans who are white would regard them as being either a part of them or greatly different from those of us who recognize and relish our difference. But what, exactly, is the nature of the difference we claim?

Black people are not born into either American citizenship or American nationality, not if these concepts have anything to do with a collective experience and a collective spirit. We are, rather, born into a generally moribund condition which exists upon the rough and precarious edge of everything that is America. For black people, American citizenship and nationality are a group obsession, the *telos* of a lifelong struggle which is rewarded only in death. And this fact is near to being an iron law. Those black people who struggle for American citizenship and nationality, for the trouble taken, die sooner (as a result of the trouble taken) or later (because of the trouble taken) with the goal nowhere in sight. Those who contrive to believe that they have succeeded in their quest for American citizenship and nationality actually succeed only in further maligning an already battered and periled identity. But the trouble begins long before one who is black will have decided whether he thinks himself an American or not. The trouble begins properly when he is born a "Negro" inside a country where most of the people are not Negroes. The child who is black learns very soon that he is a member of a "minority" group. And right away, expectations that he may be treated differently by others because of this start to develop. If the child accepts and begins to deal with this directly, he may begin to feel disadvantaged and cornered. If he is taught to ignore this fact, he may not only feel disadvantaged and cornered—he may be crushed. "The problem" either becomes undeniable, or the child becomes unrealistic, in degree or totally. But this is only the beginning of a cycle whose viciousness increases with time. Cornered or "cruising for a bruising," the black child goes to school. There he will be taught the principles of democracy and a set of social values, all of which are to be learned and accepted by faith, as they are not to be seen in practice anywhere around him. He may refute or rebel against the notions that are imposed upon him, but in so doing he becomes even less sure, as he, like the adults around him, lacks at this stage the courage or imagination to conceive of anything else. So the child listens and waits. He listens and waits for the opportunity to jump the walls (lies) around him and create the new, or else he is so frightened by what he hears and sees while listening and waiting that he consciously or unconsciously accepts the status of "minority" (unimportant, irrelevant, and so forth) and clings to the safety of voluntary servitude. Elsewhere, this is often referred to as simply a complex of inferiority or self-hatred. At the other end of the spectrum, the child who rejects all the aspects of this sordid condition and refuses to be socialized into it may either search for reasonable and constructive ways of reordering the situation (by revolting), or he may act prematurely without the benefit of forethought and be released from his affliction through victory or death. More often than not, the result is death, as there is no real plan for victory. Either way, the end result is the same: the individual is released from an intolerable condition. Either way, he has forced a showdown in which he either wins or loses. And this is preferred by many over the excruciating pain of remaining in limbo. We have, therefore, a situation in which black people in America are offered the equally unattractive choices of slavery or death, an extremely cruel dilemma, which is made all the worse by our unwise acceptance of the romantic and nonsensical slogan of "give me liberty or give me death." And why is this unwise? Simply because it makes more sense to intone that if you do not give me liberty I will give YOU death. The choice then is not between someone's giving us liberty or killing us, but between our being granted our liberty or killing someone who is depriving us of our liberty. And this is the nature and order of the trouble that begins very early for one who is born black in America.

We are still discussing identity. And the identity we are discussing is conditioned and attended by facts and circumstances which distinguish it from American identity in general. We are talking about an array of facts and experiences, blatant and subtle, that mark and condition the lives of some 25 to 50 million persons in such a manner as to make them different from all others. We are talking about every subtlety and nuance that warms, chills, threatens, or secures the life of this group. Of all those factors which condition the lives of black people in America, the most pronounced and persistent is that of powerlessness. Powerlessness that is complete, total, and absolute. There is literally no black man in America, regardless of his title or status, who may exercise the so-called rights of American citizenship and nationality in all of the fifty American states. At best, an American who is black may be able to exercise some small portion of these so-called rights in a few select areas of the country of his birth. And this is but one instance of the manifest truth that the native black population of America may in no way (other than technically) be regarded as citizens and nationals. Unfortunately, too many black people have made the mistake of assuming that, by right of their birth, American citizenship and nationality are theirs. Nothing could be further from the truth. Whenever citizenship and nationality for a native-born population becomes conditional beyond birth, it, for all practical purposes, ceases to exist. One cannot say that he is a citizen and a national when he votes and is allowed to enter public places in California, if he knows that there are certain places in Mississippi, Georgia, Alabama, South Carolina, Louisiana, Texas, and a host of other states in which he would vote or enter public places at the risk of his life. This is not the plight of people who are citizens and nationals. This is the plight of a people with fewer "rights" than foreigners. This is the plight of people who have neither country nor government to protect them. This is the plight of people who, as Huey P. Newton has said, "are slaves or subject to be enslaved at any given moment." But this has not been understood by black people. One knows that it has not been understood when, in face of yet another injustice, black people are heard to say such as, "the law has broken down," or—as one Negro leader unwittingly commented after a recent attack by Los Angeles police on the local headquarters of the Black Panther party in which two Panthers were killed—"there has been a breakdown of police-community relations." No, that is not the case. The law cannot break down for people for whom it has never worked. Such a breakdown may occur only in the case of those for whom the law once worked. It has never, in the history of America, worked for black people. Likewise, what occurred in Los Angeles was in no way representative of a breakdown in police-community relations. It was, on the contrary, an overt manifestation of relations as they have always existed between American police and members of the black community. The relationship of American police with the black community has always been one of oppressor and oppressed; one of brutal, armed police control of an unarmed, subject people. Los Angeles was par for the course, the epiphenomenon of four hundred years of black history in America.

But we are not crying again to deaf conscience. We are talking about identity and a particular political process that molds and defines it. We are talking about black people and their identity in the only sensible way that the matter can be discussed in the absence of a free and independent national black life. But what would that mean—"a free and independent national black life"—if it existed? Nought, save the power and authority to govern and all the prerogatives that follow. For black people, any day, the equal of Shakespeare's "To be or not to be?" is the question of whether we choose to govern (ourselves) or not. To govern or not to govern? That is the question for black people. To choose not to govern (ourselves) is to slavishly acquiesce in being governed by others—unjustly and mercilessly, as it is. To choose to govern (ourselves), on the other hand, would be to opt for the creation of a healthy and viable national life and to swear death to anyone who would prevent or stand in the way of such a development. And it is just, as well as healthy, to take such a stand, as anyone who could be against such a development is no credit to life or those who seek to live. And this brings us to the principles of love and peace. Given a decent chance to, most black people would love any- and everybody who would give them peace. Given no chance at all, we should die doing away with those who break the peace. And, even so, love should not be diminished, for we should love ourselves when no other people are deserving of our love—love ourselves for having done what we know to be right. There would appear to be no other way.

We must do away with the notion that there is any such thing as second-class citizenship. THERE IS NO SUCH THING AS SECOND-CLASS CITIZENSHIP. ONE IS EITHER A CITIZEN OR SOMEONE WITHOUT CITIZENSHIP. Citizenship is the highest form of camaraderie. It assumes not-too-disparate identity, trust, mutual responsibility and endeavor, common purpose and goals, all resident within and laid out upon a territory governed by people who share these. In America this breaks down as follows: Most of those who control anything are white, Anglo-Saxon Protestants (WASPS). They trust in a white God (their father), who forgives their every sin, and hold suspect the Jews who lynched him, while absolutely hating everyone who had nothing to do with it. They trust also that every other one like them will do whatever is necessary to maintain their privileged position. They endeavor to control the world and are willing to die to make it more like them. Their purpose is to defeat the Reds, to force civilization (Western, material, of course) upon the Niggers (or wipe them out if they don't dig it), and keep an eye on the Jews while rethinking what Hitler had in mind. (But, of course, the Jews have a plan for this—stay in their vanguard.) The purpose of Americans is to maximize vanity, and their goal, apparently, is to do away with everyone as fast as they can. And it is in this direction that they have progressed most. The land, of course, is not only completely controlled by them but is considered their most prized possession. It is considered theirs because they "discovered" it. And it is to keep others from sharing the land, which they know others must have to survive, that they are most willing to give their lives. Fortunately, most black people do not qualify for these, the conditions of true American citizenship above and beyond native birth. Fortunately also, the majority of us would not qualify for citizenship in the WOODSTOCK NATION (the other extreme of the American psyche), which has been hip-eloquently called for by Mr. Abbie Hoffman. (Witness the most recent attempt to construct the WOODSTOCK NATION at Altamont, California, where those people that some of us black folk believe are going to help us gain our freedom, citizenship, and nationality here in America employed the HELL'S ANGELS as their police, who, in turn, wasted no time before stabbing a black man to death.) No, this is not for a new people that wants to live in a complementary society.

When we identify the central problem of black people today as the lack of self-government—that is, a free and independent national black life—we run headlong into the contention that nationhood (for black people) is either impossible or not worthwhile: "The situation is not conducive . . ." ("How?" "Where?" "We aren't ready.") Or, "Nationalism is outmoded—we should be internationalists." Everything but effort. Such words are strange, indeed, coming from a people with a multitude of great statesmen lying in the gutters of other nations, going insane or dying of neuroses, pimping their mothers and sisters, drawing unemployment, in jail, or on the run. It is difficult, indeed, to identify a group of people anywhere on the face of earth who are more in need of independent nationhood. But there is yet another argument against it. According to some, those of us who favor independent nationhood are only seeking escape from the lifelong struggle for freedom, justice, and equality within the context of American society. In their way of seeing things, we are cowardly, shunning a struggle which, although it has not been successful after four hundred years, is bound to make us citizens "some day." (We should note that this argument dates back to the first mention by black people of returning to Africa. From the very beginning, those who thought it wise to end their forced exile were accused of copping-out on the "American Dream.") As it is, history has never been kind to those who have failed or refused to learn her lessons. For black people, the cost of not learning from history has been high, indeed. So great is the number of those who have perished, that we cannot even estimate the number of the known and unknown sacrifices to this failure. It is as if we were bound to some primordial curse which disallows our being born for any reason save to die in the name and service of others. But we think not. There are still some rather clear ways of seeing and dealing with the nature of our difficulties.

The twentieth century has been indelibly marked by several great forces. Primary among them has been the phenomenon of national statehood, the creation and the rise of broad, independent political units with territorial sovereignty and national character—a force which, naturally and in order, gave rise to mutual national antagonism (power politics) and its antithesis, internationalism. Owing in part, if not wholly, to the development of nationalism (as well as capitalism) was the rise and proliferation of imperialism and colonialism, which, again, naturally, became inextricably involved with the identity of static, undeveloped, quasinational states. That is to say, for example, that a significant part of the identity of Great Britain was that it was, among other things, for the first part of the twentieth century that country upon whose empire the sun never set. As it was, the other European states regarded this as a lofty and commendable achievement, one that they spared nothing in their untiring efforts to emulate. This meant, of course, that a huge portion of mankind was actively and brutally denied the very same thing that the Europeans were demonstrating a great willingness to kill in order to create for themselves—their identity and enough power (over their own lives) to respect their identity. And herein were sown the seeds of the turbulence and chaos that surround us today; the fecundation that would lead ultimately to millions of men crying out, as Eldridge Cleaver has, "We shall have our manhood. We shall have it or the earth will be leveled by our attempts to gain it."[1]

Other than the fact that it is Western, the exact nature and origin of twentieth-century nationalism are still very much in doubt. And, while we are aware of the importance of knowing and understanding the nature and origin of nationalism, our concern here is more immediate and is hinged only upon the fact that nationalism does exist. But so does internationalism, and it is the relationship of the two that we must try to understand. Nationalism may be seen as a centrifugal force, whose effect is to cause all bodies to move away from the center, or, in terms of the movement of people, away from a kind of "universal peoplehood," which would be a condition in which man and all that is man's (identity, wealth, culture, values, and such) would be held in common. Away from this condition, which would most assuredly be ideal, the movement is toward distinct and disparate national groups. This is the condition of nationhood, a condition in which the nations, among themselves, hold a minimum of what is man's in common (Figure 11:1). Internationalism is simply the observe of this condition. Internationalism calls, ultimately, for the total integration of all national entities into one universal entity which, because of its nature, would be unbounded (Figure 11:2).

As a general concept in the world, internationalism lacks nothing in terms of "goodness." It seems the best of all possible conditions for

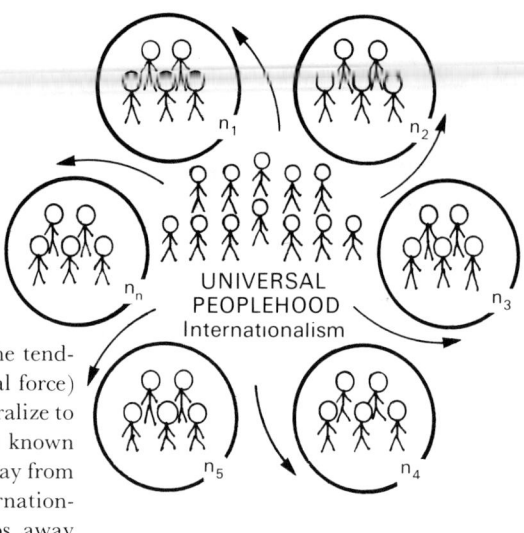

FIGURE 11:1. Illustrated here is the tendency of nationalism (a centrifugal force) to cause human groups to decentralize to form distinct groups, sometimes known as nation-states. Movement is away from Universal Peoplehood and Internationalism. Surrounding those groups away from the center are circles representing borders and boundaries, which are absent from the state of Universal Peoplehood.

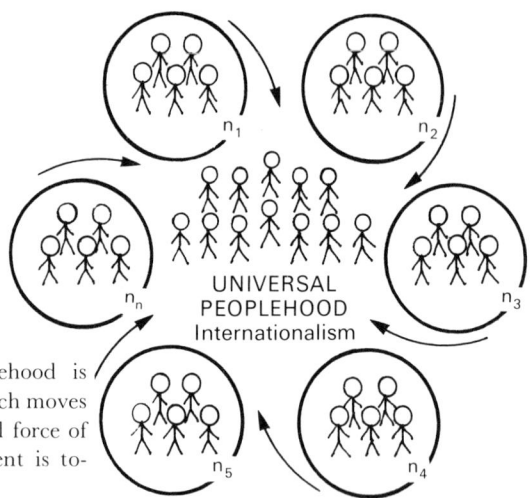

FIGURE 11:2. Universal Peoplehood is shown as a centripetal force which moves in the reverse of the centrifugal force of nationalism. Here, all movement is toward the unbounded center.

insuring the enactment of the Golden Rule. We are bound, therefore, to support such a just concept. As a *real* force in the world, internationalism has suffered immeasurably from lack of practice. We have only to witness the example of Soviet Russia to be able to fully appreciate how the lack of practice has affected internationalism as a force in the world. The future of internationalism in the twentieth century might have been presaged in Paris in 1900, when members of the Second International betrayed the principles of internationalism at the outset of World War I.[2] Likewise, Lenin, too, despite the correctness of his position (internationalism) and a life given to struggle for a just cause, was betrayed. In retrospect, it would appear that a more cautious survey of what was shaping up in the world at the turn of the century would have revealed the dangers ahead for internationalism. But that matters less at this point. What must concern us is that Lenin now rests in the soil of an affirmed, bordered, national state. And men have continued to move history (or the reverse, if you will) in the direction of more and more bordered, national states. Not only are men waging war over already-existing borders, but new lines are being drawn virtually every day, and there is flag-waving everywhere. This is clearly the century of nationalism. And the consequences have been most grave for those of us who are not nationals. We have been persistently used as either targets or cannon fodder for those who are nationals. And our present rate of attrition dictates that this must be stopped immediately.

If we are ever to stop what is occurring at present, we must first understand it. We must know exactly what our position is, and we must have both long- and short-range plans to deal with our situation. What, then, is the situation of all nonnationals, in general, and black nonnationals of America, in particular?

Essentially, we are people who are broke in a world of people rich with power. We are consequently powerless and at the mercy of those who mercilessly wield power. We stand ever upon the edge of extinction because our tormentors have no real need of us. We are, if we do not update our tactics, about to be "phased out." But such cannot be the case if we have even an ounce of self-respect and love of self left. To this we need only add a strategy, a strategy that is not mired in the abyss of petty differences and the suicidal misdirection of those oppressors who wish to save us for more oppression. We need a grand strategy for the survival of our oppressed people, above and beyond all else. Next in line, we need a specifically defined strategy for the total and complete elimination of those who can tolerate freedom for no one save themselves. This strategy should outline and direct our involvement and relationship to all peoples everywhere who love humanity and are willing to fight for the freedom of humanity. Ideology is extremely important, but it is a correct strategy that will enable us to survive. At present, we must talk about black people's being able to survive, not because we do not wish *all* PEOPLE to survive, but because it is black people whose survival is directly threatened.

We (black people) have always been internationalists. We may be (aside from the Jews, many of whom are also black) the only internationalists there are. Check our placement on the planet. We have been (are) everywhere, have been molded in every identity, have partaken of every culture, practiced every religion, and believed in everybody—save ourselves, perhaps. The time has now come to believe in ourselves. We must believe that we are not deserving of the treatment that we are currently receiving and that we are worthy of surviving. If we believe this, we can deal with the particular problems that we have in America and, in so doing, free our people (and others) elsewhere.

The particular problem that we have in America has already been described here, as has the general problem that we and people like us have in the world in general. Neither is insurmountable if we really wish to solve it.

In America, we are a numerical minority with highly conspicuous black skin and not the first right of citizenship or nationality. "They" are roughly 80 percent of the population, while we are, for the sake of those of us who believe it, roughly 20 percent of the population. And this is what really matters; the 80:20 ratio. This fact plus four hundred years of conditioning, is their mandate to do exactly what they are doing to us now, which is whatever they wish. The form of government matters less. The ratio and the conditioning remain the same. The ratio and the conditioning are the variables which must be affected if we are to survive. The 20 percent must have the weight and the significance of 100 percent, as the 80 percent now has the weight and significance of 100 percent. What I am saying here is directly related to the most basic principle of democracy: minorities ought not govern majorities. In America the racial majority has always governed and in so doing has created privilege for itself and hell for those outside its number. In accordance with this fact I am saying that, so long as men are satisfied with playing power politics (as they are now doing all over the planet, regardless of their ideologies), the worst and most dangerous thing one can be is a "minority." Those who continue to be "minorities," as long as this madness continues, may expect to continue catching hell. We (black people) must stop pretending that the lack of jobs and housing is THE PROBLEM, when the real problem is that we are a "minority." Not that these are not problems, but those deficiencies, in the end, have nothing to do with what often happens when one of us is stopped by a city policeman or a state trooper from the majority, who has been conditioned by four hundred years of history.

One or two may be a majority if they are not subject to rules made by three, four, or five. Being a part of, or subject to, three, four, or five seriously affects the manner in which one or two may behave toward three, four, or five. Fight (as they must)—win, lose, or draw—one or two have a better chance when operating independently of three, four, and five. The situation is no different from the American 80 and the black 20.

Let no one doubt for a minute that we do not know or believe that America will have to be dealt with. This is now common knowledge. The question is whether or not we will assume a position from which the fight can be carried. The fight may be carried from America's entrails by an amorphous group of unconnected victims, but the likelihood of such a group's succeeding is not great. Further still, the likelihood of their victory, should they succeed, being concretized in a meaningful freedom and justice for black people, given the 80:20 ratio and their conditioning, is less than poor.

For black people, no struggle can be truly victorious if it does not result in our possession of a fertile stretch of land (not too far from or locked from the sea) upon which all the elements fall freely. We must have a government of our own making and all the tools of elimination which will enable us to keep it that way. Nothing else will see us through the long night of the twentieth century in which men are still Americans, Niggers, Africans, Englishmen, Frenchmen, Germans, Russians, Asians, and a host of other peoples and nationalities. (If you really question this, then dig the reaction of some to the order in which these are mentioned, let alone, the reaction of those who are not mentioned. That's the way things are right now, and we have to deal with that.)

It is unfortunate that no set of ideas or terminology, save that of separatism, comes to grips with the immediate problems of black survival. The misfortune lies in the limited ability of the term *separatism* to describe what is being talked about. To be sure, much more than the need for physical separation should be denoted by whatever term one uses when speaking about solving the problem of black survival and independence. The quintessence of the matter is SELF-GOVERNMENT—the ability to give legal weight and force to the tactics of survival and independence. This is not done FOR people, it is, instead, done BY them or not at all. America and Americans are incapable of insuring black survival. It would be against everything that they are, to govern in such a manner. Government that insures the survival of the people—particularly the despised ones— is good government, and there is no good government in America.

It appears that it has been the paralyzing fear that they might have to take leave of white people that has caused the acrid responses of some blacks to separatism. Invariably, it is the members of the same throng who invoke the ageless argument that the separatists are cop-outs. To begin with, people who respond this way should know that nobody was ever talking about *their* leaving, in the first place. We have spoken of sensible members of the race (who can stand what they are) making some kind of move to check what is happening to us and to insure our survival. This does not appeal to many people who are black, and we know this. But we want to save as many of our people as we can. And we intend to be equal —equal to anyone in the United Nations, where there is no people without a country—without citizenship or nationality.

Strangely enough—or naturally enough—it is from high places in the echelons of Western white nations that we hear people decrying the antiquity and ineptness of the modern nation-state. They speak of regionalism, federalism, and, yes, some of them even speak of internationalism. They offer strong evidence that people are most capable of venturing beyond themselves once they have had the opportunity of dealing with themselves—an opportunity which they, unfortunately, had at the expense of others. While we should not have to engage ourselves in governing others in order to deal with ourselves, it may be that the ability to interact fairly and to engage in the creation of mutual government with others—to truly internationalize, that is—may have as its prerequisite the experiment of self-government. We are made mindful of this when we see that, even within like groups (take, for example, the Nigeria-Biafra situation), there appears to be a most compelling force directing men to govern within the most immediate identifiable group before entrusting that group to outside government. This would seem to indicate that nationalism, which is already up and around, has a course to run. And that course appears to be from micro to macro, from the smallest identifiable unit to the largest. But we don't have to speculate. We may settle for believing only what is happening to us. And if we do this, we see immediately what must be done. History will permit us to do only what is real.

The nature and the kind of things that have happened to black people in America will make some possible courses of action more real than others. Many individuals will attempt to tell us, the people, what is to be done. But in the end, we will know better than anyone else what works. That is what we must do.

NOTES

1. *Soul on Ice* (New York: McGraw-Hill, 1968), p. 61.
2. With signs of the coming of war everywhere, members of the Second International declared that they would not vote for the appropriation of funds for war materials in their respective governments. They declared that they, the workers of the world, would not shoot one another for the further enrichment of the capitalist classes. When World War I broke out on August 1, 1914, they not only voted the appropriations, but spared nothing in their efforts to do away with each other as nationals in the service of their respective countries. Lenin denounced them, but the deed was done.

12

Black Politics and the Kerner Report: Concerns and Direction

Jewel L. Prestage

REACTIONS TO THE report of the *National Advisory Commission on Civil Disorders*[1] have been widespread and varied, both in terms of their sources and their content. This discussion is essentially an effort to relate the *Report* to some of the theories and research findings in three areas of political science; namely, political socialization, democratic theory, and black political strategy. Any value accruing from this effort will probably be the results of the questions raised rather than directions or answers given.

POLITICAL SOCIALIZATION

One of the comparatively new and rapidly developing fields of inquiry for political scientists is political socialization.[2] Greenstein defines political socialization as ". . . all political learning formal and informal, deliberate and unplanned, at every stage of the life cycle, including not only explicitly political learning but also nominally nonpolitical learning which affects political behavior. . . ."[3]

Because political socialization has been interpreted as involving "all political learning at every stage of the life cycle" the dimensions of research possibilities are indeterminable.[4] It has been suggested that a full-blown characterization of political socialization would include classifications of: (1) who learns, (2) what is learned, (3) the agents of political socialization, (4) the circumstances of political socialization, and (5) the effects of political learning.[5]

An understanding of the political socialization function is essential to

---

Reprinted from *Social Science Quarterly* 49, 3 (December 1968): 453–464, by permission of the publisher and the author.

the understanding and analysis of any political system, and the stability and continued existence of a political system depend, in no small measure, on the extent to which the citizenry internalizes political norms and attitudes supportive of the system.[6] Political socialization, then, is induction into the political culture,[7] the means by which an individual "comes to terms" with his political system. The *Report* would seem to suggest that "coming to terms" is an especially traumatic experience for black people in America.

Examined in the context of current findings of political socialization research, the *Report* gives rise to several crucial concerns. The nature of these concerns is implicit in the observations which follow.

First, the political world of American blacks is so radically different from the political world of American whites that it might well constitute a "subculture" within a dominant or major culture. Even though there has been a great volume of writing and research on political socialization, very little has been directed to political socialization of American blacks.[8] The studies suggest that black people tend to relate rather differently to the political system and have a far greater sense of personal alienation and political futility than do similarly located whites.[9] Ghetto residents, like other citizens, tend to formulate their attitudes toward the political system largely on the basis of their contact with the system. For example, ghetto blacks believe that police brutality and harassment occur in their neighborhoods to a much greater extent than whites believe that violations occur in white areas. In Detroit, for example, 91 percent of the rioters believed anger at police had something to do with causing the riots.[10] It is not surprising that the policeman, primarily a symbol of law and order in white neighborhoods, is for ghetto people a symbol of injustice, inhumanity and of a society from which they are alien as well as alienated. Studies of white policemen assigned to ghetto areas indicate that black fears and reservations about the police may not be entirely imaginary.[11] Bobby Richardson, writing about police brutality in New Orleans, states ". . . brutality, man is a state of mine, not just a whipping with a billy, although plenty of the brothers get beat up on. They know that brutality is the way you are treated and the way a policemen will arrest one man and not another. And the way he will talk to you and treat you. Brutality is just an extension of prejudice, and it is easier to brutalize one man than it is another."[12]

Similarly, blacks tend to be less trusting of their political systems (local and national) than do their white counterparts.[13] Surveys done in Newark reveal that both "rioters" and "non-involved" blacks have a high distrust of local government with 44.2 percent and 33.9 percent, respectively, reporting they could "almost never" trust the Newark government to do what is right. In Detroit, 75 percent of the rioters and 58.7 percent of the non-involved felt that "anger with politicians" had a "great deal" or "something" to do with causing riots.[14]

Especially crucial for students of political socialization is the proportion of blacks, rioters and non-involved, who indicated that the country was not worth fighting for in a major world war. In Detroit the percentages were 39.4 for rioters and 15.5 for the non-involved, while the Newark survey revealed these sentiments on the part of 52.8 percent of the rioters and 27.8 percent of the non-involved.[15] These figures are striking, especially those related to the non-involved blacks, and would seem to indicate substantial disaffection among blacks. Similar results were ascertained in a recent study of black youth in Atlanta where 49 percent took a negative stance on the proposition, "Black Americans should be proud to be fighting in Viet Nam."[16]

Given the above data, it is interesting to note the commission's contrasting finding that rioters were not seeking to change the American system, but merely to gain full participation in it. However, the deep disaffection from the system by blacks and the continued reluctance of the system to accept blacks as full participants might lead one to question the commission's conclusion. Could it be that black rioters were attempting to change the system and to gain full participation simultaneously? Or, more directly, would not full participation by blacks in itself represent a fundamental change in the system? Such reservations regarding the goals of rioters receive some support from the recent report of Mayor Richard Daley's committee to study Chicago's riots of April, 1968. This committee reported a growing feeling among blacks that "the existing system must be toppled by violent means." This feeling was said to have its strongest expression among black teenagers, where there is "an alarming hatred for whites." Such feelings were found to be based on the attitude that "the entire-existing political-economic-educational structure is anti-black."[17]

Assuming the blacks of the ghetto have internalized the American dream of freedom, equality and justice, there is small wonder that "coming to terms" with the system has produced deep alienation, frustration and despair. Throughout the history of this country, blacks have, for the most part, been excluded from full benefits of this society. The fact that the rest of the country has experienced progressive affluence (flagrantly paraded before blacks through mass media) while blacks became poorer is a story much too familiar to belabor here. In the face of "the American dream" of equal opportunity and abundance, blacks have been forced to live "the American nightmare" of poverty, discrimination and deprivation. Despite some progress, American blacks continue to live in this "credability gap" and part of the results are distrust, estrangement and violence.[18]

Data from the Detroit survey indicate that all blacks included in the survey were not equally alienated and distrusting. Least alienated were the "counter-rioters," a major portion of whom (86.9 percent) regarded the country as worth fighting for.[19] Of this group, 88.9 percent felt that getting what you want out of life is a matter of "ability" rather than "being in the right place" as compared to 76.9 percent of the rioters and 76.1 percent of the non-involved.[20] The typical counter-rioter was described as an active supporter of existing social institutions and considerably better educated and more affluent than either the rioter or the non-involved. This would lead one to speculate that black attitudes or perceptions may be changed when "reality" changes.

Finally, the *Report* attributes responsibility for the present civil disorders to "white racism" in America, "the racial attitude and behavior of white Americans toward black Americans." The fact that a political system theoretically committed to democratic values finds itself embroiled in a major crisis resulting from undemocratic practices raises some fundamental questions regarding the real operative values of the system. How do white Americans reconcile theory and reality? What are the special problems which this situation suggests relative to political socialization of white Americans? Is resocialization of American whites a prerequisite for the fundamental policy changes recommended by the commission? A number of scholars and writers, some black and some white, have long maintained that the race problem in America is essentially a white problem, created and perpetuated by whites.[21] If the problem is to be solved it must be solved by whites. As Myrdal stated many years ago, "all our attempts to reach scientific explanations of why the Negroes are what they are and why they live as they do have regularly led to determinants on the white side of the race line."

Coming to grips with the fundamental cause of the riots, white racism, is more a task for American whites than for blacks. The process will no doubt necessitate an admission on the part of white Americans that the American dream remains a dream, that full democracy in America is yet to be realized. In short, it will entail alteration of the American political culture, a re-examination of basic values and possibly a rewriting of American history to revise the image of blacks in the minds of whites and blacks. More fundamentally, it will possibly require a restructuring of the socialization process for blacks and whites if our commitments to democratic values are to be translated into actual practices. The question for which the *Report* provides no answer is "how can this be done?" It is in the delineation of the broad outlines of such a process that political science and other social science research can possibly make its most significant contribution.

DEMOCRATIC THEORY

"Democracy is . . . characterized by the fact that power over significant authoritative decisions in a society is distributed among the population. The ordinary man is expected to take an active part in governmental affairs, to be aware of how decisions are made and to make his views known."[22]

Any attempt to view the *Report* in the context of democratic theory would seem to raise an array of tantalizing questions,[23] one of which is the relationship between *political obligation* and *consent*.

In a democracy the basis of political obligation is consent.[24] Such consent implies a high level of citizen participation in the political process or at least the unrestricted right of the interested citizen to participate. Consequently, democratic political systems have traditionally institutionalized certain structures and practices that allow for the orderly and periodic involvement of citizens in decision-making. A brief examination of the record tends to substantiate the commission's contention that throughout the course of American history, black men have been essentially "subjects" rather than "participants" in the political process.[25]

Black men arrived in America in 1619 and began what was to become a 244-year legacy of chattel slavery. Slaves were, by definition, nonparticipants in the political process. The lot of free Negroes was not markedly different from that of slaves. The end of the Civil War, the Emancipation Proclamation, and ratification of the Fourteenth and Fifteenth Amendments heralded the period of Reconstruction and relatively widespread participation in politics by black people. A return to white control and patterns of excluding Negroes from southern politics followed the Compromise of 1877 and withdrawal of federal troops from the South. Southern states revised their constitutions to deny the franchise to Negroes and as the Negro entered the twentieth century, his political future looked dismal and bleak.[26] Since 1900, blacks have staged an uphill battle in quest of full participation in the body politic. Most significant among legal victories for blacks have been the outlawing of white primaries in 1944, the passage of Civil Rights acts in 1957, 1960, and 1964, the Anti-Poll Tax Amendment in 1963 and finally the Federal Voting Rights Act of 1965.[27]

Perhaps the most reliable source of information on current black registration and voting in the South is the Voter Education Project of the

Southern Regional Council. According to its director, Vernon Jordan, the 1965 Voting Rights Act has had a marked impact on voter registration among southern Negroes. He states that significant gains have come in Alabama, Louisiana, Georgia, South Carolina, Virginia, and Mississippi. In Mississippi, Negro registration jumped from 8 percent to nearly 60 percent in just two and a half years.[28]

The most recent figures on voter registration supplied by the Voter Education Project are presented in Table. 1.

TABLE 1. VOTER REGISTRATION IN THE SOUTH, WINTER-SPRING, 1968

	White Registered	Percent White VAP[a] Registered	Negro Registered	Percent Negro VAP[a] Registered
Alabama	1,119,000	82.7	271,000	56.3
Arkansas	616,000	72.4	121,000	62.8
Florida	2,194,000	83.8	293,000	62.3
Georgia	1,450,000	80.6	334,000	54.5
Louisiana	1,122,000	87.0	301,000	58.5
Mississippi	655,000	88.9	264,000	62.5
North Carolina	1,555,000	77.5	293,000	53.2
South Carolina	567,000	63.6	183,000	49.3
Tennessee	1,434,000	80.6	225,000	71.7
Texas	3,532,000	72.3	540,000	83.1
Virginia	1,200,000	63.9	247,000	56.6
TOTALS	15,454,000	76.9	3,072,000	61.2

Source: Voter Education Project, News, 2 (June, 1968).
[a]VAP=Voter Age Population

Also noteworthy is the election of over 200 blacks to public office in the South since the Voting Rights Act was passed.[29] There are presently 50 blacks holding local, parish, and state offices in Louisiana, all elected since 1965.[30]

These accelerated advances in black registration and election are indeed impressive, but they do not eradicate the voting problem. With the exception of Texas, black registration percentages are still below white percentages in all the states included in the Voter Education Project survey, and in many areas blacks still experience substantial difficulties in gaining the franchise. Also, the number of blacks holding statewide positions in government and political parties is in no way proportionate to the number of blacks in the population.

Wilson observes, "that the political participation of the Negro in the North is significantly higher than in the South but even so is lower than than that of most other Northern population groups."[31] It ought to be pointed out that low participation in the North cannot be attributed to the type of legal restrictions historically operative in the South. Social science surveys have indicated that persons with low socioeconomic status tend to vote less than persons of higher socioeconomic status.[32] In addition, Negroes in the urban North are more geographically mobile than whites and are less likely to be able to satisfy residence requirements for voting. Nonpartisan elections, candidates running at-large and weak party organization also contribute to low turnout among low income voters. And it could well be that "the extent to which an individual feels effective as part of the institutionalized process may well determine the degree to which he participates in those processes. In sum, the individual's perception of his personal effectiveness should be supportive to the values he places on participation."[33] Thus, while there are no legal deterrents to Negro voting in the North, the cultural deterrents (income, education, occupation) are attributable to the system. That is, the prevailing social, economic and educational arrangements operate in a manner which relegates Negroes to this status, and as long as Negroes face these artificial barriers it is reasonable to assume that their level of political participation will not change.[34]

The extent of constraints on black participation, North and South, would seem to suggest an absence of consent by blacks and thus possible relief from obligations traditionally incumbent upon citizens in a democracy. Of interest in this connection is a recent re-examination of the principles of obligation and consent and related problems rendered by Pitkin.[35]

Pitkin, in a highly provocative treatise, holds that obligation depends not on any actual act of consenting, past or present, but on the character of the government. If it is just government, doing what a government should, then you must obey it. If it is unjust, then you have no such obligation. Or, your obligation depends not on whether you have consented but on whether the government is such that you ought to consent to it. Are its actions consistent with the type of government men in a hypothetical state of nature would have consented to establish and obey? Pitkin's study would suggest that any assessment of the riots and the rioters would of necessity involve grappling with these kinds of concerns.

The propensity among blacks to disobey certain basic canons of the political system has produced strains in the system which threaten to destroy its very foundation. Could this propensity derive fundamentally from the unwillingness of the system to incorporate blacks as full partners in the political process? Cook has projected that "on the empirical level, a tradition of exclusion from participation in the political system breeds disrespect for, and disloyalty to, that system."[36] "Men rarely question the legitimacy of an established order when all is going well; the problem of political obligation is urgent when the state is sick. . . ."[37]

Does exclusion from participation, coupled with exclusion from benefits of "the good life" of the system, not only remove the obligation to obey, but also give rise to the obligation to disobey or revolt? These queries are relevant, but they are also difficult in as much as they solicit precise guidance in specific and varied kinds of situations. Pitkin underscores the inadequacy of classical democratic theory as well as her own theory on consent by noting that both provide insufficient cues for determining what authority to resist and under what conditions. In the same way, both provide only imperfect guidelines for assessing and evaluating the consistency between civil disorder of the magnitude of riots and the obligation of citizens to obey the authority of society invested with the duty of enforcing the law.

BLACK POLITICAL STRATEGY

Scoble suggests that Negro leadership and politics represent a quest for effective political power. Negro politics can be best understood if viewed as pursuit of power and influence over authoritative policy decisions.[38] On the other hand, Wilson, in a recent article on the subject, writes, "Because of the structure of American politics as well as the nature of the Negro community, Negro politics will accomplish only limited objectives. This does not mean that Negroes will be content with those accomplishments or resigned to that political style. If Negroes do not make radical gains, radical sentiments may grow."[39] The crucial problem of the black man in the American political arena seems to revolve around the magnitude of the needs of the black people, (as set forth in the *Report* and elsewhere) in relationship to the limited potential of politics as a vehicle for ministering to those needs.[40] More succinctly put, it now seems incumbent upon black men to decide if politics, in the traditional sense, is now more of an irrelevancy rather than an imperative in the search for solutions to their problems. If politics is relevant, then what types of strategies will best serve the needs of the black community, North and South? If irrelevant, what are the alternatives?

Questions of strategy are significant and there are those who feel that this aspect of the black protest movement has not received sufficient attention from leaders in that movement. In fact, the alleged absence of a programmatic element in radical politics in America today, especially the black protest movement, provoked Lasch to state, "the very gravity of the crisis makes it all the more imperative that radicals try to formulate at least a provisional theory which will serve them as a guide to tactics in the immediate future as well as to long range questions of strategy."[41] Along the same general lines, Crozier points out that America is now committed to the omnipotence of reason and the black protest movements are out of step with that development. Very pointedly, he reflects that "it is no longer possible to make good through mere numbers, through the vote or through manual labor, but only through the ability to play the game of modern calculation. And in that area the Negro is still fundamentally disadvantaged. The more rational the society becomes, the more he loses his foothold."[42] Could it be that traditional politics characterize the black subculture while a more rational-calculating variety of politics has long been the pattern in the dominant political culture?[43]

The literature of the discipline and popular periodicals are replete with suggestions of appropriate strategies and/or programs for solving the race problem. Some of the more popularly suggested and researched strategies include black-liberal white coalitions, black-conservative white coalitions, fluctuating or *ad hoc* coalitions, separate black political parties, Black Power, ghetto power.[44] No examination of this proliferation of literature can be made in this limited commentary. Nor will any full-blown theory or strategy be offered. However, it does seem reasonable to submit that any strategy designed to redefine the status of black people in America must of necessity be devised with certain considerations.

First, political strategy for blacks must take into account the difficulties inherent in being a numerical minority. Minority strategy must be highly flexibly based, to a large degree, on the fluctuating attitudes and actions of the white majority in any given setting. It must also be directed toward overcoming traditional constraints on the exertion of effective power by Negroes endemic to the black community itself. Second, any therapeutic strategy must acknowledge the reality that blacks in the ghetto already constitute a "separate society,"[45] and must address itself seriously to black charges of control by "alien, outside" agents. Indigeneous control of the ghetto and similar demands cannot be summarily dismissed as, for example, "old wine in new bottles."[46] Third, given the general apathy and insensitivity of whites toward problems of blacks, it seems reasonable to suggest that any meaningful gains for blacks will come as a result of *demands,* supported by evidence of black willingness to cause great inconvenience to the community at large if these legitimate demands are ignored. Fourth, it might be that the commission placed too much emphasis on the material aspects of the black man's problem (and the material aspects are indeed important) and did not devote enough attention to such psychological needs as dignity, self-respect and identity and to the relationship between the latter and any corrective actions, political or otherwise. Taking these psychological dimensions into account will probably necessitate innovations in and restatements of traditional concepts and theories regarding democracy, civil disobedience, protest, and other forms of political activity. New tactics, new rhetoric and new sources of leadership will most probably emerge and must be accommodated by the system.[47] Fifth, and in a similar view, it would seem that black strategy and black strategists ought not be constrained to political alternatives if these alternatives prove to be mostly dysfunctional for blacks, and there is a growing body of opinion which holds that they may well be. Finally, the magnitude of the problems faced by blacks is such that the correctives must be radical. If radical programs are not adopted, the Kerner Report may be more a prelude to, rather than a summation of, the worst race riots in the history of this nation, for there seems to be little reason to believe that black rioters will be satisfied with anything less than radical corrective action.

NOTES

1. National Advisory Committee on Civil Disorders, *Report of the National Advisory Commission on Civil Disorders* (New York: Bantam Books, 1968) (hereafter referred to as the *Report*).

2. Major studies include Herbert Hyman, *Political Socialization* (Glencoe, Ill.: The Free Press, 1959); Fred Greenstein, *Children and Politics* (New Haven: Yale University Press, 1965); Gabriel Almond and Sidney Verba, *The Civic Culture* (Boston: Little, Brown and Company, 1965); Lewis Froman, "Personality and Political Socialization," *Journal of Politics*, 23 (May, 1961), pp. 341–352; David Easton and Robert D. Hess, "Youth and the Political System" in Seymour M. Lipset and Leo Lowenthal, eds., *Culture and Social Character* (New York: The Free Press of Glencoe, 1961), pp. 226–251; David Easton and Robert D. Hess, "The Child's Political World," *Midwest Journal of Political Science*, 6 (Aug., 1962), pp. 229–246; Roberta Sigel, "Political Socialization: Some Reactions on Current Approaches and Conceptualizations," paper read at the 62nd annual meeting of the American Political Science Association, New York City, September, 1966; John J. Patrick, "Political Socialization of American Youth: A Review of Research with Implications for Secondary School Social Studies," High School Curriculum Center in Government, Indiana University, Bloomington, Indiana, March, 1967, mimeographed paper; Jack Dennis, "Major Problems of Political Socialization Research," *Midwest Journal of Political Science*, 12 (Feb., 1968), pp. 85–114.

3. Fred Greenstein, "Political Socialization," in *International Encyclopedia of the Social Sciences* (New York: Crowell-Collier Macmillan Publishing Company, 1968); Roberta Sigel defines political socialization as "the gradual learning of the norms, attitudes, and behavior accepted and practiced by the ongoing political system." See Roberta Sigel, "Assumptions About the Learning of Political Values," *Annals of the American Academy of Political and Social*

Science, 361 (Sept., 1965), pp. 1–9; of political socialization, Gabriel Almond writes, "What do we mean by the function of political socialization? We mean that all political systems tend to perpetuate their cultures and structures through time, and that they do this mainly by means of the socializing influences of the primary and secondary structures through which the young of the society pass in the process of maturation." See Gabriel Almond and James Coleman, eds., *The Politics of Developing Areas* (Princeton, N.J.: Princeton University Press, 1960), p. 27.

4. The varied nature of such studies may be discerned from the foci of the following studies: Philip E. Converse and George Dupeux, "Politicization of the Electorate in France and the United States," *Public Opinion Quarterly*, 26 (Spring, 1962), pp. 1–23; Fred Greenstein, "Sex-Related Political Differences in Childhood," *Journal of Politics*, 23 (May, 1961), pp. 353–371; M. Kent Jennings and Richard Niemi, "Family Structure and the Transmission of Political Values." *American Political Science Review*, 62 (March, 1968), pp. 169–184; Heinz Eulau, William Buchanan, Leroy G. Ferguson, and John C. Wahlke, "The Political Socialization of American State Legislators" in John Wahlke and Heinz Eulau, eds., *Legislative Behavior: A Reader in Theory and Research* (Glencoe: The Free Press, 1959); Edgar Litt, "Civic Education, Community Norms and Political Indoctrination," *American Sociological Review*, 28 (Feb., 1963), pp. 69–75.

5. Fred I. Greenstein, *Children and Politics* (New Haven: Yale University Press, 1965), p. 12.

6. Almond and Coleman, *Politics of Developing Areas*, p. 31.

7. Almond and Verba state, "When we speak of the political culture of a society, we refer to the political system as internalized in the cognitions, feelings and evaluations of its population." Almond and Verba, *The Civic Culture*, p. 13.

8. See Dwaine Marvick, "The Political Socialization of the American Negro," *Annals of the American Academy of Political and Social Science*, 361 (Sept., 1965), pp. 112–127; and Bradbury Seasholes, "Political Socialization of Negroes: Image Development of Self and Polity" in William C. Kvaraceus, ed., *Negro Self-Concept: Implications for School and Citizenship* (New York: McGraw-Hill Book Company, 1965), pp. 52–90.

9. See Dwaine Marvick, "The Political Socialization." When Negro respondents were matched with whites (counterpart groups) having similar socioeconomic characteristics, Negroes expressed considerably less confidence that they would receive "equal treatment" from governmental officials or from the police.

In a study of Gary, Indiana, James T. Jones found that more Caucasian children than Negro children agreed that "A person owes his first duty to the community and the nation and next to himself." James T. Jones, *Political Socialization in a Midwestern Industrial Community* (Ph.D. diss., Department of Political Science, University of Illinois, 1965), p. 228.

Roberta Sigel found that Negro children were considerably more upset and worried than white children over the assassination of President Kennedy. These differences maintained themselves even when partisanship and socioeconomic status were taken into account. Roberta Sigel, "An Exploration into Some Aspects of Political Socialization: School Childrens' Reaction to the Death of a President" in Martha Wolfenstein and Gilbert Kilman, eds., *Children and the Death of a President* (Garden City: Doubleday and Company, 1965), pp. 34–69.

10. The *Report*, p. 178.

11. See the *Report*, p. 306. From a study by Albert Reiss, director of the Center for Research on Social Organization, University of Michigan, "In predominantly Negro precincts, over three-fourths of the white policemen expressed prejudice or highly prejudiced attitudes toward Negroes. Only one per cent of the officers expressed attitudes which could be described as sympathetic towards Negroes. Indeed, close to the one-half of all the police

officers in predominantly Negro high crime rate areas showed extreme prejudice against Negroes. What do I mean by extreme racial prejudice? I mean that they describe Negroes in terms that are not people terms. They describe them in terms of the animal kingdom."

12. Robert Richardson, "Every Black Man is My Brother," *New Orleans Magazine*, 2 (June, 1968), pp. 30–31; and see also Eldridge Cleaver, "Black People and Police Routine," *Black Politics: A Journal of Liberation*, 1 (April-May, 1968), pp. 33–36.

13. Marvick, "Political Socialization of the American Negro," "The Political Socialization," pp. 112–127.

14. The *Report*, p. 178.

15. *Ibid.*

16. James E. Conyers and William Farmer, *Black Youth in a Southern Metropolis* (Atlanta: Southern Regional Council, 1968), p. 13.

17. "Survey of Chicago Riots Reveals 'Black Racism,'" *Baton Rouge Morning Advocate*, August 8, 1968, p. 12-D.

18. "Characteristically, violence has been employed by those groups in the political system which feel that they have least to lose from chaotic upheaval, and which face an enormous gap between possessions and expectations." See Gabriel Almond and Bingham Powell, *Comparative Politics: A Developmental Approach* (Boston: Little, Brown and Company, 1966), p. 82.

19. The *Report*, p. 178.

20. *Ibid.*, p. 176.

21. See James Baldwin, *The Fire Next Time* (New York: The Dial Press, 1963); Gunnar Myrdal, *An American Dilemma* (New York: Harper and Row, 1944); and *Ebony Magazine* (special issue) "The White Problem in America," 20, August, 1965.

22. Almond and Verba, *The Civic Culture*, p. 19.

23. For critical commentary on this general subject see Lane Davis, "The Cost of Realism: Contemporary Restatements of Democracy," *Western Political Science Quarterly*, 17 (1964), pp. 37–46; Jack Walker, "A Critique of the Elitist Theory of Democracy," *American Political Science Review*, 60 (June, 1966), pp. 285–295; Robert Dahl, "Further Reflections on the Elitist Theory of Democracy," *American Political Science Review*, 60 (June, 1966), pp. 296–305. See also Joseph Tussman, *Obligation and the Body Politic* (New York: Oxford University Press, 1960).

24. For an extensive treatment of the principle of consent in the American political experience see David W. Minar, *Ideas and Politics: The American Experience* (Homewood, Ill.: The Dorsey Press, 1964), Ch. 4.

25. "Subjects" are those individuals who are oriented to the political system and the impact which its outputs, such as welfare benefits, laws, etc., may have upon their lives, but who are not oriented to participation in the input structures. "Participants" are those individuals who are oriented to the input structures and processes, and engage in, or view themselves as potentially engaging in, the articulation of demands and the making of decisions. See Almond and Powell, *Comparative Politics*, p. 53.

26. For a detailed account of this period, see John Hope Frankling, *From Slavery to Freedom* (New York: Alfred A. Knopf, 1967).

27. See *Revolution in Civil Rights*, 3rd ed., (Washington, D.C.: Congressional Quarterly Service, 1967).

28. Vernon E. Jordan, "New Forces of Urban Political Power," *The New South*, 23 (Spring, 1968), p. 47.

29. United States Commission on Civil Rights, *Political Participation* (Washington, D.C.: U.S. Government Printing Office, 1968), p. 15.

30. These include 8 constables, 9 justices of the peace, 11 party executive committee

members, 5 school board members, 6 city and town councilmen, 10 police jurors and only one statewide officer, a member of the state House of Representatives. Source: List of Negro Elected Officials of Louisiana prepared for Workshop for Louisiana Negro Elected Officials held at Southern University, Baton Rouge, Louisiana, July 13, 1968.

31. James Q. Wilson, "The Negro in American Politics: The Present" in John P. Davis, ed., *The American Negro Reference Book* (Englewood Cliffs, N.J.: Prentice-Hall, Inc., 1966), p. 431.

32. See Angus Campbell *et al.*, *The American Voter* (New York: John Wiley and Sons, Inc., 1964).

33. James T. Jones, *Political Socialization in a Midwestern Industrial Community*, pp. 218–219.

34. This point is developed in Philip Meranto, "Negro Majorities and Political Power: The Defeat of an All-Negro Ticket in East St. Louis" prepared for Herbert Hill, ed., *The Revolt of the Powerless: Negroes in the Cities* (New York: Random House, forthcoming); in earlier studies similar projections had been made regarding Negro registration and voting in the South. Donald R. Matthews and James W. Prothro, "Social and Economic Factors and Negro Voter Registration in the South," *American Political Science Review*, 57 (March, 1963), pp. 24–44. On the national scene, there are one black U.S. Senator and five black Representatives (Adam Powell excluded). About 80 blacks were among over 2,600 delegates and alternates at the 1968 Republican Convention and some 301 were among 5,611 delegates and alternates at the Democratic Convention. "Has the GOP Written off Black Votes," in *Pittsburgh Courier*, nat'l ed., August 17, 1968, p. 1; and "Negro Delegates to Confab Shows Gain, Chairman Says" in Baton Rouge, *Morning Advocate*, August 15, 1968, p. 18-A.

35. Hanna Pitkin, "Obligation and Consent—I," and "Obligation and Consent—II," *American Political Science Review*, 59 and 60 (Dec., 1965 and March, 1966), pp. 990–999; pp. 39–52.

36. Samuel D. Cook, "The Negro and the American Political System: Obligation and Resistance," (unpublished paper presented at the Conference on Political Obligation and Resistance to Authority, Gatlingburg, Tennessee, April 18–20, 1968), p. 1.

37. S. I. Benn and R. S. Peters, *Social Principles and the Democratic State* (London: George Allen and Urwin, 1959), pp. 299–300.

38. Harry Scoble, *Negro Politics in Los Angeles: The Quest for Power* (Los Angeles: Institute of Government and Public Affairs, University of California, 1967), p. 2.

39. See James Q. Wilson, "The Negro in Politics" in Kenneth B. Clark and Talcott Parsons, eds., *The Negro American* (Boston: Houghton Mifflin Company, 1966), p. 444. He notes that "American political institutions provide no way for the organized political pressure of a particular disadvantaged group to reshape in any fundamental sense social and economic conditions. . . . That politics seems irrelevant to their daily pre-occupation is not necessarily an expression of neurotic withdrawal . . . but may well be the rational conclusion of a reasonably well-informed citizen." Also, see Carey McWilliams, "Protest, Power and the Future of Politics," *Nation*, 206 (Jan. 15, 1968), pp. 71–77.

40. On the changing nature of the black protest, see Bayard Rustin, "From Protest to Politics: The Future of the Civil Rights Movement," *Commentary* (Feb., 1965), pp. 25–31.

41. Christopher Lasch, "The Trouble with Black Power," *The New York Review of Books*, 10, February 29, 1968, p. 14.

42. Michel Corzier, "America Revisited: The Lonely Frontier of Reason," *Nation*, 206 (May 27, 1968), p. 693. See also Harold Cruse, *The Crisis of the Negro Intellectual* (New York: William Morrow and Company, Inc., 1967).

43. This writer's personal ambivalence on this question leads to the belief that some effort to apply developmental theory to the study of black politics in America would seem to provide interesting and meaningful research possibilities.

44. On the white conservative-black coalition in Atlanta, see Edward C. Banfield, *Big City Politics* (New York: Random House, 1955), pp. 18–36. The coalition of blacks with liberal whites in Houston, Texas, is reported by Harry Holloway, "Negro Political Strategy: Coalition or Independent Power Politics," a paper in this issue of the *Quarterly*. See also Ronald Moskowitz, "Education and Politics in Boomtown," *Saturday Review*, February 17, 1968, pp. 52–54, 66–67. James W. Wilson suggests that blacks form coalitions on an issue-to-issue basis. See "The Negro in Politics" in Parsons and Clark, *The Negro American*, pp. 434–435. Also see Bayard Rustin, "Black Power and Coalition Politics," *Commentary*, 42, (Sept., 1966), pp. 35–40; Stokely Carmichael and Charles V. Hamilton, *Black Power: The Politics of Liberation in America* (New York: Random House, 1967); Floyd McKissick, "Programs for Black Power" in Floyd B. Barbour, ed., *The Black Power Revolt* (Boston: Porter Sargent Publisher, 1968), pp. 179–181; Hubert M. Blalock, Jr., *Toward a Theory of Minority Group Relations* (New York: John Wiley and Sons, Inc., 1967).

45. Kenneth B. Clark, *Dark Ghetto* (New York: Harper & Row, 1965).

46. See W. H. Ferry, "Blacktown and Whitetown: The Case for a New Federalism," *Saturday Review*, June 15, 1968, pp. 14–17.

47. In the last decade, black sit-ins, mass marches and general obstruction of operations of various governmental and educational enterprises have become commonplace. These tactics have found widespread acceptance by nonblack groups such as students against university administrations and protestors against the draft. It would seem reasonable to suggest that similar creativity with regard to tactics will characterize the black struggle in the future.

13

Black Administrators and Higher Education

Roosevelt Johnson

IN THE WAKE of black consciousness, black power, black studies, the free speech movement, and the "relevancy explosion" on college campuses, a need for more black administrators has become undeniably apparent. The question which must be answered without too much delay is, how are the desperately needed administrators going to become prepared to cope with the charges which the black college students have placed before the predominant white college campuses across the continent?

The non-black has traditionally risen from the ranks of the faculty to dean, vice-president, and culminated his ascension with the presidency of a given institution. However, with the immediate demand before higher education for more black administrators to serve the recently recruited black students, the black scholar contingency cannot climb the administrative ladder in such a precise order. The customary order of entering the administrative framework within higher education will have to be re-evaluated, re-defined, re-oriented, and the need reconciled if a legitimate effort is going to be made to assist the black students once they reach the predominantly non-black campus.

The major thrust of this writing will be an analysis of the current problem facing higher education vis-à-vis black administrators, the current state of higher education (a caricature which is difficult to elucidate), and some suggestions for possible improvement of its deplorable condition. It is my intention not to cover the broad spectrum of higher education, including both black and white institutions, but rather to deal with the phenomena of the white institutions which are, as we all know, hard put to come up with some vehicle to fulfill the national purpose confront-

---

Reprinted from *The Black Scholar* (November 1969) by permission of the author and the publisher.

ing them today—getting black folk into the main stream of higher learning. A lot, perhaps not enough, has been said about the problems of the "Negro institutions." I would like to beg off discussing Negro colleges this time, but some would say that Negro institutions, traditionally speaking, would be one and the same as white colleges, as regards black administration.

As it stands now the black administration at non-black institutions is manifested in several individuals who occupy "window dressing positions." They are the recently acquired black manikins who are brought out on special occasions, say like on "Mother's Day," to do a special job of seducation for very esoteric audiences. These audiences and special occasions, can run the gamut, from seeing a press release about the institution's involvement in the plight of the black community (in most cases, a sham) to displaying the new fire extinguisher to dash out blazes which frequently result as a corollary of black and white basic encounter sessions—and I have no reference to the ones which are conducted by the Human Relations Committee.

They are usually consigned to one of the following pseudo-administrative type "jobs": an admissions officer—to concentrate upon the ghetto schools with platitudes sent by the institutional power structure; a black counselor in the advisement office, if the institution has one, to handle the "militant advisee"; an assistant to the Director of the Student Center to keep the Director up on the latest dances and inform him of what soul records should be on the music box and an assistant to the Chancellor to act as the integrating agent in his public retinue.

Usually the extent of the black administrator's power and decision-making ability is relegated to a private conference with his superior to advise him on how to handle some trivial confrontation between two ethnic group social fraternities and possibly to act as a "go-between" when the black students get up to their necks in absurdities and rebel by taking over a dean's office or perhaps, depending upon the extent of the oppression, a building.

If per chance one has been sensitive enough to note that I have left out the Director of the Black Studies program, then it is fitting to draw the conclusion that the reader's aptitude on the question of blacks and higher education is exceptionally elevated. This exclusion of the Black Studies Director is intentional. Why? The reason is quite simple—not enough has been done in this area, at this point, to elaborate upon the fate of these aborning administrators to speak of their efficacy; they represent a possible break-through on this whole business of blacks and higher education.

However, the Black Studies Director must be ever conscious of the tremendous task which lies before him at every writing of the memoranda requesting budget revisions, at every conference with the black student pressure groups calling upon him, conscious of the vicarious needs of the white faculty calling upon him for possible teaching positions, and especially tuned in to the brother approaching him in the dashiki who espouses blackness but whose goals may be the antithesis of the whole movement. Although the outcome of the Black Studies Director's role in higher education is too new to be evaluated, his daily operation will be tremendously formidable and challenging.

Back to the business at hand, that of trying to illuminate what I had reference to when I alluded to the terminology of "window dressing." Well, it certainly does not take an intelligence quotient of 150 to know the quaint psychology of having-one-of-the-enemy-on-our side: we have seen this type of operation since silent movies. Let us take a look at the movies that we currently see on the late, late show, for example, to get a better picture of the predicament. When one sees re-runs of *Ramar of the Jungle*, and other such antiquated movies, the psychology becomes all too clear to the sensitive black. As far as I am able to remember, Ramar, the great white physician, always had along "Willie Willie, the ignorant looking black," to talk to the natives in the many dialects of which he displayed competent knowledge, so that Ramar, in the event of danger, could call upon Willie Willie to offset aggression so that he could go about his business of performing experimental medicine on the tribes he came into contact with. Think about this for a second and let the full effect grab you.

Willie Willie, for all intents and purposes, had to have been a very gifted individual to go about the Mother Country and talk all of those languages to keep Ramar alive. Well, the same situation is apparent today on the modern American multiversity—the good native black brother has been hired, in most cases, to keep the great experimenter alive via his interactions with the hostile young "natives" from the alien tribe across the railroad, which the colonial power structure has admitted to the "king's courtyard"—college campus U.S.A. In the final analysis, seeing that Willie Willie was so intelligent and had so much insight into the customs of all the tribes, he should have, in fact been hired, not as a guide, but, to put him on parity with Ramar, as a professor of cultural anthropology. Show me an employed black man and I'll show you an under-employed man!

I insist that when blacks are brought into the polluted mainstream of higher education to perform these "window dressing roles" that these roles can serve as a positive correlative of just how far blacks have gone in the United States since Reconstruction—we have gone, intervally speaking, not one hash mark up on the scale of social progress. The Reconstruction was a farce and I would submit that, at this point the business of black administrators in the higher educational arena today is just as much a farce. We are constantly dangled out in front of the benevolent foundations, those very well-deserving edifices, as though we were some sort of "black carrot" to attract some foundation's investigator. The investigator, not too recently removed from an impoverished situation himself, is apt to become enraptured with our plush offices and the administration's "mouthing" of a black enrollment to equal that of the national proportion of the black population, so much that he is prone to grant funds to the institutions at hand, thinking that a concerted effort is really being made in an attempt to achieve that goal.

The "window dresser" is usually placed in some conspicious "cubby hole," where he must be seen by the public, and is given some perfunctory "job." I know of an assistant to a Director of Financial Aid at a leading Mid-Western university whose sole purpose for being there, he feels, is to act as a countervailing agent in the event of some confrontation by the black students on that campus. He is virtually without any power and the decisions he has to make are unbelievably frivolous. He has the authority to assign part-time jobs which have been designated by some tacit systematic method as being for the black students on this particular campus—janitorial, cafeteria, and odd job work at faculty members' homes. In terms of having the authority to make the decisions considered to be important to the students, he is administratively emasculated. He, for example, has nothing to do with the granting of the National Defense Loans, the state grants, the achievements awards, the voting upon scholarship recipients, nor can he approve an emergency loan of, say, five dollars.

I ask, is this administration? To further make the situation appalling is the self-realization on his part of the role he is having to play. This is truly a dilemma! What is he to do? If he speaks up, he is very likely, says he, to be "professionally" castrated and the pursuit of his advanced degree forfeited. If he continues to be docile, he will not last another year with the pressure being exerted upon him by the factions of the black students on the campus who are unquestionably aware of his behavior, which is in some instances, interpreted as cowardice.

What is the responsibility of a quasi-administrator, who is black and/or Negro, whatever the case calls for, who is directing a large program in the Mid-West which is handsomely funded by one of the leading foundations in the country and who does not have control of his budget? How can he wear the title of Director of anything when, in fact, he cannot direct his secretary to purchase a postage stamp without the approval of some uninvolved, uninterested, glory-seeking white superior? I would assert that implicit in any administrative role is the presence of a budget commensurate with the responsibility of role. In saying this, one could conclude that the absence of control of money indicates the circumvention of black administration.

Any newly recruited black administrator must go into the interview situation pointing out the principles he has within him that are not negotiable. This administrator must know from the word "go" that doing a good job and having job security are not postively related when it comes to the black administrator. That doing a good job is important and must be striven for cannot be overemphasized. However, if a good job means taking demeaning roles and engaging one's self in sophisticated "shuffling," then the job is not good enough to be done.

Not only are white administrators across the country playing a teasing game with the black administrators at the "knowledge factories," but the black students are giving them a fair share of hell in their own right. However, I am not at all sure that some of the black students are acting rationally when they accuse the black administrators of "selling out to the system" when, on certain occasions, it appears as though he is "acting a little white." Let's face it: we all have little white orientation in us. That militant student who is usually pointing his finger at that black compromiser would be hard put to explain his presence on the "lily white" campus which he is trying to reform. So much for that. The point is this: the black administrator is caught in a game of double jeopardy between the hustle of the white power structure and the young, vicious, energetic, and answer-seeking black warriors. He is caught in a web of hostility which is relentless in either quarter and it is compelling upon him to cope with every traumatic second and emerge immaculately free of any psychological ramification or anxieties of having betrayed his dual responsibilities—a case of academic administrative ambivalence.

A more common role played by black administrators is that of Director or Coordinator of the remedial or compensatory programs on the campus such as the Upward Bound Program, the Education Opportunity Programs, Educational Talent Search, etc. True, these positions should be held by blacks if the largest percentage of the students enrolled in such programs is black. No matter, however, what the case may be vis-à-vis a particular minority, it is important that these positions be held by nonwhites. Accordingly, this black individual, if there is not an identity crisis, is apt to have (aboriginal or soulful) insight into the problems of the "high potential" recruits.

To further emphasize this sensitiveness, will one please concern himself with this thought? All of us black administrators now holding Ph.D's and other high caliber white credentials, know full well the disciplines and subject-matter area where we encountered the most difficulty. Namely, in most cases, English composition and mathematics, and I have no quarrel with any brother who might want to disagree with my assessment of the areas of difficulty—to each his own. However, I would hold tenaciously to these two areas. If we know that these are the areas in which we have encountered difficulties, should not our counseling and development of the special curriculums take the same into account? It certainly should. That is, if that certain indigenous soulful concern has not been crucified out of the particular administrator by the white ethnocentric curriculums across the nation.

If a brother administrator is willing to come to grips with himself and reconcile his close natural association and physical attributes of remarkable similarity with the students so enrolled in his program—in short, if he identifies—he does not have to have that many meetings with the black students to ascertain what they want; he knows what they want! What's more, he is capable of articulating needs to the institutional power structures in such an eloquent manner that they are apt, if they have legitimate intentions, to respond with rapidity.

All too often, regrettably, too many of our black administrators fortunate enough to move into one of the alluded-to positions, forget from whence they have come. Although there is probably some self-hate syndrome immediately beneath the surface, there is no reason for such a total "deblackification" so prevalent in and around certain "cities of intellect." For in the words of Saint Malcolm X, when addressing an audience at a leading Eastern university after having received sharp and cutting remarks from a Negro Ph.D. who was in the crowd, said he, in essence, "Do you know what they call you, Ph.D.? A nigger." This is to say that all of those brothers who are "neo-toms," and Oreo's turning into vanilla wafers will not be saved when all of the acting is over, and the circumstances lead to the final confrontation. The oppressive, dehumanizing, institutional racism that they are helping to nourish will make no effort to distinguish in the degrees of blackness—at the moment of truth, it is black survival against psychological genocide.

Get those "soulful insights and aboriginal traits" out front and put them to use for the sake of liberating the black minds of our well-meaning, often too naive, black brothers and sisters who are calling upon us the best way they know—a native way. The black rebels on college campuses are resorting to primitive ways to deal with a primitive mode of oppression, via the conditioning of minds by educating one away from his identity.

The failure of the white educational system, relative to the black constituency, has been pre-supposed. It has failed! The directors of these black programs must take heed and come to the naked conclusion that they must try something new and that they must be the agent which will shock the Institutional power structure into a new mentality predicated on the axiom that blacks will not be educated as usual. That there is more than one way of performing the same task is an adage which our forefathers believed. To the extent that we realize the uncompromising flexibility and validity implicit in such a cliché we will achieve in renovating and innovating the current curriculum patterns in higher education.

Black administrators of the compensatory programs on the various campus must grapple with this whole problem of remediation and lead in innovation. Is it not true that all study is a remedial experience? A remedy for something that one does not know or has a deficit in? Posing this question, I would then ask, can we afford to wait to remediate in the traditional sense of the term in an effort to ameliorate the conditions of the black "high potential" student? I, personally, do not think that we can tackle this problem of remediation and compensatory education in the traditional sense. If we continue upon the thesis that the path to liberation of the mind is through the currently established curriculums, which have been with us since the University of Paris and Medieval Period and which have been geared to an elitist society, we will continue to search into a darkness so pervasive that the radiant red blood from 350 years of lynching cannot illuminate it.

It is pressing upon all black administrators in remedial programs to equip themselves with a diversified body of curriculum development and go to war with the central, oh yes, conservative administration and push for compensatory programs that will offer the participants some type of prorated credit toward graduation. I will contend that we cannot, at this point, ask our undergraduate brothers and sisters to engage themselves in programs of compensatory and remedial education which will not afford them any credits toward the baccalaureate degree. I am not so obstinate that I would insist that the participants receive full load credits each semester or quarter (it would be nice though) but I am saying that they must receive some credit for the work on which they are expending a tremendous amount of time. I will offer no specifics in this case; let every institution assess its own milieu and adapt its program to that particular environment.

That black administrators should direct compensatory programs cannot be overstressed, but the ultra significant, important positions into which blacks must be placed, without too much gradualism, have to do with the decisions and policy-making for the entire university. Power must be available which will afford black America an opportunity to effect significant educational change. There must be actions instead of motions, realism instead of rhetoric, and power in place of ambassadorial platitudes and euphemisms. That is, positions which make themselves felt in such areas as curriculum planning with intracomponent colleges and divisions, personnel of the professional and para-professional nature, academic policy, rank and tenure, management of all aspects of the university.

I will contend that it is contradictory to pass legislation, appropriate funds, recruit and enroll black students who, for some asinine reason, have been tagged "high risk," if no instrument is available whereby their needs can be communicated to the higher echelon of the college administration and, for heaven's sake, the faculty. Where this instrument is lacking, turbulences are in the making and some type of "undesirable" confrontation will ensue in a subtle or blatant fashion, depending upon the severity of the incident which triggers the charge. The conspicious exclusion of blacks from the viable and legitimate administrative roles is one of the central, underlying forces which have detonated most of the campus explosions where black students were involved.

With the exception of a very few cases of campus activity during the last academic year, the principle cry heard after a confrontation was that the students did not utilize the proper protocol to make their needs known to the administration. How, pray tell, will these students be able to discern the different roles and functions of university offices when the multiversities are growing to such magnitude that the mail clerk and the plumber are the only ones who know where the offices are? Of course, this is not true in all cases, but for the large campuses where activity erupted this will hold true in more cases than one.

If, we come to grips with the university's socio-historical developments and study its origin in the U.S. we will discover that this particular institution has grown only one way—horizontally. Therefore, it would behoove us, the black administrators, not to work for change which will call for a redevelopment of a college or a department within a university. Rather, we will have to work for additional departments and/or institutes which will be grafted onto the existing structure. White faculties are by nature conservative; white administrations have, at one time, been white faculty; the board of trustees, in a number of cases, represent the alumni, who are conservative; and the alumni are the personifications of arch-conservative views. Calculating such a homogenous group yields a monolithic index. Taking this tremendous impasse into serious account, no alternative is left but to add some instrumentality onto this monolith, an instrument which will receive its impetus from a viable external pressure group —black America.

The black structure pressure organizations on campuses are attempting to do their part to "negotiate" for constructive change, but they are "only" students in the eyes of the faculty and administration, and to further emphasize the point—only black students. There needs to be some modifications made in the triangle of students, faculty, and administration which comprise the university.

There is no use in recommending the "playpen" student governments as the answer. That simply will not work. It appears to me that in addition to permitting students to sit on the board of trustees, a new movement, we must now place tactful statesmanship right out front and ask at institutions where the black enrollment is increasing, that black students be placed on the policy working bodies within the institutional framework. This ought not be a "show" position; it should, rather, be a position whereby the needs of the black constituency can be articulated to the individuals who are professing meager knowledge of the black man's plight. These students should be in a position to exercise full voting rights on these key policy bodies.

There is no use in our "rappin" about who the institution is for, for we will not come to any consensus on this topic. The faculty will say it's for research, the students will say it's for teaching, the administration is apt to espouse any number of reasons for its being, but one can rest assured that none of these bodies will express a position that it is for society as a whole. If, perhaps, they could bring themselves to a point of serious deliberation about the concept of society, they would learn that the black spectrum is definitely a part of the society and by virtue of our being a part we deserve a role in the process of making decisions about our destiny.

The white power structure has always honored administration via subgroup pressure. It is now incumbent upon them to come to the realization that the temporal trend within this country makes it essential for them to come around to a new way of thinking and effectuate a receptiveness to the emerging sub-group pressures: the black community generally, and in higher education, the young black students who are not cognizant of any changes which have been made to enhance the black condition.

In some cases, it would not be possible for the black students to constitute this vehicle of communication. In these situations, it would be wise to include, by any means necessary, a black faculty member or administrator on one of these bodies in an attempt to keep the university community, at large, attuned to the needs and stresses of the black students on the campus. This individual ought to have rank within one of the departments and should not be linked officially to the black student pressure group on the campus. (By virtue of his blackness, however, he will inevitably be thought of, by certain quarters of the faculty, as being a part of the "conspiracy" to over-throw the system of higher education within the United States.) For all intents and purposes, this black faculty member will serve as a professional sensitizing agent to keep the administration and the faculty honest in their endeavors to educate the black students.

Again, tradition must be laid aside if a serious effort is going to be made to institute some instrument for communication. Tradition would have us wait two decades for the newly acquired black students to establish themselves for positions on these faculty councils and other machinery found on college campuses, which would put us in an inoperable position. An arbitrary edict must come forth and direct the college to select individuals who are black and carry rank, to immediately become parts of that machinery. I would suggest, wherever a reluctance is discovered on campuses to make policies which will effect immediate change, that that institution is a bigoted caricature of a university or college.

At institutions where the Board of Trustees are espousing a doctrine of "concern for black student enrollment," a position of Vice-President, Vice-Chancellor for Minority Group Affairs should be established. To many, the ones living in retrograde, this idea could sound unrealistic. To them, I would say that perhaps it is better for them to research the development of student personnel administration in higher education and learn of the factors influencing the development of specific areas into established components of higher education; student personnel administration was an effort to ensure a harmonious college life for the student. At one time the president performed all of the administrative functions of the college. As administrative needs grew, more personnel had to be sought. Thus, the dean of students, the counselor, health services, registrar, etc., became meaningful parts of the college community as the temporal needs became apparent. There is now a temporal need—a need for black representation at the decision and policy-making level in colleges and universities. Having such will benefit the faculty and administration as well as the student, to whom the most worthy consideration must be given.

I envision such a position as that of Vice-President or Vice-Chancellor for several reasons. Ordinarily, these individuals would report directly to the president of the institution who in turn would go directly to the Board of Trustees. Unless the president is some omnipotent god, he is apt to give this position academic "carte blanche" in its realm of operation. Concomitant to this position would be *power*. This individual should have a budget commensurate with his title and responsibility. This individual should have enough power to effect the administrative changes which would derive from his title and responsibility. This individual should be answerable only to the President.

In the organizational structure this administrator should be on the line directly beneath the President of the institution with authority lines leading into all segments of the university community, as these would have to do with meeting the needs of the American Minority Group Student. His services should be called upon by the other vice-presidents or chancellors whenever any situation arises concerning the minority students on campus. I am informed of the fact that there are now several institutions who are employing vice-presidents and chancellors for Foreign Students' Affairs. I insist that it is wrong to employ individuals in this capacity to deal with aliens when so many descendants of the men who built this country are standing around with an unquenchable thirst for a higher education.

The writer envisages this black administrator working on an executive and administrative parity with the chief academic officer, the one under the President, of the University. If this happens to be the Dean of the Faculty, then he should work congruently with him; if this is the Academic Vice-President, then he should work congruently with him; if he should be the Academic Chancellor, then he should work congruently with him; the desirability of having this black officer working at the top of the vertical hierarchy is obvious.

If one would note, in the above, the emphasis on the word "academic" or "faculty," it should become apparent the significance I bestow upon the academic framework of the university. The university is positively related to academe. If we were to remove the concept of academe, we would not have a college or university. Therefore, taking that assertion into account, one must conclude that academe defines all segments of the university. If this is the case, and I believe it to be, all other offices, departments, schools, institutes, etc., are merely ancillary machinery necessitated by the student's central purpose for having attended college —to master academic material.

No office, it appears to me, could justify its reason for being if it were not for the academic framework of the university. Advancing this concept a bit further, I would assert that all offices, departments, and schools are, or should be, answerable to the top academic officers of the university or the college. In the final analysis, it is uncontrovertibly necessary for the black administrator recruited and hired for this position to have the authority and decision-making ability commensurate with that of the chief academic officer under the President of the university.

There is not enough time to wait for a generation of Ph.D.'s to be exuded into the main stream of higher education in an equal manner to satisfy the caprices of the white institutional power structure. No, we cannot wait! There is also reason to believe, by looking at most of black scholars today, that the acquisition of the Ph.D. is leading the black away from teaching and personal involvement rather than into this involvement. The actualization of this critical situation is leading any number of us to believe that we must now impress upon the white institutional power that good teaching and research are not necessarily positive correlatives with Ph.D. With all of the countries represented in the whole of American Higher Education, it must behoove us to push to get some African-Americanism represented in the diversified relics which we find alienating us today.

The one simple way of instituting this change into higher education is by refusing to cater to the whims of the white institutional power structure. When they go into the academic euphemism about wanting only blacks with Ph.D.'s, we must keep the truth right out front, that because of the social injustices and racism, we are unable to come forth with this cadre of Ph.D.'s which most of them are well aware of our not having. Whenever white administrators ask for blacks with that terminal degree to fill a position, that is a true sign of a "cop out" and we must realize that we have been hit again with the "qualification syndrome"—remember Willie Willie. We must refuse to go along with the "qualificatitis" which the white administrators are constantly trying to ram down our parched throats. That is, the symptoms which show the signs of equating academic qualifications with the Ph.D. degree in order to enter the bureaucratic "city of intellect," must be rediagnosed and reacted to in a pervasively different manner.

Back to the point of black Ph.D.'s being educated away from the personal involvement. This brings to mind a conference I attended recently in Atlanta, Georgia, where black educators were assembled from across the country to deal with and develop new perspectives in black education and to come up with creative solutions. While I am not at liberty to quote the number of Ph.D.'s present (it would be a guess), I can say that very few of the supposedly nationally known black scholars were present. Black people at that conference came with deep convictions and hopes of acquiring new and meaningful knowledge, but to their dismay, they were left without the knowledge of some of our foremost black writers and scholars to help them with their attempts to legitimate and viable change. To you all, where were you?

That particular episode could easily serve as food for thought on the subject of the mentality which a number of black scholars must have on the college campus—the Ph.D. black scholars. Therefore, we must take a different bearing as to how we are going to provide the needed black administrators on the predominantly white college campus. And after having found some type of solution to this problematical situation, we must interpret it to the existing institutional powers and be obstinate in our belief that the road down which we have chosen to travel must be one navigated by our cognition. I say it can be done!

This is being stressed for those unrealistic and antipathetic majority group administrators who feel to date that the only blacks who are qualified to become members of their institutions must have all the makings of the archaic conceptualization of the "super Negro." The time has now come in higher education when the criteria for selection of black administrators will have to be re-defined in black terms and with black standards of excellence. Engendering the principle of "preferential treatment" as the primary criterion for selection, will be a step in the right direction for breaking the cycle which has enmeshed the black psyche in a deep woven web of inferiority caused by abandonment neurosis, oppression, and social injustices.

THE INSTITUTE FOR BLACK COLLEGE ADMINISTRATORS

Robert J. Wert, one-time Executive Associate, Carnegie Corporation of New York, said in *Current Issues in Higher Education,* 1959, "Most presidents have had no particular preparation and a few, at least, will never miss it. Either they are instinctively good administrators or they have worked on their own to learn administrative theories and practices." In view of this statement concerning college presidents, I would think that a similar statement could be made about individuals of lesser line authority in a college organizational structure. In the future as in the past, I would venture to say that administrators will continue to become so without any formal training.

However, to tranquilize the whims of many "majority group" administrators, I submit the following as a means for aspiring black administrators to supply evidence of their qualifications as a black administrator in higher education. Please learn that the writer feels that this plan is offered to meet the immediate needs. It has been said that we are witnessing a social revolution. Thus, a revolution is supposed to encompass a magnitude of abrupt changes. Anything taking a conventional or traditionalistic path in an attempt to make changes is, then, a reformation. To keep in pitch with the crescendo of the militant symphony of unrest on college campuses, the academic conductors must move the baton of change with extreme rapidity.

The Institute for Black College Administrators should be held at universities and colleges centrally located by geographic regions throughout the nation. Perhaps to have them housed at several centers for the study of higher education would be as good a place to initiate them as any. The Institute for Black College Administrators should be administrated by black academicians who have shown their ability to be creative and effective. These institutes would have to be instructive and have some academic format of transmitting knowledge. Therefore, all platitudes about having equal time for "rappin" will have to be dispensed with. We must assume that certain individuals have more knowledge and experiential background and implicit in such an assumption would be the proposition that one can learn something from another.

If predominantly white universities are legitimately interested in recruiting black administrators, they should be capable of recruiting aspiring black college administrators and financing their periodic formal training in order to keep abreast of the trends in higher education as seen from a black perspective. Not only would the institute, which could be held each summer, be beneficial to the black administrators, and scholars, but it should strengthen the white colleague as well.

If the Department of Health, Education, and Welfare is serious about the Higher Education Act, then I feel that this governmental agency should be of some financial assistance in an endeavor of this nature. The benefits of such a program would stimulate black individuals who are not in higher education to enter the "closed corporation" without having to resort to redundant types of learning activities which their professional fields covered in their undergraduate and graduate curriculums.

The format would be that of a common course where the learning activities and workshops would run the gamut of all phases of Administration in Higher Education from the black perspective. The participants would assemble at the said universities for a period of twelve weeks. The individuals attending would register in advance and would have the option of participating in the institute for credit or no credit. Each visiting professor would have a two to three day stay at the respective campus for presenting and leading the learning relative to his expertise and topic.

In the main, these learning activities would be in the art and the science of Administration in Higher Education. Inherent in this type of format would be the socio-historical development of the American Higher Educational System to gain insights as to how the system developed, thus affording the participants an opportunity to formulate their own theories about possible solutions to the problems which are universal in higher education. The influences of Holland, Scotland, and Germany would be systematically studied to indicate the many piece-meal components of the system of higher education in the United States of America.

A vital knowledge to any college administrator is the financial administration in higher education. As I am sure that no black administrator will have a long while before he will be involved in the system to such a degree that he will learn all of the sources of income for the "closed corporation," I, then, cannot over-emphasize the importance of knowing all of the ramifications of budget preparation and control.

The whole area of student personnel administration will have to be studied and solutions to problems dealt with from a black perspective. It is staggering to witness the vastness of this particular phase of higher education and look at how enormously it has grown during the twentieth century. However, we must realize that it must grow even more to incorporate within it the black man's plight. This administrative area must be systematically studied and researched in our institute. These alluded-to areas must be built into the proposed institute with a plan carefully prepared and earnestly addressing itself to the stated hypothesis—if given a chance, the black can be an effective administrator in higher education.

There would be research possibilities. Each participant would be presented with a topic on which he could do research for the academic year to be completed and ready for submission at the onset of the following summer institute. For this work credit would be given by the sponsoring institution.

The administration of the institute would also have the responsibility of coordinating an internship for black administrators.

The major thrust of such a program would be the immediate availability of black college administrators at the beginning of each academic year. The program would entail enough flexibility to attract blacks who are currently employed outside of higher education. It would afford an ongoing opportunity for research on the various areas of higher education from the black perspective. It would be of tremendous assistance in providing the personnel which the growing community college demands.

In conclusion, the problem is irrevocably upon us and nothing less than a program which will show tangible, legitimate yields in the shortest period of time, will do in trying to meet the needs of the ideological, politically energetic black students presently enrolling on American college campuses.

14

Blacks and Conservative Political Movements

Hanes Walton, Jr.

CONSERVATISM AS A doctrine appeared early in America. The English settlers of the American colonies brought it with them. Many had knowledge of the philosophy and ideas of Edmund Burke and of the aristocratic foundation of the English society. In that land of ordered hierarchy, the higher governed the lower, the few controlled the many, and good overruled evil. In other words, society was directed by the best, the refined, and the cultured.

Therefore, with at least a fundamental understanding of conservatism, all the early English settlers had to do was to adapt it to the American context. And this they did in time. Conservatism, as a defense of the status quo against major changes in the economic, social, or political institutions of society, became entrenched before the close of the nineteenth century.[1] Once entrenched, the doctrine of conservatism influenced both thought and action.[2] Conservative leaders and movements soon began to appear on the American scene. And these movements, as well as the leaders, have continued to evolve and adapt themselves within the changing American context to retain their viability.[3] Basically speaking, then, American conservative thinking is identifiable in our social, economic, and political thought and actions.

Today in American politics the term *conservative* has no precise meaning, but the general conservative position on issues has been one that is fairly "consistently opposed to governmental regulation of the economy and civil rights legislation, and in favor of state over federal action, fiscal responsibility and decreased governmental spending and lower taxes."[4] With this in mind, then, one could raise the questions, What kind of

---

Reprinted in revised form from *Quarterly Review of Higher Education Among Negroes*, October 1969, by permission of the author.

people then would support a conservative political movement? What stake would they have in supporting such a movement? and finally, What ethnic group or minority group would support such a movement? Answers to the first questions are numerous and complex. But the latest question is the least known and explored. The purpose of this article is to inquire generally into black conservatism, and specifically into why black people would support conservative political movements. This inquiry, however, doesn't seek final answers but, at least, some tentative conclusion and generalization until a larger and more conclusive study can be made of the area.

BLACK CONSERVATISM

The roots of black conservatism are ambiguous and complex.[5] But its beginnings developed from the black man's odysseys in this country. In sum, black conservatism is an outgrowth of black reactions to slavery, segregation, and discrimination in America. It can only be understood and recognized in this fashion because outside this framework of the American experience there isn't anyplace to turn for an explanation. Moreover, even if the roots of black conservatism could be traced beyond these shores, the impact of the American culture would certainly have so modified those pre-American roots as to render them somewhat insignificant.

However, it is true that blacks were also aware of aristocratic traditions in their African kingdoms.[6] But the influence of these feudal structures upon their thinking is not known, nor is the degree of this aristocracy among the various blacks who were brought to America known.[7] In other words, the number of black aristocrats and blacks with aristocratic thinking who survived the "middle passage" and made it to America is unknown. Moreover, the influence of this group upon black thinking is also unknown. Thus, for all intents and purposes, black conservatism emerged on the American continent. And in this place, then, black conservatism grew from a number of sources.

The existence of a free black population, North and South, during the era of slavery permitted the emergence of a relatively wealthy black middle class. This group of blacks acquired property, money, plantations, and slaves, as did whites.[8] They also acquired, in the South, a bourbon aristocratic tradition whereby they placed themselves apart not only from the slaves but also from other free blacks of lesser means.[9] They became involved in maintaining the status quo because their societal position rested on it.[10] In fact, very few blacks aided in any kind of conspiracy with the slaves to overthrow the slavocracy.[11]

In the North, the free black population, through its numerous conventions, considered first its disabilities and how to remove them. All blacks did not participate in the abolition movement, and only a few developed some race consciousness and some concern for the slaves.[12]

Among the slave population in the South, a division existed between house and field slaves. This division was created by the privileges and rights which the house slaves acquired. The house slave, having received a modicum of education to manage the necessary household chores, having the right to wear the cast-off clothes of the master, and in many cases being of a lighter hue than the field slave, felt better off than his brethren in the field.[13]

In fact, the house slaves had a stake in the status quo. Their position in the social milieu of the plantation rested upon maintaining the social system. And when slaves plotted to overthrow their masters, or revolt, it was in many cases the house slave who turned the fledgling insurrectionists in. In essence, their interest was in preventing a change in the status quo.

In addition to these groups which had an interest in maintaining the status quo were the black nationalists.[14] The relationship of early black nationalists to conservative thinking was in their policy of separatism. In other words, the free blacks who advocated separation, colonization, and separatism, in effect, accepted the system. They, in a manner speaking, did not desire to change the status quo, but more or less only to effect changes in it. But all black nationalists cannot be thought of as black conservatives. Only later, when the civil-rights movement became full grown were black nationalists looked upon as conservatives.[15]

Therefore, prior to the Civil War a secure economic status, privileged positions based on color, education, and minimal freedom, as well as black nationalism in a limited sense, provided the basis for black conservative thinking. After the war, these bases continued, for the most part. Many of the black politicians of Reconstruction had a disdain for the black masses,[16] while the secure blacks of the north in effect accepted the system and preached merely for some changes within it.

However, Reconstruction and the era after it brought sudden change. Each swift change created catastrophic conditions in the black community. Basically, black leadership looked to the future in Reconstruction. As for the masses, there was some attempt to go back to work for their former masters. When Reconstruction ended, the post-Reconstruction era brought in a completely new situation, and confusion abounded among both the masses and the black leadership. Neither knew what to do.

The ideas of old reappeared. H. M. Turner, Pop Singleton, and others espoused separation and separatism, while Booker T. Washington argued for accommodation.[17] Monroe Trotter, W. E. B. DuBois, and James Weldon Johnson, in the footsteps of Frederick Douglass, urged blacks to continue to struggle for full equality. They argued that integration would bring about a complete answer to the black problem in America. And with their intellectual skill, white financial backing, and a powerful organization, they made themselves heard and felt. The National Association for the Advancement of Colored People set the course for black Americans. It also set the course for black thought.[18]

Integration, in effect, became liberalism. It was accepted as a liberal idea, and accommodation, separation, and nationalism became conservative positions. In other words, any doctrine, idea, or leader that didn't push for integration was seen as conservative or Uncle Tom.[19] And any black who did become an integrationist became a hero, a militant, a liberal. Those who pursued integration at a slow pace or in a grdual manner were considered more or less moderate.

In this vein, black nationalists or separatists like Garvey were denounced as visionaries or utopians. Garvey's ideas were considered reactionary and destructive to the black masses. In short, he was looked upon as a reactionary conservative. The black Communists and Socialists who espoused the idea of a Black Republic, the Forty-Ninth Staters, the Black Muslims, and recently the advocates of Black Power have been looked upon as black conservatives. They have wanted a status quo ante. Or, at least, they have accepted the system and sought only minor changes.

In regard to the present-day advocates of Black Power, a chief tenet of their doctrine has been black separatism, which they have espoused as a goal in opposition to integration. This, then, has cast their thinking into an anti-liberal mode. Some black social scientists have labeled them just plain, old conservatives in the mode of Booker T. Washington—who have finally accepted the system.[20] The argument goes that they want all-black communities in which they will seek improvement, rather than in the system at large.

In sum, the base of black conservatism changed in America. At first it had an economic and strategical foundation, but later it shifted from this to an emphasis upon a goal. The policies and philosophy of black leaders were measured in terms of their achieving a final solution for the black problem, and that solution had to be integration. Black conservatism, thus has a goal as well as an economic and strategical foundation. In this light we can view black support of conservative political movements.

BLACKS AND CONSERVATIVE POLITICAL MOVEMENTS

In light of my foregoing analysis, black conservatives, for one reason or another, do exist. And they have supported conservative political movements.

There is on record the fact that blacks—under coercion—supported the pro-slavery Native American party in 1838 and the Democratic party in Louisiana just before the Civil War.[21] After the war some blacks supported the Southern Democratic party in numerous localities across the region. There are also some indications that blacks willingly fought for the Confederacy and willingly aided in erecting its defenses.[23]

"Even during Reconstruction some Southern Negroes had supported the 'Conservatives' or Democrats." According to Professor A. Meier, these blacks "were genuine conservatives because of their close connections with paternalistic upper-class whites, others were disillusioned with Republican corruption, and some were chiefly political opportunists."[23] Moreover, "after Reconstruction Southern Negroes who stood with the Democrats tended to be of the old servant class, or successful, conservative farmers and businessmen who identified their interests with those of upper-class whites."[24] In addition, some blacks during the post-Reconstruction era, supported independent conservative political movements like the Readjusters and Funders.

When the Republican party split into two factions in the South (a Lily-White faction and a Black and Tan faction), numerous blacks in many of the southern states supported the Lily-White groups.[25] And in some cases these blacks went with the Lily-White groups to contest the regular Black and Tan faction on the point of adequate racial composition at national Republican conventions. The same thing happened in 1968 when one black joined the regular, white Mississippi delegation, enabling them to contest the Loyal Democratic party of Mississippi, which was in reality more balanced.[26]

In the start of the twentieth century, one could find blacks supporting Woodrow Wilson in the 1912 election campaign, even though he shunned such support.[27] There have also been many black supporters and votes for the Socialist party, with its announced racism. In this category, one can also find similar supporters of the Conservative and racist-oriented Communist and Prohibition parties.[28]

In 1948 the white supremicist Dixiecrat party found black supporters.[29] And racist governors and senators, both North and South, have through the years also received some support from the black community. A case in point is the governor of Alabama George C. Wallace, who received black votes for his first term in office.[30] Moreover, 179 blacks voted for arch-conservative Lester Maddox (who later chased blacks away from his restaurant at pistol-point and then closed the restaurant in order to avoid serving blacks under the 1964 Civil Rights Act) in Atlanta's 1961 mayoralty race.[31]

In the North, a black conservative joined with white conservatives to form a Conservative party in New York in 1961. In May 1964 the Conservative party nominated that black man, George Schuyler, to run for Congress in the Eighteenth District in New York, which was represented by Adam Clayton Powell. He ran on a platform opposed to civil rights and to Martin Luther King's nonviolence and blamed "the Harlem race riots on the incessant encitement of civil-rights leaders." He polled 637 votes, a total of 0.6 percent of the votes cast.[32]

Voting in Eighteenth Congressional District
(Manhattan, Harlem), 1964.[33]

Candidates	Votes
Adam C. Powell (D)	94,222 (84.6%)
Joseph Bailey (R)	11,621 (10.4%)
Allen Lewis (Liberal)	4,851 (4.4%)
George Schuyler (Conservative)	637 (0.6%)

Six hundred votes gives one an idea of the number of black conservatives that can be found even in a ghetto area.

With the coming of the 1964 presidential election, in which presidential candidate Barry Goldwater made a forthright conservative appeal, black supporters in a small degree joined his campaign.[34]

However, the most recent example of a conservative movement was the 1968 campaign of George Wallace. Wallace's American Independent party from the outset found black supporters. In Butler County, Ohio, a black, Alvin D. Smith, editor of the ultraconservative newspaper the *Butler County American*, took it upon himself to establish the county George Wallace Club.[35] And during Wallace's campaign, Smith campaigned actively for him throughout the county.

In Alabama, several blacks spoke out to the effect that they truly supported Wallace and his movement.[36] In addition, they even promised to vote for him. Wallace received 0.1 percent of the black votes in this election.

During this campaign, Black Power advocates suggested that candidates like Wallace and Lester Maddox should receive black votes because if these men were elected, it would show the true character of the American people—that is, their racist nature. And this, then, would unify the black community and bring about people-hood.[37]

But beyond the individual blacks who have supported conservative political movements lies support from the black newspapers. Earlier, when the sit-in movement began, several black newspapers came out editorially against them.[38] And an analysis of black papers in the 1968 election revealed that one paper was pro-"law and order" in its editoral policy and otherwise conservative. This paper was one of those which had opposed the sit-ins. In other words, then, even parts of the black press are somewhat conservative because of their financial backing.[39]

The upshot of this analysis is that some blacks have always since the Civil War supported conservative political movements. They have, because of necessity, expediency, ideological commitment, and economic standing, opposed any changes in the status quo.

CONCLUSION

In America black conservatism is tied to the legacy of the black experience. Numerous blacks found the ante-bellum status quo to their liking. Some found that their societal positions were such that they didn't want to see change come in any social, economic, or political institutions.

After slavery and the Civil War arose the caste system of segregation, and segregation also found its black supporters.[40] Numerous blacks, especially black businessmen and, in large measure, the entire black middle class, acquired a "vested interest in segregation."[41] Behind the wall of segregation blacks created such institutions as black churches, businesses, schools, libraries, and hospitals. These institutions enriched their black ministers, businessmen, teachers, and other professionals. And these blacks have come to feel that they have an exclusive right to enjoy the social and material rewards to be derived from the status quo.

If the walls of segregation were removed, these blacks with a vested interest in the system would have to compete with whites, and competition could remove some of those blacks which the segregated system has elevated. Therefore, some blacks who have a vested interest in the system end up trying to maintain it.[42] They redouble their efforts, to maintain the status quo because it means a continuation of their rank and social privileges. Thus, they become conservatives because of their desire to maintain their present societal position.

Other blacks become conservatives because they have accepted the white man's word that we are inferior and are entitled to an inferior status.[43] While still some blacks accept conservatism because of necessity —coercion or its intellectual stylishness. Hence, conservative political movements, despite the anti-black rantings of their candidates or their overt or covert racism, will continue to find a minimal number of black conservatives who will ardently support them.

NOTES

1. For insight into the development of American conservatism, see: Clinton Rossiter, *Conservatism In America* (New York: Knopf, 1962), pp. 67–198; Peter Viereck, *Conservatism Revisited* (New York: The Free Press, 1962), pp. 121–159; Alan P. Grimes, *American Political Thought* (New York: Holt, Rinehart and Winston, 1960), pp. 478–510.
2. Grimes, *American Political Thought*, pp. 486–489.
3. See Russell Kirk, *The Conservative Mind: From Burke to Santayana* (Chicago: Regency Press, 1953).
4. Jack C. Plano and Milton Greenberg, *The American Political Dictionary*, 2 ed. (Holt, Rinehart & Winston, 1967), p. 4.
5. There has never been a study of black conservatism in America. In fact, all blacks have been looked upon as being liberals—that is, in favor of integration—and when some blacks have rejected this goal, they have been thought of as Uncle Toms, idealists, visionaries, or Communists. For a brief insight into the nature of black conservatism, see James Graham Cook, *The Segregationists* (New York: Appleton-Century-Crofts, 1962), the chapter on the "Dark Segregationists," pp. 305–344.
6. For a thorough discussion of ancient African civilizations, see Margaret Shinnie, *Ancient African Kingdoms* (New York: St. Martin's 1968), and B. Davidson, *Lost Cities of Africa*, (Boston: Little, Brown, 1959). For insight into the social structure of some of the tribes which inhabited early kingdoms, see M. Fortes and E. E. Evans Pritchard, *African Political Systems*, (New York: Oxford University Press, 1963).
7. Blacks who were brought to American didn't come from any single ethnic group. "They were from a number of groups and from many different tribes with different languages, customs, traditions and ways of life."—James Comer, "The Social Power of the Negro," in *The Black Power Revolt*, ed. F. Barbour (Boston: Horizons, 1967), p. 73. For a listing of the tribes, see E. Franklin Frazier, *The Negro in the United States*, (New York: Macmillan, 1949) pp. 4–5.
8. For an analysis of the free black slave-owners, see Carter G. Woodson, *Free Heads of Families in the United States in 1830*, (Washington, D.C., Associations Press, 1925). For an overall view of free blacks and their accumulations in early America, see Frazier, *The Negro*, Chapter 4, pp. 59–81.
9. See Leon Litwack, *North of Slavery: The Negro in the Free States, 1790–1860* (Chicago: University of Chicago Press, 1961).
10. See E. Franklin Frazier, *The Black Bourgeoisie* (New York: The Free Press, 1957).
11. For an analysis of American slave revolts, see H. Aptheker, *American Negro Slave Revolts* (New York: International, 1943). In fact, only one free Black led a major slave revolt —Denmark Vessey.
12. Frazier, *The Negro*, pp. 79–81.
13. Frazier, *Black Bourgeoisie*, and *The Negro*, pp. 53–58.
14. Howard Brotz, ed., *Negro Social and Political Thought 1850–1920* (New York: Basic Books, 1966) pp. 1–5.
15. Kenneth B. Clark, "The Present Dilemma of the Negro," *Journal of Negro History* January 1968, pp. 7–8.

16. Harold F. Gosnell, *Negro Politicians: The Rise of Negro Politics in Chicago* (Chicago: Phoenix, 1967), p. 5.
17. Charles E. Silberman, *Crisis in Black and White* (New York: Random House, Vintage, 1964), pp. 125–134.
18. Silberman, *Crisis*.
19. Silberman, *Crisis*.
20. Clark, "The Present Dilemma," pp. 7–8.
21. Hanes Walton, Jr., *The Negro in Third-Party Politics* (Philadelphia: Dorrace, 1969), p. 28.
22. Lewinson, *Race, Class and Party* (New York: Oxford University Press, 1932), pp. 17–45.
23. Meier, *Negro Thought in America* (Ann Arbor: University of Michigan Press, 1963), p. 26.
24. Meier, *Negro Thought*, p. 27.
25. See Hanes Walton, Jr.'s, "The Politics of Black & Tan Republicanism," a paper presented at the 54th annual meeting of the Association for the Study of Negro Life & History.
26. Hanes Walton, Jr., *Black Political Parties* (New York: The Free Press, 1970), Chapter 3.
27. Walton, *Third-Party*, p. 95.
28. Walton, *Third-Party*, pp. 38, 72.
29. Walton, *Third-Party*, p. 103.
30. H. Holloway, *The Politics of the Southern Negro* (New York: Random House, 1969), p. 154.
31. C. Stone, *Black Political Power in America* (Indianapolis: Bobbs-Merrill, 1968), p. 48.
32. George S. Schuyler, "Teaching Negro History Is Questionable," *Globe Democrat*, August 13, 1968, in *Black America*, ed. Richard Resh (Boston: D.C. Heath, 1969), pp. 257–260. See also Schuyler's *Black and Conservative* (New York: Arlington House, 1966), pp. 347–348.
33. Complete returns of the 1964 election by congressional district, *Congressional Quarterly Special Report*, March 26, 1965, p. 494.
34. Walton, *Third-Party*, p. 104.
35. It might be important to note that Smith was the only black in the club and that he was elected president and held several meetings in his home.
36. Walton, *Third-Party*, p. 81.
37. H. Rap Brown, *Die Nigger Die!* (New York: Dial, 1969).
38. Louis E. Lomax, *The Negro Revolt* (New York: Harper & Row, 1962), p. 220.
39. Brown, *Die Nigger Die!*, p. 41.
40. E. Franklin Frazier, "Human, All Too Human: The Negro's Vested Interest in Segregation," *The Survey Graphics* January 1947, p. 74.
41. Frazier, "Human," p. 99.
42. Frazier, "Human," p. 75.
43. Cook, *The Segregationists*, pp. 307–308.

PART FOUR

The Future of Black Politics

15

Measuring Black Political Power

Chuck Stone

In general, we understand by "power," the chance of a man or of a number of men to realize their own will in a communal action against the resistance of others who are participating in the action.

MAX WEBER

IN THE AMERICAN political system, organizations and interest groups wield power, individuals don't. Individuals can affect power outside organizations only if they possess charisma, that undefinable quality of body and spirit reserved for a few "world historical individuals." Such charismatic leaders must still, however, rely on followers, and eventually these followers become institutionalized into some form of organizational structure.

If organizations are the true power brokers in society, then political parties represent summit political power. Their power is measurable by the number of elections they win, the number of public officials they elect, and the amount of control they can exercise over the administration of government. Because the state is the supreme power in any society, that organization which controls the government controls the state. Political parties control governments. The power of political parties is measured by the degree of sovereignty they exercise over the heads of government, its appointees, its domestic and foreign policies, and its dispensation of patronage.

The measurement of the political power of an ethnic group, an economic class, or another interest group is far more difficult. Such a group's claims of political achievements are usually exaggerated and extravagantly publicized. On occasion, they have been able to establish a direct connection between the defeat or election of a candidate inimical or responsive to their wishes. But this group's ability to deliver the vote of

---

From *Black Political Power in America*, copyright © 1968, by C. Sumner Stone, reprinted by permission of the publishers, The Bobbs-Merrill Company, Inc.

its members is not always subject to scientific verification. Their leaders may fervently endorse a particular candidate or polity. But the group's members, by their decision at the polls, will vote diametrically opposite to the official position of the interest group. For example, in the Gary mayoralty election of November 1967, the labor union leaders in Gary publicly endorsed the Democratic candidate, a negro. In a political race governed by strong racial overtones, white steel workers from the Gary steel mills ignored the official posture of their labor leaders and instead gave 89 percent of their vote to the white Republican candidate.

This is a classic example of the social variables that impinge on the consciousness of individuals, forcing them to structure a priority of loyalties and then decide which loyalty will determine their political decisions. As the distinguished Lebanese philosopher and statesman Charles Malik has written: ". . . man has other loyalties than his loyalty to the state. He has his loyalty to his family, to his religion, to his profession; he has his loyalty to science and to truth. These loyalties are equally exacting as the loyalty to the state."[1]

Thus, a white Roman Catholic living in an integrated city neighborhood whose children attend integrated schools is not likely to respond as antagonistically to his church's call for more integrated schools as is a white Roman Catholic living in a wealthy suburb where no negroes live or attend school. Nor are union members of an industrial union with a large percentage of negroes likely to be as determined to bar union participation of negroes as the racially exclusive crafts unions.

Throughout the history of American politics, various interest groups have tended to follow rather than reject the advice of their leaders in tacit fealty to the pragmatic doctrine that to do otherwise would dilute the group's credibility and power. Interest groups have sought political power through five methods:

1) Political oscillation—threatening to take their votes to another candidate or party.

2) Proportionate control of policy-making jobs in government—placing its members in sensitive positions in order to influence public policy favorably toward their interests.

3) Retribution—punishing politicians through a "backlash vote" for opposing the group's interests.

4) Educational propaganda—influencing other members of the electorate to a sympathetic adoption of the group's point of view through the use of pamphlets, meetings, and public statements.

5) Lobbying in Congress and state legislatures for legislation which promotes the group's interest or against legislation which threatens the group's survival and political power.

Of these five methods, the first and second have tended to dominate the activities of most interest groups. The possibility of other groups determining the outcome of an election as the result of a "backlash" and the confluence of other groups also lobbying with equal effectiveness for a piece of legislation decrease one group's ability to claim sole credit for such accomplishments. With very infrequent exceptions, negroes have been unsuccessful in all five methods.

Occasionally, they have managed to rally friends to their cause—the passage of civil-rights laws, the creation of the open society—but their success has stemmed more from their activities outside politics (demonstrations, marches, sit-ins) rather than within the framework of the political system. One of the greatest tragedies of the civil-rights movement has been its inability—or maybe its lack of understanding—to transmit the fervor of civil-rights activities into political activity.

Civil-rights demonstrators make good marchers, but poor politicians.

Civil-rights leaders can get up a good boycott, but they can never get out a good vote.

Civil-rights laws provide for equality of opportunity, but do not ensure equality of results.

Equality of results is what the science of politics is concerned with.

Because they have never concerned themselves with real power in society, civil-rights leaders have danced on the fringes of the political and economic apparatuses that control society.

As already stated, they have feared that any diligent seeking of real political power, resulting in the possible displacement of sympathetic politicians, might in turn alienate those politicians. But politicians are not primarily concerned with any ethnic group's rights as much as they are concerned with their own right to survive.

In one of the most perceptive columns ever written about this paradox, Mike Royko, a white columnist for the *Chicago Daily News*, commented in his April 5, 1967, column the day after a Chicago primary:

. . . black power was available in sizable quantities in Chicago Tuesday. And a person didn't have to march, sing, riot or boycott to get it.

It was inside the voting machine. By pulling a lever or using a pencil, the Negro could have thrown a scare into City Hall.

Instead Chicago Negroes went out and gave something like 80 to 85% of their vote to Mayor Richard J. Daley; about 10% to John Waner and just a dib and a dab to Dick Gregory. And Daley didn't even campaign in the Negro areas.

I'm not saying they shouldn't have voted for Mayor Daley. If he is their man —fine. But is he their man? If so, they show it in strange ways.

They should remember that the city was in an uproar most of last summer because the civil rights wing of the Negro population was marching to protest the way the Negro was being treated by the mayor's administration.

It was the mayor's house that was being picketed for the last couple of summers. It was the administration's school system that they boycotted and raged against.

It was the mayor's police department that was accused of being unkind to Negroes. The mayor's firemen were the ones shot at and stoned. And it was his fire department that was accused of being segregated.

... The inconsistency mounts when you consider that the poorest Negro areas —the most riot-inclined areas—were where Daley got his best support. He didn't do much better in his own neighborhood than he did in some West Side wards.

...

And finally, if there is a leader of Chicago's Negroes, he is Richard J. Daley, that rosy cheeked Irishman from the Back of the Yards. . . .

So this summer, don't sing me that old refrain of "black power." The voting machine was listening Tuesday, but he couldn't hear you even humming.

While Royko's analysis defines the peculiarity of the Chicago political machine with its tyrannical control over the electorate because of the crime syndicate's enforcement powers, it is a fact that the black vote has not always predictably followed its best civil-rights interests. Black voters have invariably been more slavishly loyal to a political machine with its built-in hostility to their best interests than other ethnic groups. Nevertheless, the classical myth—and fear—of the black vote as a balance of power in close elections has persisted.

In some quarters, recognition has been given to the appointment of negroes to high office for the first time (member of a federal agency, the Cabinet, the U.S. Supreme Court, etc.) as an example of the potency of the black vote.

High-level negro appointments are still rare, and, because they are, they must be categorized as symbolic appointments. Symbolic negro appointments do not control power. Usually, they are more honorific than substantial and are extremely impressive to black people. The appointment of a negro does not guarantee any improvement in the economic, educational, or political conditions of the black masses, however. Not a single additional negro receives an increase in his wages because one negro is appointed to the Supreme Court.

Worse still, the symbolic negro appointment is ofttimes a promotion to a higher position. In such an instance, the promotion is valueless because negroes have gained no new political power.

When Carl Rowan was promoted from Ambassador to Finland to the directorship of the United States Information Agency, a negro was not appointed Ambassador to succeed him. Negroes thus lost that appointment. They gained no power. This has occurred repeatedly in government, particularly under the Johnson administration. The appointment of Thurgood Marshall to Solicitor General and then to the U.S. Supreme

Court does not mean an accretion of political power because one negro has simply been rotated between jobs.

The only way in which black people can develop political power in government is to be able to control the hiring processes. This they have never been able to do. When negroes have been placed in top-level positions, they have usually refused to hire other negroes.

As other ethnic groups have achieved political power, they have expanded their power base by bringing members of their own group into the bureaucratic mainstream of government. Certain departments, certain job classifications have become the exclusive province of certain ethnic groups. In certain agencies, an Irish Catholic has been expected to head that department, just as certain specialties have been reserved for Jews. The success of an ethnic group in maintaining exclusive dominion over certain policy-making jobs as well as reserving an unspecified percentage of jobs for their group is the true exercise of ethnic political power.

Once they have been appointed to high positions, negroes have shied away from hiring other negroes in the belief that a quick and perceived upswing in the number of negro employees would tend to increase the possibilities for resegregation. The civil-rights movement's philosophical emphasis on integration has taken its psychic toll of negro office-holders.

Moreover, negro office-holders have usually been appointed either to positions that control little patronage or with an understanding that their hiring policies would be governed by other ethnic and political considerations.

There is also the elation many black people have felt in being a "first" or even an only negro within a department. For them to encourage the employment of other negroes within their departments or the appointment of negroes to similarly high positions would be to diminish the honorific distinction of their achievement.

Given the paucity, then, of black appointments to high office, analyses of negro political power have been confined to measuring the black vote. Because of their high visibility and physical confinement to ghettos, negro voting strength has been more easily measured than that of other ethnic groups.

The vast majority of black people in any city live in definable areas—in New York City, Harlem; in Chicago, the South Side and the West Side; in Philadelphia, the North Side; in Los Angeles, Watts. To rely on the vote as the sole standard of measurement of negro political power is sterile. The electoral process is merely one step in the acquisition of power, and votes do more than simply elect officials. Votes guarantee a favorable disposition of an ethnic group's aspiration and demands. Votes should ensure that the members of a particular group will be appointed in significant numbers in the policy-making councils of government. Votes are judgeships, commissionerships, governorships, mayorships, Congressional seats, aldermanships, superintendencies, political party chairmanships, government contracts, Federal aid, construction projects, and political contributions. Consequently, discussion of any group's voting strength as the sole measurement of its political power neglects the realities of politics and misunderstands the relationship of government to pressure groups.

PROPORTIONAL POLITICAL PATRONAGE

The most important indices of a group's political power are its numerical percentage of the population and its percentage of the vote during an election. For example, an ethnic group might comprise 20 percent of the population in a city but regularly deliver, on the average, only 10 percent of the vote. Somewhere between these two percentages should lie the accommodation by the party organization and its control of the government to the demands of the particular ethnic group.

Nationally, black people comprise approximately 12 percent of the population. In America's thirty largest cities, the proportion of negroes in the population ranged from a low of 4 percent in Minneapolis, Minn., and 5 percent in Phoenix, Ariz., to a high of 66 percent in Washington, D.C., and 47 percent in Newark, N.J.[2]

PROPORTION OF NEGROES IN EACH OF THE 30 LARGEST CITIES,*
1960 AND 1965 ESTIMATED

City	1960	1965	City	1960	1965
New York, N.Y.	14	18	Pittsburgh, Pa.	17	21
Chicago, Ill.	23	28	San Antonio, Texas	7	8
Los Angeles, Calif.	14	17	San Diego, Calif.	6	7
Philadelphia, Pa.	26	31	Seattle, Wash.	5	7
Detroit, Mich.	29	34	Buffalo, N. Y.	13	17
Baltimore, Md.	35	38	Cincinnati, Ohio	22	24
Houston, Texas	23	23	Memphis, Tenn.	37	44
Cleveland, Ohio	29	34	Denver, Colorado	6	9
Washington, D.C.	54	66	Atlanta, Ga.	38	44
St. Louis, Mo.	29	36	Minneapolis, Minn.	2	4
Milwaukee, Wis.	8	11	Indianapolis, Ind.	21	23
San Francisco, Calif.	10	12	Kansas City, Mo.	18	22
Boston, Mass.	9	13	Columbus, Ohio	16	18

City	1960	1965	City	1960	1965
Dallas, Texas	19	21	Phoenix, Ariz.	5	5
New Orleans, La.	37	41	Newark, N.J.	34	47

*Although these figures are from a joint report prepared by the Bureau of the Census and the Bureau of Labor Statistics in October 1967, titled "Social and Economic Conditions of Negroes in the United States," they are for the year 1965. Newark officials and various city agencies concerned directly with urban renewal and race relations agree that in 1967 Newark had a majority of negroes in its population—52 percent for 1967.

Two unanswered questions about black political power are: (1) What are the political circumstances that in 1965 enabled New York City, with an 18 percent black proportion, and Los Angeles, with 17 percent, to have one black Congressman each among its Congressional delegation, while twelve other cities, all with proportionally larger black populations, have none? (Baltimore, 38 percent; Cincinnati, 24 percent; Cleveland, 34 percent; Dallas, 21 percent; Houston, 23 percent; Indianapolis, 23 percent; Kansas City, 22 percent; Memphis, 44 percent; Newark, 47 percent; New Orleans, 41 percent; Pittsburgh, 21 percent; and St. Louis, 36 percent.)

2) What combination of racial cohesion and political organization enabled the Detroit black electorate to elect *two* black congressmen in 1964 with a black proportion of 34 percent, while five cities with larger black proportions were unable to elect even one?

Part of the explanation for the absence of black congressmen from Memphis, New Orleans, St. Louis, Baltimore, and Kansas City are the Southern traditions and orientations of these cities. Black voters have yet to exhibit the fierce independence and black pride that would unleash a black leader who could whip ambition together into a phalanx of bloc voting in exchange for black spoils—i.e., a congressional seat.

But the election of black congressmen is only one facet of black political power in a city. Black state senators and representatives, black city councilmen or aldermen, black city and state judges, black heads of city departments (commissioners, etc.), black members of boards of education, black key figures in the state and city political organizations, and other honorary appointments that recognize the individual power and importance of black community leaders comprise a more accurate measurement of the ethnic group's political power.

The first law for measuring the political power of an ethnic group is that there must be a direct relationship between the proportion of its vote in an election or its proportion of the population—whichever is higher

—and its proportion of all political jobs and elective offices.

This is the theory of proportional equality, and . . . practically every other ethnic group in America has been able to develop political power at the national, state, and local levels commensurate with its proportion of the population.

STONE'S INDEX OF PROPORTIONAL EQUALITY

Political power can be quantified and measured by the proportion of elective offices and jobs in specific areas. Stone's Index of Proportional Equality establishes minimum standards for measuring the political power of an ethnic group. There are six factors, which include the proportion of the ethnic group within a city in the following areas of political activity: (1) U.S. congressmen; (2) city councilmen and aldermen; (3) state representatives; (4) heads of municipal departments; (5) judges (at the city, state, and national levels); and (6) members of the board of education.

Again, . . . the Irish, the Italians, the Jews, and the Poles have all developed political control in several cities where they are numerically strong by dominating in all six areas. A political canon of the Irish when they first became active in politics was: "It is better to know the judge than the law."

The reason all city departments are included in this standard of measurement is the tendency for black appointments of department heads to be concentrated in the weaker, or "human relations" and "welfare," departments. Black people are rarely appointed as heads of the departments that control finance, real estate, construction, city contrasts, public works, buildings, and taxes. Instead they saturate the departments of welfare, human relations, and education. There is little political power in these departments.

Thus, if black people constitute 10 percent of the vote or 10 percent of the population and are given 10 percent of the jobs and elective offices in a city and state administration, and if this 10 percent is concentrated in the lower-paying positions or unimportant elective offices, then black people in that situation do not have political power.

As of 1967, negro political power at the federal level was insignificant, with the exception of two appointments, Housing and Urban Development Secretary Robert C. Weaver, one of the twelve members of the President's Cabinet, and U.S. Supreme Court Justice Thurgood Marshall, one of nine Associate Justices.

But using the black national proportion of 12 percent for 1966 as a base index, the relationship of this proportion to negroes' total political participation in the federal legislative, executive, and judiciary branches of government can be assessed. It is important to keep in mind the national proportion of 11 percent in any kind of analysis of black political activity.

U.S. CONGRESS, 1966

Of 435 U.S. Representatives elected to the 89th Congress in 1966, only six, or 1.3 percent, were black. Compare this proportion, for example, to the number of Jewish congressmen. In 1966, Jews comprised 3 percent of the population—5,600,000 out of 200,000,000—and also constituted 3 percent (15 Jewish congressmen) of the Congress.

Of one hundred senators, one, or 1 percent, was black (the first to be elected since 1881).

Thus, nationally, it is mournfully obvious that negroes can exert very little influence as legislators in the U. S. Congress. Rather, they must rely on a tenuous alliance with committed white liberals or white congressmen with significant black constituencies to secure the passage of legislation designed to elevate the economic and educational standards of black people.

White congressmen with substantial black constituencies are not going to be influenced unless their districts are politically unstable and tend to swing back and forth between the two parties. Only in such instances, if the negro vote cohesively acted as a balace of power to guarantee the election of a congressman, and if he, in turn, recognized this fact, would he be responsive to negro demands.

But, of the ninety-six congressmen who have a 20 percent or greater black constituency, sixty-five are southerners. Because of a traditional pattern of massive racial intimidation and oppression through murders, bombings, and economic reprisals, negroes still have not registered or voted in numbers approximating their proportion. Even where they have voted, they still have tended to simplistically (lazily) accept the lesser of two white evils rather than cut the umbilical cord of white subordination by voting for a strong black challenger. This happened in the Memphis, Tenn., October 5, 1967, primary. In a seven-man race for mayor, one of the candidates was black state representative A. W. Willis. Although the registered black vote was exactly one-third of the total number of Memphis votes (80,033 out of 235,303), a united vote behind one negro candidate could have placed him in the final run-off, assuming a split white vote among the other six candidates. Memphis negroes instead voted for the incumbent white mayor, and even gave a substantial proportion of their votes to a former white mayor. Willis ran a poor fourth. He subsequently charge that Memphis negroes had been brainwashed all their lives. During his campaign, he declared that the campaign was raising for the first time "the real problems of racial inferiority. The Negro has been taught to be inferior. He thinks the white man's ice is colder, his sugar is sweeter, his medicine is better."

In most southern communities, black people will also support a racist congressman who, despite his consistent antinegro votes in Congress, looks after his black constituents with the same benevolent paternalism of the old plantation owner. Negroes in South Carolina's Sixth Congressional District have continued to vote for Representative John L. McMillan, even though he was known as one of the staunchest opponents of home rule for the District of Columbia because of its black majority. In Tampa, Fla., not one negro publicly criticized Tampa's Representative Sam M. Gibbons for leading the move to strip Representative Adam Clayton Powell of his powers as chairman of the Education and Labor Committee in September 1966.

If Congress is a microcosm of the white racism that continues to dominate the United States, congressional staffs show the same loving affection for this pattern. Of the five black congressmen, four have negro women as administrative assistants. Representative John Conyers has a white administrative assistant, as does Senator Edward W. Brooke. Until his exclusion from the Congress, Adam Clayton Powell was the only man in either the House or the Senate to have a black man as an administrative assistant. He had two. His first was Livingston Wingate, who later became executive director of Harlem's antipoverty program HARYOU-ACT. The second was myself. Powell was also the only congressman to employ black people in several capacities as professional staff members. Not only was his special assistant a black, but the chief clerk of the committee, Miss Louis Maxienne Dargans, and the education chief, Dr. Eunice Matthews, were black.

None of the other 535 representatives and senators has black legislative assistants. One Indiana congressman assigned such a title to one aide, but on closer investigation, it was revealed that the aide was, in fact, a very intelligent office boy who performed routine office chores instead of drafting bills and doing legislative research.

There is a plethora of negro secreatries on Capitol Hill, but only because there is a shortage of secretaries. Although the average congressman is a racial bigot, he is also a pragmatist. So, negro secretaries are hired, if for no other reason than to keep the office running.

Of the sixteen Senate committees and the twenty House committees, only one committee in the House, as of 1967, had a professional negro staff member. She is Mrs. Christine Ray Davis, staff director of the House Government Operations Committee, whose chairman is William L. Dawson. Mrs. Davis was the first negro to become a staff director of a congressional committee. She has served as the top staff member of that committee since 1949, when Dawson became its chairman and she was appointed chief clerk. During 1952–53, when the Republicans were in control of the House, she was a minority staff consultant, and in 1954, when Democrats resumed control of the House, she was appointed staff director.

The unwritten law against black pages in the House and Senate was broken in the first half of the Eighty-ninth Congress, in 1965, when Lawrence W. Bradford, Jr., of New York City, became the first black page in the Senate and Frank V. Mitchell, Jr., of Detroit, Mich., became the first black page in the House. Oddly enough, both boys were sponsored by Republicans, who secured their appointments.

U.S. CONGRESS, 1968

For the Ninety-first Congress beginning in January 1969, there will be a new high of eight black congressmen and possibly nine, depending upon what happens in the Third Congressional District in Chicago, where a white congressman is being seriously challenged for the first time by a black man.

Adam Clayton Powell has announced his intention to run again and, barring a most cataclysmic unforeseen event, will be re-elected, as will the other five black congressmen. Two new black congressmen will come from Cleveland's newly formed Twenty-first Congressional District, and Brooklyn's newly formed Twelfth Congressional District representing that community's black ghetto, Bedford-Styuvesant.

The Deomcratic candidate for Cleveland's new congressional district is Louis Stokes, brother of that city's black mayor, Carl B. Stokes. While the Democratic candidate for Brooklyn's Twelfth Congressional District had not been nominated as of this writing, that race portends excitement with the entry of former CORE executive director, James Farmer, who has been endorsed by both the Liberal and Republican parties. Although not a Brooklyn resident, Farmer is expected to wage a strong race because of his famed civil rights role.

U.S. EXECUTIVE

Of the many public exercises that have seemed to delight the southern heart of President Lyndon Baines Johnson, none has been carried off with more P. T. Barnum fanfare than the announcement of a "first negro appointment." So much carnival hoopla has attended these sessions that the impression has been gained that this President, who, as a congressman, vigorously fought against civil rights for negroes, "has done more for the cause of civil rights" than any other President "in our history."[3]

The spectacular appointments of the first negro Cabinet member, Robert C. Weaver, as Secreatry of the Department of Housing and Urban Development on January 18, 1967, Andrew F. Brimmer as the first black governor of the Federal Reserve Board, Thurgood Marshall as the first black Solicitor General in the Department of Justice and the first black Supreme Court Justice, and Mrs. Patricia Harris as the first black woman ambassador (to Luxembourg) have created the external appearance of a government where black people are taking giant steps forward in helping to run their country.[4]

In the history of American politics, no greater charade has been played by any President. The fact is that these showcase appointments have not substantially changed the administrative and policy-making patterns of government.

Again, bearing in mind that blacks comprise 11 percent of the national population, the progress of negro employment in the higher councils of the Federal government can be measured. In the executive Office of the President, the following is the breakdown of black positions, as of 1967, among the top positions listed in the Congressional Directory of the Ninetieth Congress, First Session, but revised for subsequent changes in the latter part of the year:

Office	Number of Top Positions	Number of Negroes
White House Office	25	0
Bureau of the Budget	26	0
Council of Economic Advisers	4	0
National Security Office	7	0
Central Intelligence Agency	5	0
National Aeronautics and Space Agency	6	0
Office of Economic Opportunity	16	1
Office of Emergency Planning	16	0
Office of Science and Technology	5	0

Office of Special Representative for
Trade Negotiations   15   0
TOTAL   125   1 (1 percent)

Were it not for the one black executive in the Office of Economic Opportunity, the eleven offices within the Executive Office of the President would be lily-white.

Of the forty-four largest federal independent agencies, only one—the Equal Employment Opportunity Commission—is headed by a *"Negro,"* Clifford Alexander, Jr., a colorless and mediocre lawyer who was previously a Deputy Special Counsel to the President with no precise administrative responsibilities. Typical of the excessively cautious federal civil servant, Alexander climbed slowly through the ranks by becoming a faceless negro who neither made controversial comments nor militantly condemned the injustices against negroes in American society.

Of the 183 commissioners, members of the boards and the executive directors or administrators of these forty-four independent agencies, only seven, or 3 percent, were negroes: Mrs. Frankie Muse Freeman, of the U.S. Commission on Civil Rights; Clifford L. Alexander, Jr., chairman, and Samuel C. Jackson, member, of the Equal Employment Opportunity Commission; Dr. G. Franklin Edwards, member of the National Capital Planning Commission; Howard Jenkins, Jr., member of the National Labor Relations Board; Dr. Kenneth W. Clement, member of the National Selective Service Appeal Board; and Dr. Andrew F. Brimmer, governor of the Federal Reserve Board. No independent agency in the federal government is headed by a black staff members.

A third index of the exclusion of negroes from the policy-making and executive positions of government is indicated by the number of negro assistant secretaries and deputy assistant secretaries. This is the administrative level at which Cabinet departments are compartmentalized into operational units of responsibility.

Of the 220 assistant secretaries and deputy assistant secretaries in the twelve Cabinet departments and the Army, Navy, and Air Force, only five, or 2 percent, are negroes. These five negroes are concentrated in only four departments: State, Labor, Health, Education and Welfare, and Agriculture: Samuel Z. Westerfield, Jr., Deputy Assistant Secretary of State for African Affairs; Mrs. Charlotte M. Hubbard, Deputy Assistant Secretary of State for Public Affairs; George L. P. Weaver, Assistant Secretary for International Affairs in the Department of Labor; Shelton

B. Granger, Deputy Assistant Secretary of HEW for Education, International Affairs; and Alfred L. Edwards, Deputy Assistant Secretary of Agriculture for Rural Development and Conservation.

Thus, there is not a single negro among the 130 assistant or deputy assistant secretaries in the Departments of the Treasury, Defense, Army, Navy, Air Force, Justice, Post Office, Interior, Commerce, Housing and Urban Development, and Transportation.

Two of the federal government's most powerful negroes who do not have Assistant Secretary or Deputy Assistant Secretary status are Miss Barbara Watson, Acting Administrator of the State Department's Bureau of Security and Consular Affairs, and Edward C. Sylvester, Jr., Director of the Labor Department's Office of Federal Contract Compliance. Both make critical decisions which respectively shape America's foreign and domestic policies. Miss Watson has been the target of intensive lobbying by white industrialists with heavy investments in Africa and Mr. Sylvester has been the constant target of the various construction trades unions which have resented his rulings requiring nondiscriminatory union practices in order to work on federal projects.

This pattern of "white-out" for negroes, however, is far more entrenched than the obvious executive levels would indicate.

Within the twelve Cabinet departments, there are no black staff executives or appointees in the eleven top positions of the U.S. Mission to the United Nations, the twenty-six top positions in the Agency for International Development, the twenty-three top positions in the Peace Corps, the eleven top positions in the Internal Revenue Service, the eleven top positions in the Bureau of Customs, the fifteen top positions of the Office of the Comptroller of the Currency, and the seven top positions of the Secret Service.

In the twelve Cabinet Departments, there are *no negroes* in any of the policy-making or responsible administrative positions in the Coast Guard, Office of Merchant Marine Safety, Director of Defense Research and Engineering, the Joint Chiefs of Staff, Defense Atomic Support Agency, Defense Communications Center, Defense Contract Audit Agency, Defense Intelligence Agency, Defense Supply Agency, Office of Civil Defense, the Army Staff, the Navy Administrative Staff, Naval Office of Civilian Manpower, Naval Office of the Comptroller, Naval Office of Information, Office of Naval Research, Naval Office of Program Appraisal, Office of the Judge Advocate of the Navy, Navy Appellate Review Activity, the U.S. Marine Corps, Naval Bureau of Medicine and Surgery, National Naval Medical Center, Office of the Chief of Naval Operations, Bureau of Naval Personnel, Naval Air Systems Command, Naval Ordnance Systems Command, Naval Ship Systems Command, Naval Electronic Systems Command, Naval Supply Systems Command, Naval Facilities Engineering Command, U.S. Naval Station, Air Force Office of Information, the Air Staff, Comptroller of the Air Force, Deputy Chief of Staff for Personnel, Deputy Chief of Staff for Plans and Operations, Deputy Chief of Staff for Programs and Resources, Deputy Chief of Staff for Systems and Logistics, Deputy Chief of Staff for Research and Development, the Immigration and Naturalization Service, Bureau of Prisons, Board of Parole, the Federal Prison Industries, Inc., the Post Office's Bureau of Personnel *(despite the fact that negroes comprise an estimated 40 percent of Post Office employees)*, the *Post Office's* Office of General Counsel, Bureau of the Chief Postal Inspector, Bureau of Research and Engineering, the *Interior Department's* Fish and Wildlife Service, Geological Survey, Bureau of Indian Affairs, Bureau of Land Management, Bureau of Mines, National Park Service, Bureau of Reclamation, Office of Territories, Bureau of Outdoor Recreation, Federal Water Pollution Control Administration, the *Agricultural* Stabilization and Conservation Service, Commodity Credit Corporation, Federal Extension Service, Foreign Agricultural Service, International Agricultural Development Service, Consumer and Marketing Services, Commodity Exchange Authority, Rural Development and Farmers Home Administration, Forest Service, Rural Electrification Administration, Soil Conservation Service, Economic Research Service, Statistical Reporting Service, Office of Budget and Finance, Office of Information, Office of Management Services, Office of Personnel, Office of Plant and Operations, Office of the General Counsel, Office of the Inspector General, *Commerce Department's* Office of Business Economics, Bureau of International Commerce, Office of Foreign Commerce Activities, Business and Defense Services Administration, Bureau of the Census, Maritime Administration, National Bureau of Standards, Patent Office, Bureau of Public Roads, National Highway Safety Agency, *Labor Department's* Labor-Management Services Administration, Office of the Solicitor, the Wage and Labor Standards' Bureaus and Divisions, the Food and Drug Administration, Vocational Rehabilitation Administration, the Public Health Service, Bureau of Disease Prevention and Environmental Control, Bureau of Health Manpower, Bureau of Health Services, National Institutes of Health, National Institutes of Mental Health, Social Security Administration, Welfare Administration (this is a particularly ironic form of racial discrimination since such a large proportion of Negroes are on public welfare), the Housing and Urban Development's Federal National Mortgage Association, and the HUD Regional Offices.

The appointment of a black assistant secretary, or Cabinet official, or member of a commission makes front-page news. The nonappointment of black people as administrators, assistant administrators, deputies, office managers, and to the thousands of administrative categories that make policy for the U.S. government is not news. And the exclusion pattern of black people from the apparatus of policy-making and responsible positions in the Federal government, with the exceptions already listed, is as rigid and as racially determined as ever. Racial bigotry in America begins at the White House.

THE FEDERAL COURTS

There are 480 Federal judgeships.[5] These include the nine in the U.S. Supreme Court, eighty-eight in the eleven Judicial Circuits of the U.S. Court of Appeals, 342 in the U.S. District Courts, and forty-one in the five Special Courts (U.S. Court of Claims, U.S. Court of Customs and Patent Appeals, U.S. Customs Court, Tax Court of the United States, and the U.S. Court of Military Appeals).

Of these 480 federal judgeships, eleven, or 2 percent, are held by black people:

U.S. Supreme Court	Thurgood Marshall
U.S. Court of Appeals	
District of Columbia Circuit	Spottswood W. Robinson, III
Third Judicial Circuit	William Henry Hastie
Sixth Judicial Circuit	Wade Hampton McCree, Jr.
U.S. District Courts	
District of Columbia	William B. Bryant
Illinois (Northern)	James B. Parsons
New York (Northern)	Mrs. Constance Baker Motley
Pennsylvania (Eastern)	Leon Higginbotham
Virgin Islands	Walter A. Gordon
U.S. Customs Court	
	Scovel Richardson
	James L. Watson

Judge Hastie was the first negro in the history of the United States to be appointed to a federal court. President Roosevelt appointed him in 1937. Judge Parsons became the first negro in 1961 to be appointed to a Federal District Court. President Kennedy made the appointment.

The generally conservative orientation of the federal courts, compounded by the dual standards of justice for blacks and whites of southern judges, has been one of the factors most acutely inhibiting the negro's quest for racial equality. Invariably, the burden of proof of discrimination, intimidation, denial of constitutional rights, or simple denial of the most elementary exercise of his rights rested on the negro.

In making federal appointments, Presidents, as a matter of political courtesy or to minimize the risk of disapproval, clear their prospective choices with senators, congressmen, or state officials in a region, depending upon which wields the most power. Naturally, southern officials will seek to influence the appointments of southerners. And 99 percent of all white southerners, even in 1967, are hard-core racists.

The historical pattern of justice dispensed firmly, but unequally, for negroes in the South can be traced to the racial orientations of the judges appointed. Only with rare exceptions have southern judges been able to break through their southern backgrounds and render decisions which guarantee the constitutional rights of negroes. One such rare exception, which electrified the black community, was the ruling by a South Carolina U.S. District Judge, J. Waites Waring, on July 12, 1947, that South Carolina's exclusion of negroes from Democratic primaries was a de facto denial of the right to vote. Judge Waite's decision was upheld by the U.S. Circuit Court of Appeals, and the lily-white primaries of South Carolina's Democratic party were dead forever. After his ruling, Judge Waring was acclaimed as one of the negro community's new heroes and was honored and feted by a variety of negro and interracial organizations throughout America.

THE REVOLVING-DOOR NEGRO

The thesis can be advanced, of course, that negroes have made phenomenal progress in government and politics in the Kennedy and Johnson administrations, compared to previous gains. There is a persuasiveness to the argument that negro political power measured at 3 percent is a three-hundredfold increase over 1 percent. Yet, a close examination of many federal appointments reveals that frequently the same negro has been appointed to two or even three history-making positions during the course of his career. While the historical value of the racial breakthroughs has been acclaimed for their favorable impact on the state of race relations, the rotation of two or three appointments within the career of one negro means that negroes have not acquired any additional political power, nor has there been an accretion of policy-making positions for black people in government.

Those negroes who have been appointed to a series of high-level federal appointments by a President are what are known as "revolving-door negroes." They are used by the President to initiate a racial breakthrough in several areas. After they have been appointed to their new position, a negro is never appointed to their previous position. The "revolving-door negroes" do not add more negroes to the policy-making positions in government. Instead, they add more status to the individual achievements of that particular negro appointee. His personal pride is increased, not the political power of his race.

This is not an indictment of the negro accepting a series of such appointments or even an indictment of the negro's personal ambitions. Rather, the inability of a President to find an additional black man for a high-level federal appointment is the harshest indictment of that President's limited approach to the solution of the racial problem. It is the President who makes the decision that he has sufficient respect for only one or two negroes to fill the various positions to which they are appointed. The "revolving-door negro" is simply another manifestation of the racism inherent in the office of the President of the United States. While the "revolving-door negro" is utilized most successfully and exploited with the greatest fanfare by one President, it is nonetheless possible for two or three Presidents to appoint the same negro to a variety of prestigious positions because this particular "negro leader" has established impeccable credentials to national leadership or personal achievement.

Historically, a "revolving-door negro" could be a militant, or he could be one who was forthright and uncompromising in his fight for equality. More often than not, however, he was usually the safest the congressional traffic could bear without provoking a united opposition to the appointment. In the Johnson administration, the "revolving-door negro" has either been an "Uncle Tom" or one who could be counted upon not to cause any serious emotional dislocation of the body politic. Still a southerner by temperament and in his relations with negroes, President Johnson has gravitated toward those negroes who did not make him feel personally uncomfortable and who could assure him that everything he was doing in the area of race relations was right, good, and proper. Thus, one of Johnson's favorite negroes, to whom he often turned for advice, was the moderate-conservative executive secretary of the NAACP, Roy Wilkins.

Probably the first "revolving-door negro" in the federal appointive process was that brilliant and legendary "father of the protest movement" and the intellectual forerunner of the Black Power philosophy, Frederick Douglass. Douglass was appointed first by President Grant in 1871 to be the secretary of the Santo Domingo Commission. In 1877,

President Hayes appointed Douglass as Federal Marshal for the District of Columbia, and in 1881, President Garfield appointed him Recorder of Deeds for the District of Columbia. In 1889, President Harrison named him Minister Resident and Consul General to Haiti. In Douglass' case, not only were his appointments well deserved, but there was a paucity of men of his incredible intellect and personal charisma. There were other negroes on the national scene who could have held these jobs and administered them with the same degree of competence as Douglass. But Douglass was unquestionably one of the most distinguished black men of his day, and his appointments were a justifiable recognition by the federal government of his contributions to progress. What the series of Douglass appointments did do, however, was to lay a kind of prior claim by negroes to that office and to endow the office with new respectability and remove it from the category of "for whites only."

The second nationally prominent revolving-door negro was William H. Hastie, a scholarly lawyer and former dean of Howard University Law School. In 1940, President Roosevelt appointed him a civilian aide and race-relations adviser to Secretary of the Army Henry Stimson. In 1943, Hastie did something that very few negro Federal appointees have ever had the courage to do—he resigned in protest against an Army decision to establish a segregated technical training school at Jefferson Barracks, Mo. His unusual display of personal courage apparently did not injure his promising career, and in 1946 Hastie was named Governor of the Virgin Islands by President Truman. In 1949, President Truman nominated Hastie to be the first black member of the U.S. Circuit Court of Appeals, where he now serves with distinction.

While President Kennedy was the first President to make many historic appointments for negroes within one administration, he appointed few "revolving-door negroes" because of his determination to avail himself of a quantity of competent negro appointees.

On the other hand, President Johnson has shown a propensity for keeping the black revolving door whirling constantly. Of the twenty-eight major appointments during the first four years of his administration (including the first negro to the U.S. Supreme Court, the first negro director of the U.S. Information Agency, the first negro Cabinet member, and the first negro woman ambassador), six were "revolving-door negroes," Thurgood Marshall, Robert C. Weaver, Carl T. Rowan, Clifford L. Alexander, Andrew F. Brimmer, and Hobart Taylor.

The "revolving-door negro" process may knock down racial barriers, but it does not build up racial political power. Thus, the proportion of negroes in policy-making positions in government is increased at an agonizingly sluggish pace. Had black people recognized earlier the built-in element of political retardation in the "revolving-door negro" process and complained about its efficiency in delaying a true accretion of black political power, they might have been able to move rapidly into the higher councils of Federal power.

THE STATES

Negro political power as reflected by state representatives, elected and appointed state officials, and judicial appointees varies with individual states. For the most part, however, negroes have not been successful at the state level in striking any remote balance between the proportion of negro elective offices or appointments and their proportion in the population.

As of the November 1967 elections, thirty states had black state legislators in either the lower house or the senate.

As of 1967, only Connecticut had an elected official among the five top state offices of governor, lieutenant governor, secretary, treasurer or controller, and attorney general. He is Gerald A. Lamb of Waterbury, the state treasurer, who was nominated in 1962 on the Democratic ticket after the Republicans had already nominated a negro attorney from Hartford, William Graham. Lamb defeated Graham in a Democratic sweep and was subsequently re-elected for a second term in 1966.

As of 1967, only three states had negroes in the state cabinet—New York, California, and Ohio. At the time of these appointments, all three states had Republican governors (Nelson A. Rockefeller, New York; Ronald Reagan, California; and James A. Rhodes, Ohio).

As the following table indicates, negro membership in thirty state legislatures was 127 out of a total of 657 or 4.4 percent in 1967. Illinois led with the largest number of negro state legislators (thirteen) in the lower house, but Missouri negroes should be regarded as possessing more political power in the state legislature since their twelve negro members constituted 11.1 percent of the total in the lower house, compared to Illinois's negro legislators, who constituted only 7.3 percent. When these two percentages are related to the percentage of the two states' negro population—Missouri, 9.0 percent and Illinois, 10.3 percent —we see that the legislative power of Missouri negroes is appreciably greater.

As the electoral patterns in the loyalties of negroes in the last twenty years have indicated, the overwhelming majority of elective offices have been held by Democrats.

Progress in the short span of seven years in the state legislatures has kept pace with the strident urgency of the civil-rights movement. As of

Extent of Negro Representation in State Legislative Bodies in U.S. (1966–67)*

state	in State Lower Houses total members	negro members	negro percent of total	in State Senates total members	negro members	negro percent of total	negro percent of total population
Michigan	110	9	8.1	34	3	8.8	9.2
Illinois	177	13	7.3	58	4	6.8	10.3
Missouri	163	12	7.3	34	1	2.9	9.0
Ohio	127	9	6.5	33	2	6.0	8.1
California	80	5	6.2	40	2	5.0	5.6
Tennessee	99	6	6.0	—	–	—	16.5
Georgia	205	12	5.8	54	2	3.7	28.5
Delaware	35	2	5.7	17	1	5.8	13.6
Maryland	123	7	5.6	29	2	6.9	16.7
New York	150	8	5.3	58	3	5.1	8.4
Pennsylvania	210	10	4.7	50	1	2.0	7.5
Indiana	100	4	4.0	40	1	2.5	5.8
New Jersey	50	3	6.0	21	1	4.7	8.5
Colorado	65	2	3.0	35	1	2.8	2.3
Nevada	37	1	2.7	—	–	—	
Oklahoma	119	3	2.5	44	1	2.2	6.6
Arizona	80	1	2.5	—	1	—	3.3
Nebraska	43	1	2.3	Unicameral Body			
Kentucky	100	2	2.0	—	–	—	7.1
Iowa	108	2	1.8	—	–	—	0.9
Connecticut	294	4	1.3	36	1	2.7	4.2
Texas	150	2	1.3	31	1	3.2	
Massachusetts	240	3	1.2	—	–	—	2.2
West Virginia	100	1	1.0	—	–	—	4.8
Washington	99	1	1.0	—	–	—	1.7
Wisconsin	100	1	1.0	—	–	—	1.9
Kansas	125	1	0.8	40	3	7.5	4.2
TOTALS	3281	126	3.8	657	31	4.4	

*Statistics were compiled by Ernest Calloway and published in the November 25, 1966, issue of the *Missouri Teamster*. It is one of the most comprehensive studies ever undertaken of negro state representation. As has been already indicated earlier, three Deep South states —Virginia, Louisana, and Mississippi—elected negroes to state legislatures in 1967, thus bringing the total of the states that have negro state representatives to 30.

1960, there were only an estimated thirty state representatives and six state senators.

There is still a political blackout of negro state legislators in the Southern states of Alabama, Arkansas, Florida, and South Carolina, even though negroes are, respectively, 30 percent, 22 percent, 18 percent, and 35 percent of the population. As of 1967, the Bureau of the Census estimated that 55 percent of the country's black people still lived in the South.

As is true for the Federal judiciary, the judiciary of most states have traditionally barred negroes from their higher courts. As of 1967, there were no negroes in any of the state supreme courts or highest courts. The negro judge occupying the highest state judicial position is Harold A. Stevens, a Justice of the Appellate Division of the Supreme Court of New York State. (The highest court in New York State is the Court of Appeals, which hears cases from the Appellate Division of the Supreme Court.)

According to a study made by California State Senator Mervyn M. Dymally in 1967, published in the *Christian Science Monitor* on November 4, 1967, there were eight negroes serving on state college governing boards.

In summary, the pattern of negro political power in the state executive, legislative, and judicial branches is one of weakness. The greatest power is exhibited in the legislatures and there is a near absence of any negro representation in the state courts. As will be demonstrated in the case studies of the cities, negro political power has been most successfully orchestrated in the cities. Here, the black vote, as a balance of power and as cohesive bloc to elect black officials, has realized its fullest expression.

Rarely, however, has the negro vote been organized by negro politicians or been responsive to their leadership as a punitive force. Blindly loyal and as affectionately faithful as an overgrown sheep dog, the black vote has lain at its white master's feet, lapping up the small bones of patronage tossed its way. When the master has commanded the vote to exhibit its fidelity, it has stirred itself from the fireplace of its second-class status, risen slowly, and lumbered to the polls to vote without question or discrimination. After the vote, it has returned to its preferred place by the smoldering coals of contentment and lazily waited for a few more tiny bones of patronage to keep it amused as a substitute for the large delights enjoyed by other ethnic groups.

There are two classic examples of the black vote defying the expected pattern of behavior. In one instance, it successfully switched parties to elect a mayor. In another instance, it supported a negro candidate at the risk of causing the defeat of a liberal white candidate, but did so deliberately to teach the white politician a lesson.

The first instance, one of the very few remarkable displays of outright Machiavellian maneuvering by a negro politician, occurred in 1928 in Memphis, Tenn., under the astute and shrewd generalship of Robert R.

Church, one of America's most brilliant black politicians.

The incumbent Democratic mayor, Rowlett Paine, had been elected in 1923 with the help of negro votes by promising certain improvements in the black community and a cessation of police brutality against negroes. Subsequently, these promises were not fulfilled to the satisfaction of negroes. Compounding their disappointment was the construction of a garbage incinerator only a few hundred yards away from a negro high school and a negro amusement park, despite their organized protests. Negroes angrily struck back. Church threw the full weight of his organization and political skills to the support of Watkins Overton, the Democratic nominee for mayor, against the Republican nominee supported by Paine. Church led a voter-registration drive among negroes and it was this expanded vote that was credited with the election of the Democratic candidate, Overton.[6]

The political ingredients of this particular election are a fascinating study in power politics. A powerful Republican negro politician turned his back on the nominee of his own party in a southern city, crossed over to the Democratic party to support its nominee, organized a vote drive, and brought the black vote with him to defeat the nominee of his own party! That is a classic example of black political power in the most splendid exercise of its retributive energies to make a point.

A second instance of black political power operating for a different purpose—the recognition of demands in an election or the deliberate scuttling by negroes of an entire slate to cause its defeat—occurred in Houston in 1956. Samuel Lubell describes what happened:

> In Houston, Texas . . . a loose sort of understanding existed under which Negroes joined with labor unions and other "progressive" groups in supporting "liberal" candidates. When the 1956 campaign for the school board started, the liberal leaders wanted to avoid the segregation issue, believing that raising it meant certain defeat. When this view was presented to Carter Wesley, who published a string of Negro newspapers in the Houston area, he insisted the segregation question be met head on. Declaring "it's time to stand up and be counted," Wesley demanded the coalition run a Negro as one of its candidates. When the coalition refused, a Negro entered the race independently. He was defeated, along with the entire liberal slate.
>
> "We knew he couldn't win without liberal support," explained Wesley, "but we showed them they could not win without us either.[7]

That commitment to "us" among black politicians has been as much a political rarity as attendance by Alabama's George Wallace at a meeting of the Student Nonviolent Coordinating Committee.

Black voters have not yet developed the political sophistication of retribution to the extent other ethnic groups have. A politician voting against the state of Israel will lose 95 percent of the Jewish vote. A legislator voting to sever diplomatic relations with Italy would lose 95 percent of the Italian vote. A politician who is an uncompromising advocate of birth control would be treated just as uncompromisingly at the polls by Irish Catholic voters. Yet, at the 1964 Democratic National Convention in Atlantic City, very few black delegates protested when the segregated Mississippi delegation was seated and the Mississippi Freedom Democratic party's predominantly negro delegation was rejected. Despite the tense emotionalism of this issue and the fact that the MFDP voted unanimously to reject the so-called compromise plan offered by the Credentials Subcommittee, there was little black delegate support for the Mississippi negroes. Racial loyalties were overcome by political chains.

An almost shocking example of the black voters' lack of ability to discern loyalty to the cause of advancing the interests of his ethnic group occurred in the April 1964 Democratic primary in Chicago.

Running for re-election in the Sixth Congressional District was Representative Thomas J. O'Brien, an elderly fourteen-term congressman. Ill for several months prior to the primary, O'Brien had been unable to campaign in the predominantly black district on the West Side. Running against him was a young black woman who had long been active in civic and civil-rights programs. On primary day, Congressman O'Brien died. But that did not matter to the black voters in his district. They went out anyway and voted for a dead white man over a live colored woman, re-electing O'Brien.

Loyalty, whether it derives from a religious or a racial background, is the most important element in building a powerful bloc vote. After loyalty, the ability to punish enemies is next. The four most important elements in building a powerful voting bloc are: (1) ethnic loyalty at any cost; (2) the ability to promise punishment and make good on the promise; (3) the capacity to switch political loyalties at any given time on any issue; and (4) the ability to secure jobs and important policy-making appointments for members of that voting bloc.

Political switching involves ticket-splitting, a habit that not only has eluded black voters, but has evaded the intelligence of most white voters. Thus, while it was logical for negroes to vote for Kennedy in 1960, it was not equally consistent for them to vote for Democratic southern racists. Had the black vote, critical in Texas, South Carolina, and Illinois, which provided the margin of victory in those three states and thus Kennedy's election, voted for the local or state Republicans who were not so antagonistic to black ambitions as their Democratic opponents, the white political bosses would have acquired a new respect for—and fear of—black voters.

The last element, the ability to secure jobs for its members, has been the area of greatest weakness among negroes. This is because black voters have been brainwashed with the sterile value of their vote as a balance of power.

The voting process must relate to the governmental process. Unless the black vote has been able to guarantee a significant increase in jobs, better housing, high-level appointments, and more modern educational facilities, then the vote is useless as a force for negro progress.

Although the black vote in the South has increased from a 1940 low of approximately 85,000 to a 1966 comparative high of 2,700,000, there has been no comparable increase in black political strength in the legislatures, the courts, and the state policy-making positions. With the exception of Georgia and Texas (and in 1967, Virginia, Louisiana, and Mississippi, which each elected the first negro to their state legislatures since Reconstruction), Southern negroes have been unable to make the political impact of their vote felt at the state level. Thus, the mere announcement of a dramatic increase in negro voter registrations is meaningless unless it is juxtaposed with a comparable increase of black judicial and executive appointments and elective offices.

Nor is there evidence to date that this increase in the Southern black vote has influenced the Southern white vote toward a more liberal posture on equal rights for negroes. Thus, in 1966, the two most segregationist candidates in the race for governor of Georgia, Republican Howard H. Callaway and Democrat Lester G. Maddox, polled the largest number of votes in their respective primaries. Any candidate for office in the Deep South who has dared to take a remotely liberal position on the race question has been defeated and will continue to be defeated unless there is a sufficiently large black voting bloc that can ensure his victory in combination with a small number of liberal white votes. This has happened in Atlanta, where the liberal Democrat Charles Weltner was elected to the House of Representatives in 1962 with nearly solid support of Atlanta's black voters, who comprised 38 percent of the electorate.

Until black voters begin to demand more jobs and appointments for their support, politicians will continue to seek the black vote only as a necessary balance of power to guarantee the margin of victory. Until black voters develop the kind of sophistication that the Memphis negroes exhibited in 1928, when they switched political parties to punish an official who had reneged on his promises, white political bosses will have no respect for the black vote. Until black voters are secure enough and militant enough to demand that white politicians take a strong liberal stand on the racial issue, even at the risk of defeat, the white politicians will continue to compromise and postpone the inevitable day of full black participation in the administration of American democracy.

NOTES

1. Extracts from the Proceedings of the United Nations Commission on Human Rights, 1947.

2. As of 1967, the six black U.S. Congressmen (including Adam Clayton Powell, who was excluded from the Ninetieth Congress on March 10, 1967) came from the five largest cities, New York City (Powell), Chicago (William L. Dawson), Los Angeles, Calif. (Augustus Hawkins), Philadelphia (Robert N.C. Nix), and Detroit (Charles C. Diggs, Jr., and John Conyers). All six are Democrats.

Although these figures are from a joint report prepared by the Bureau of the Census and the Bureau of Labor Statistics in October 1967, titled "Social and Economic Conditions of Negroes in the United States," they are for the year 1965. Newark officials and various city agencies concerned directly with urban renewal and race relations agree that in 1967 Newark had a majority of negroes in its population—52 percent for 1967.

3. From the brochure "This President . . . Is Doing More," published in 1967 by the Democratic National Committee.

4. The author had lunch with Louis Martin, Deputy Chairman of the Democratic National Committee, a few days after Secretary of Defense Robert S. McNamara's appointment to the presidency of the World Bank had been announced. Martin said that he received a telephone call from a very prominent southern white politician, who growled into the phone, half-jokingly but with just enough rancor to indicate his belief in the possibility: "What nigger have you got lined up for the Secretary of Defense job now?"

5. Administrative Office of the United States Court, Washington, D.C.

6. Paul Lewinson, *Race, Class and Party*, (New York: Grosset and Dunlap), p. 141.

7. Samuel Lubell, *Black and White* (New York: Harper & Row, 1964), p. 70.

Black Political Life in the United States: A Bibliographical Essay

Lenneal J. Henderson, Jr.

LITERATURE ON OR related to black political life in the United States is fast accumulating. Articles, analyses, periodicals, biographies, autobiographies, general works, and anthologies already abound; daily there appears new work which demands addition to the list. This essay is a guide for readers who wish to delve further into general or particular aspects of black political life. It is in no way all-inclusive; the profusion of new literature and the many current programs of reissuing the out-of-print classics in this field would not allow that. However, the attempt is to set down works under general categories of emphasis which will enable readers to specialize in their selection. General studies are divided into works dealing with black political life before 1960 and after 1960; more specialized works are grouped under the categories of the law, political parties, urban politics, community organizations, and biography. For further research into black political life, useful bibliographies, periodicals, and organizations are listed, also. More bibliographical material is included in most of the works mentioned herein, and the reader is encouraged to consult those listings, as well.

GENERAL STUDIES

Black Political Life Before 1960

There is no general history of black political life which extends from its genesis to the contemporary United States. But there are several general histories of black people in the United States which illuminate many aspects of the history of black political life. John Hope Franklin's classic *From Slavery to Freedom: A History of the Negro People in the United States*

(3rd ed. New York: Random House, Vintage, 1967) towers above most general works in the field. The book's great assets are its thoroughness, its clarity, and its delineation of underlying political themes. Franklin successfully ties together the political aspects of the African, Carribean, and American dramas over slavery, of the slave trade, of the origins of American slavery, and of black participation in seminal colonial institutions, in the Revolutionary War, and in the many major historical events and trends which followed. Herbert Aptheker's prodigious anthology *A Documentary History of the Negro People in the United States* (New York: Citadel, 1965), published in two volumes, is an unparalleled source of documents and papers, which include black petitions for freedom during the long era of slavery, personal statements by slave rebels, black petitions for equal educational and economic opportunities, and the minutes, statements, and resolutions of early black political gatherings, conventions, and organizations. Another acclaimed general work on the history of black people in the United States is Lerone Bennett's *Before the Mayflower* (Chicago: Johnson, 1964). Bennett's skillful blowups of major historical events are made fascinating by his poetic and clear literary style. A good synopsis of black history is found in Kenneth G. Goode's *From Africa to the United States and Then . . .* (Glenview, Ill.: Scott, Foresman, 1969). Goode travels the long road of black history in Africa and later in the United States up to the present in 168 pages. There is obviously no time for in-depth treatment of any one historical period here; however, for detail the reader can refer to the many specialized works on particular historical periods.

On the colonial American period, Winthrop Jordan's *White Over Black: American Attitudes Toward the Negro, 1550–1812* (Baltimore: Penguin Books, 1969) is the leading work. The utility of Jordan's work is heightened by its historical depth, lucidity, and, most important, its interdisciplinary character. It is certainly a psychosociological study which throws light on an obscure colonial malady. Aptheker's *Negro Slave Revolts in the United States, 1526–1838* (New York: International Publishers, 1939) refutes well the myth of black acquiescence in slavery. W. E. B. DuBois's exhaustive study of the slave trade, *The Suppression of the African Slave Trade to the United States, 1638–1870* (Cambridge, Mass., 1896; Reprint, New York: Dover, 1970), remains among the best accounts of the political struggles over that trade. John H. Russell's *The Free Negro in Virginia, 1619–1865* (Baltimore; Reprint, Westport, Conn.: Negro Universities Press, 1969) theorizes that blacks were servants before they were slaves and makes occasional references to a few attempts by blacks to influence politics in Virginia. Adele Hast's "The Legal Status of the Negro in Virginia, 1705–1765" (*Journal of Negro History* July 1969) also sheds light on the use of slavery as a legal and political issue. Despite his disparaging statement that "after all, Negroes are only white men with black skins," Kenneth Stampp's monumental *The Peculiar Institution: Slavery in the Ante-Bellum South* (New York: Knopf, 1956) does well in tracing the growth of slavery and the use of enslaved black men as political objects from early colonial times to the period just before the Civil War.

On the Revolutionary era, Benjamin Quarles's *The Negro in the American Revolution* (Chapel Hill: University of North Carolina Press, 1961) remains the most fascinating work about this period of black political usury, but see also George H. Moore's *Historical Notes on the Employment of American Negroes in the American Army of the Revolution* (New York, 1862). And Charles A. Beard's *An Economic Interpretation of the Constitution of the United States* (1913; Reprint, New York: Macmillan, 1935) gives good background on the issue of slavery at the Constitutional Convention.

On the pre-Civil War era, particularly on the disposition of the institutions of slavery, Eugene D. Genovese's *The Political Economy of Slavery* (New York: Random House, Vintage, 1965) is a major work which cleverly examines the confluence of the economic and political aspects of slavery. The struggles of free blacks during this period are explored in Leon Litwack's *North of Slavery: The Negro in the Free States, 1790–1860* (Chicago: University of Chicago Press, 1961); E. Franklin Frazier's *The Free Negro Family* (Nashville: Fisk University, 1932; Reprint, New York: Arno, 1968) is a thin but incisive sociological treatment of black family life and its influence on other facets of black life at that time. That era was rich with the growth of black organizations and conventions. John W. Cromwell describes the earliest of these organizations in *The Early Negro Convention Movement* (Washington, D.C., 1904); see also Bella Gross, "The First National Negro Convention" (*Journal of Negro History* October 1946). On the growth of the colonization organizations, see Philip J. Staudenraus's *The African Colonization Movement, 1816–1865* (New York: Columbia University Press, 1961) and H.N. Sherwood's "The Formation of the American Colonization Society," (*Journal of Negro History* July 1917). On the abolition movement, see Herbert Aptheker's "Militant Abolitionism" (*Journal of Negro History* October 1941) and his superb *The Negro in the Abolitionist Movement* (New York: published by the author, 1941). For a lucid and eloquent presentation of a black abolitionist ideology, see David Walker's *Appeal in Four Articles* (in David Walker and Henry H. Garnet, *Walker's Appeal and Garnet's Address to the Slaves of the United States of America*. New York: Arno, 1969). Add to these the many slave narratives nicely summed up in the chapter-by-chapter bibliographies of Franklin's *From Slavery to Freedom*, mentioned previously. An important article which outlines conflicts between black and white abolitionists is found in Benjamin Quarles's "The Breach Between Douglass and Garrison" (*Journal of Negro History* April 1938). Other works concerning this period are mentioned under the biography and autobiography sections of this bibliography.

The Civil War period was a pivotal time in the history of black politics. The war itself was an expensive use and result of sectional politics, which again had the black man as political object. For a good general reference on the black man's involvement in the Civil War, see George W. Williams's *A History of the Negro Troops in the War of the Rebellion* (1888; Reprint, Westport, Conn: Negro Universities Press, 1970). Benjamin Quarles's *The Negro in the Civil War* (Boston, 1953; Reprint, New York: Russell & Russell, 1968) is a valuable reference on this period, and the intricate relationship of black troops and the Union government is well described in Fred Shannon's "The Federal Government and the Negro Soldier, 1861–1865," (*Journal of Negro History* October 1926). A serious student of black political history in this period should read the several biographies of Abraham Lincoln for further insight into the relationships between black political fate and the politics of the Civil War. Chief among these is Carl Sandburg's *Abraham Lincoln*, of which several editions are available. But the more important relationship is between Lincoln and the Emancipation Proclamation. Lerone Bennett's "Was Lincoln A White Supremicist?" (*Ebony*, September 1968) is a jolting reconsideration of the benevolent role Lincoln played in the issuance of the great document. John Hope Franklin's *Emancipation Proclamation* (New York: Doubleday, 1963) is a perceptive and fascinating recreation of the political circumstances in which the document was issued. Other works of interest on the proclamation include Charles H. Wesley's "Lincoln's Plan for Colonizing the Emancipated Negro" (*Journal of Negro History*, January 1919) and Harry S. Blakiston's "Lincoln's Emancipation Plan" (*Journal of Negro History* July 1922).

The Reconstruction failure following the Civil War brought fundamental changes in the character of black political life in the United States. It marked a tortuous change in the status of black people from that of political objects to that of oppressed political activists. No student of black political life can ignore this period. Good factual information is found in Chuck Stone's *Black Political Power in America* (New York: Bobbs-Merrill, 1968), Franklin's *From Slavery to Freedom*, and Bennett's *Before the Mayflower* (both mentioned previously). A major work, suspect for its clearly Marxist approach to the Reconstruction era, is W. E. B. DuBois's *Black Reconstruction in America, 1860–1880* (New York: Meridian, 1935; Reprint, Russell & Russell, 1956). The most important works on this era deal with the lives and politics of the parade of black politicians, journalists, educators, and advocates active between 1865 and 1901. Among these Lerone Bennett's *Black Power U.S.A.: The Human Side of Reconstruction* (Baltimore: Penguin, rev. ed. 1962) is the most well-written, detailed, and fascinating work, as it brings entertaining glimpses of many black political actors together with a discernible historical theme. A disturbing account of the "white backlash" to Reconstruction policies is found in Forrest G. Wood's *Black Scare: The Racist Response to Emancipation and Reconstruction* (Berkeley and Los Angeles: University of California Press, 1970). John Hope Franklin's *Reconstruction After the Civil War* (Chicago: Univeristy of Chicago Press, 1961) and Kenneth Stampp's *The Era of Reconstruction 1865-1877* (New York: Knopf, 1965) reinterpret the central political importance of Reconstruction for the political status of blacks. C. Vann Woodward's *The Strange Career of Jim Crow* (New York: Oxford University Press, 1966), particularly Chapter 1, is among the best accounts of the birth of "Jim Crow" practices and legislation during the Reconstruction era. The works of black politicians and advocates during Reconstruction also provide an essential collection of insights on this era: John R. Lynch's *The Facts of Reconstruction* (1913; Reprint, New York: Arno Press, 1968), a fascinating and observant account of Reconstruction and Mississippi, and T. Thomas Fortune's *Black and White: Land, Labor and Politics in the South* (1884; Reprint, New York: Arno Press, 1968), a bitter denunciation of rampant white racism during Reconstruction from the pen of a prominent black journalist, are two examples of such work. Of equal interest are studies of state and local politics and policies during Reconstruction. Two representative short works on this aspect of the period are found in Louis R. Harlan's "Desegregation in New Orleans Public Schools During Reconstruction" [*American Historical Review* 67 (April 1962): 663–675] and Vernon L. Wharton's "The Race Issue in the Overthrow of Reconstruction in Mississippi" (*Phylon* Fourth Quarter 1941). Wharton's monumental *The Negro in Mississippi, 1865-1890* (Chapel Hill: University of North Carolina Press, 1947) should also be consulted. Works addressed specifically to electoral aspects of Reconstruction politics[1] are: Luther P. Jackson, *Negro Officeholders in Virginia* (Norfolk, Va., 1945); Samuel D. Smith, *The Negro in Congress, 1870-1901* (Chapel Hill: University of North Carolina Press, 1940); Alrutheus A. Taylor, "Negro Congressmen a Generation After," (*Journal of Negro History* April 1922); G. David Houston, "A Negro Senator" (*Journal of Negro History* July 1922); William A. Russ, "The Negro and White Disfranchisement During Radical Reconstruction" (*Journal of Negro History* April 1934); R.H. Woody, "Jonathan J. Wright, Associate Justice of the Supreme Court of South Carolina, 1870–1877" (*Journal of Negro History* April 1933).

The overthrow of Reconstruction policies and the black political activity they allowed is described well in Bennett's *Before the Mayflower*. C. Vann Woodward's *Reunion and Reaction: The Compromise of 1877 and the End of Reconstruction* (Gloucester, Mass.: Peter Smith, 1951) goes deep into the circumstances which ended in a curious bargain between President Hayes and opponents of Reconstruction in 1876 and 1877. The demise of Reconstruction politics and the compromises which expedited it, moved the status of black people back toward that of being political objects. Some of the rationalizations for this regression into segregation and degradation are found in a fascinating anthology, I.A. Newby's *The Development of Segregationist Thought* (Homewood, Ill.: Dorsey, 1968), particularly the essays by Claude Bowers, Frank Clark, William Graham Sumner, and Thomas W. Hardwick.

The noisy collapse of Reconstruction was followed not so much by a total collapse of black political activity as a recession into political dormancy. Chased from electoral politics, black political activity became more manifest in protest and special-interest organizations. W. E. B. DuBois's *The Souls of Black Folk* (New York: Fawcett, 1903) captures the black reaction to this way in which the century closed. One essay, "On the Dawn of Freedom," prophesied that the major political problem of the twentieth century would be "the problem of the color line." Another piece, "On Mr. Booker T. Washington and Others," is a moving abstract of the platform of the Niagara movement, a handful of black professionals and intellectuals who were opposed to much of the ideology of the prevailing black leadership. DuBois rightly sensed the spiritual strains of black thought and feeling at this time in the essay, "Our Spiritual Strivings." Such strains linked weary blacks, battered by the setbacks of Reconstruction, to Africans reeling under the depravations of European imperialism. The year 1900 was the occasion of the first Pan-African Conference, in which DuBois was involved. His role is described in Clarence G. Contee's "The Emergence of DuBois as an African Nationalist" (*Journal of Negro History*, January 1969). But the central fact of this era was the decline of black political rights. V. O. Key's classic *Southern Politics* (New York: Random House, 1949) makes brief mention of this in its early chapters. Chapter 5 of Paul Lewison's cogent *Race, Class and Party* (New York: Grosset and Dunlap, 1932; Reprint, Russell & Russell, 1963), cites racial and class disfranchisement as two mutually aggravating problems in the post-Reconstruction era. August Meier's *Negro Thought in America, 1880–1915* (Ann Arbor: University of Michigan Press, 1963) is a provocative work on the impact of the demise of Reconstruction on black ideology, which unfortunately is conceptually perforated in some chapters.

The era before World War I, ending with the passing of Reconstruction, the birth of a new century, and the ascendancy of the Progressive movement was a period of political incubation for blacks. Several black interest groups were founded which have survived to the present. Mary W. Ovington's *How the National Association for the Advancement of Colored People Began* (New York: 1914) and Robert L. Jack's *History of the National Association for the Advancement of Colored People* (Boston, 1943) are pioneering but somewhat vainglorious works on the history of the NAACP. A more recent work by a prominent black poet, Langston Hughes, is *Fight for Freedom: The Story of the NAACP* (New York: Norton, 1962). For the first twenty-three years of the NACCP (1910–1933) W. E. B. DuBois was Director of Research and Publications, a position which included the editorship of the *Crisis* magazine, still the official publication of the organization. For a fine collection of some of his editorials, see *W. E. B. DuBois, An A B C of Color* (New York: International Publishers, 1970). L. Hollingsworth Wood outlines the purpose and direction of the early Urban League in "The Urban League Movement" (*Journal of Negro History* January 1924). Chapter 5 of Hanes Walton, Jr.'s *The Negro in Third-Party Politics* (Philadelphia: Dorrance, 1969) is an incisive discussion of the black man's relationship to Progressive movements.

World War I and its aftermath brought the increased urbanization and politicization of black people. No student of black politics can ignore the emergence of Marcus Garvey during those years. His famous conflicts with W. E. B. DuBois are referred to in Colin Legum's *Pan Africanism* (New York: Praeger, 1965). His political ideology is best pieced together in Amy Jacques Garvey's *The Philosophy and Opinions of Marcus Garvey* (New York: Atheneum, 1969), as well as in E. David Cronon's *Black Moses: The Story of Marcus Garvey and the Universal Negro Improvement Association* (Madison: University of Wisconsin Press, 1965). White riots against blacks and black riots against whites are frequently mentioned in most histories of this period; Arthur I. Waskow's *From Race Riot to Sit-In: 1919 and the 1960s* (New York: Doubleday, 1966) is a good reference on this. On black leadership perspectives, see Abram L. Harris's "The Negro Problem as Viewed by Negro Leaders" (*Current History* June 1923), and Horace M. Bond's "Negro Leadership Since Washington" (*South Atlantic Quarterly* April 1925). The major work on black migration into cities, an event of decisive impact on the future development of black political life, is Emmet J. Scott's *Negro Migration During the War* (1923; Reprint, New York: Arno, 1969).

There is a strange dearth of literature on the political aspects of the "Harlem (or "Negro") Renaissance." Most connections between the literary mood of this movement and its influence on the political thought of blacks in the period must be drawn from reading the poetry, novels, plays, and essays of blacks who were writing between the end of World War I and the Depression.

Perhaps the confluence of the residue of the Negro Renaissance cultural awakening and the sharp deprivations caused by the Depression sparked the increase in political activity among black people during the period of the New Deal. Black political activity also diversified in this period, becoming significant electorally, ideologically, organizationally, and administratively. Urbanization provided a new forum for black political activity with a new issue base. Harold F. Gosnell's classic *Negro Politicians: The Rise of Negro Politics in Chicago* (Chicago: University of Chicago Press, 1935) is a masterful analysis of the black political leadership which rose from the quagmire of South Side Chicago to enter the labyrinth of power politics in the city. The book perceptively identifies forces in big-city politics which both cause and are caused by black political life: electoral maneuvering, bossism, interest-group formation, and party affiliation. Its glimpses of the North's first two black congressmen, Arthur Mitchell and Oscar dePriest are more than laudable. Its skillful tracing of connections between black politics and black teachers, policemen, civil servants, federal workers, and the underground perhaps is not anachronistic. Finally, the work does not overlook the ties between Chicago's black South Side in the early days of the Depression and the strains and strands of historical influences which preceded it. Ralph Bunche's "The Negro in the Political Life of the United States" (*Journal of Negro Education* July 1940) is a tempered, scholarly, and perhaps too comprehensive capsule of black political status in the United States in the late 1930s. Among the first essays to worry about black political clout in the cities was Harold F. Gosnell's "The Negro Vote in Northern Cities" (*National Municipal Review* May 1941). A new but essential part of black political activity which emerged in the 1930s and 1940s was black participation in administrative agencies and committees. Lawrence J.W. Hayes's *The Negro Federal Government Worker* (Washington, D.C., 1941) is a good work on the roles of black government advisers in this period. Much will also be found in John P. Davis's "Blue Eagles and Black Workers" (*The New Republic* November 14, 1934). Early chapters in Samuel Krislov's *The Negro in Federal Employment* (Minneapolis: University of Minnesota Press, 1967) describe briefly and clearly the evolution of committees, commissions, and agencies for equal employment opportunity in the federal government during these years. Bernard Sternsher's *The Negro in Depression and War: Prelude to Revolution 1930–1945* (Chicago: Quadrangle, 1969) is a good collection of essays on the observations of blacks in the "Black Cabinet" and on the activities of black pressure-group organizations in these decades. No reference to this period should overlook these black organizations and movements. Wilson Record's *Race and Radicalism: The NAACP and the Communist Party in Conflict* (Ithaca, N.Y.: Cornell University Press, 1963) is not only a worthwhile examination of the tensions between the two organizations, but it is also a good glimpse into the activities of the NAACP during the 1920s and 1930s. Black labor problems in this period were at the heart of many political struggles. Among the best works on these problems are Charles H. Wesley's *Negro Labor in the United States* (New York: Viking, 1927; Reprint, Russell & Russell, 1967); Brailsford R. Brazeal's *The Brotherhood of Sleeping Car Porters: Its Origin and Development* (New York: Harper, 1946); Horace Cayton and George S. Mitchell's *Black Workers and the New Unions* (Chapel Hill: University of North Carolina Press, 1939; Reprint, College Park, Md.: McGrath, 1969); Lester B. Granger's "The Negro—Friend or Foe of Organized Labor?" (*Opportunity* May 1935); Herbert Hill's "Labor Unions and the Negro: The Record of Discrimination" (*Commentary* December 1959), and A. Phillip Randolph's "The Trade Union Movement and The Negro" (*Journal of Negro Education*, January 1936). Other works on black political history and problems in this period are: C.A. Bacote's "The Negro in Atlanta Politics (1869–1955)" (*Phylon* Fourth Quarter 1955); Ralph Bunche's "The Negro in the Political Life of the United States" (*Journal of Negro Education* July 1941); John G. Van Husen's "The Negro in Politics" (*Journal of Negro History* July 1936); William M. Brewer's "The Poll Tax and the Poll Taxers" (*Journal of Negro History* July 1944); and James A. Harrell's "Negro Leadership in the Election Year 1936" (*Journal of Southern History* November 1968). The politics of war were integral to the period, and the participation of blacks in the armed services became a political issue then as it is now. For treatments of this, see particularly W.Y. Bell, Jr.'s "The Negro Warrior's Home Front" (*Phylon* Third Quarter 1944) and Richard M. Dalfiume's *Desegregation of the U.S. Armed Forces: Fighting on Two Fronts* (Columbia: University of Missouri Press, 1969), which focuses on the tortuous desegregation of the armed forces before and during World War II. For a richly methodological work, steeped in survey research data, see Leo Bogart's *Social Research and the Desegregation of the U.S. Army* (Chicago: Markham, 1969). A summary overview of "the Negro policy" of the several branches of the armed services during World War II is given in Paul C. Davis's "The Negro in the Armed Services" (*Virginia Quarterly Review* October 1948).

The postwar period was a rich preface to the political struggles of black people during the 1950s. For a succinct overview of the major developments, see Rayford W. Logan's *The Negro and the Post-World War: A Primer* (Washington, D.C.: University Place Book Shop, 1945) and Louis Ruchames's *Race, Jobs, and Politics* (New York: Columbia University Press,

1953). The political forces in and around the Fair Employment Practices Commission are discussed in Louis Kesselman's *The Social Politics of the FEPC* (Chapel Hill: University of North Carolina Press, 1948). A good overview of the political disposition of black people at that time is found in Henry L. Moons *Balance of Power: The Negro Vote* (New York: 1948; Reprint, Kraus, 1970). A monumental and highly acclaimed work on this subject is V.O. Key, *Southern Politics* (New York: Random House, Vintage, 1949), a book whose major flaw is its assumption that blacks were relatively passive political actors.

The 1950s were rich with black political activity; see particularly: Rosaline Levenson's "The Negro Vote in California," Master's thesis, Institute of Governmental Studies, University of California at Los Angeles, 1953; Harold C. Flemming's "Resistance Movements and Racial Desegregation" [*The Annals* 304 (March 1956): 44–52]; J. A. LaPonce's "The Protection of Minorities by the Electoral System" [*Western Political Quarterly* 10 (June 1957): 318–339]; and Arthur M. Schlesinger, Jr.'s *The Politics of Upheaval* (Boston: Houghton Mifflin, 1960), pp. 598–600. On the emergence of the politics of protest, see: Martin Luther King, Jr.'s *Stride Toward Freedom: The Montgomery Story* (New York: Harper, 1958) and *Why We Can't Wait* (New York: Harper & Row, Torchbooks, 1963); Louis Lomax's *The Negro Revolt* (New York: Harper, 1962) and *When the Word Is Given . . .* (New York: New American Library, 1964); Charles Silberman's *Crisis in Black and White* (New York: Random House, 1964); Lerone Bennett's *Confrontation: Black and White* (Chicago: Johnson, 1965); Alan F. Westin's *Freedom Now!: The Civil Rights Struggle in America* (New York: Basic Books, 1964); Kenneth B. Clark's *The Negro Protest* (Boston: Beacon, 1963); and William J. Brink and Louis Harris's *The Negro Revolution in America* (New York: Simon and Schuster, 1964). On the student protest movements at the close of the 1950s, see Howard Zinn's *SNCC: The New Abolitionists* (Boston: Beacon, 1960).

Black Political Life from 1960 to the Present

Several good general works which bridge historical and recent aspects of black political life are available: Chuck Stone's *Black Political Power in America* (Indianapolis: Bobbs-Merrill, 1968), written in a live, witty style, is abundant in historical detail, first-hand insight, and issue perspective. Matthew Holden, Jr.'s two volumes, *The White Man's Burden* and *The Politics of the Black Nation* (San Francisco: Chandler Publishing Co., 1972), are a monumental contribution to the study of black political life. Holden's work successfully brings together theoretical issues of concern to political scientists and ideological issues of concern to political activists. Everett Carl Ladd's *Negro Political Leadership in the South* (Ithaca, N.Y.: Cornell University Press, 1966) is concerned with leadership selection, leadership styles (conservative, moderate, militant, and the like), and organizational foci (welfare, protest, electoral) in the South. Harry Holloway's *The Politics of the Southern Negro: From Exclusion to Big City Organization* (New York: Random House, 1969) is a strong methodological contribution to the study of black political life, as is James Prothro and Donald R. Matthews's popular work, *Negroes and the New Southern Politics* (New York: Harcourt Brace Jovanovich, 1966). Matthews and Prothro's work is an exhaustive study of black and white attitudes in the South on race and on civic participation, in which socioeconomic attributes, community structure, attitudes, cognition, and other variables are examined. James Q. Wilson's *Negro Politics: The Search for Leadership* (New York: The Free Press, 1960) is primarily a study of black politics in Chicago, which raises issues of national interest from the perspectives of black politicians. Edward Clayton's *Negro Politicians* (Chicago: Johnson, 1964) is a good guide to some of the issues and personalities in the world of black politics in the early 1960s. Stokely Carmichael and Charles V. Hamilton's *Black Power: The Politics of Liberation in America* (New York: Random House, Vintage, 1967) was thought to be the black-power position paper of the late 1960s; while falling somewhat short of that, it nevertheless presents a political perspective for black politicians and thinkers which has not been without influence. *Political Participation*, a report of the United States Commission on Civil Rights (Washington, D.C.: Government Printing Office, 1968) presents the issue from the perspective of the United States Commission on Civil Rights. *The Black Man in American Politics: Three Views* (Washington, D.C.: Metropolitan Applied Research Center, 1969) consists of three essays by Kenneth B. Clark, Julian Bond, and Richard G. Hatcher; as the work of activists with somewhat different roles in black political life, these pieces are mandatory reading for persons interested in current opinions among black politicians. Mack H. Jones's *Black Schoolboard Members in the South* (Atlanta: Southern Regional Council, 1971) is a skillful and perceptive analysis of issues and dilemmas of black political life in the politics of education. *Revolution in Civil Rights* (Washington, D.C.: Congressional Quarterly Service, 1968) is a good store of information on legislation, court decisions, school desegregation, and other matters germane to black political life. Mervyn Dymally's *The Black Man in American Politics* (Los Angeles: Urban Affairs Institute, 1969) is an excellent study guide for teachers and scholars, alike. The annual *National*

Roster of Black Elected Officials (Washington, D.C.: Joint Center for Political Studies) is a compendium of information on black elected officials throughout the nation. Other articles of good perspective and orientation on issues are: Julian Bond's "The Negro in Politics" (*Motive*, May 1968); J. Erroll Miller's "The Negro in National Politics," St. Clair Drake's "The Patterns of Interracial Conflict in 1968," Daniel C. Thompson's "The Civil Rights Movement, 1968"; and Edward F. Sweat's "State and Local Politics, 1968," all four collected in the anthology *In Black America* (Los Angeles: Presidential Publishers, 1968); and Simeon Booker's "Black Politics at the Crossroads" (*Ebony*, October 1968).

Good anthologies on black political life include: Richard P. Young, *Roots of Rebellion: The Evolution of Black Politics and Protest Since World War II* (New York: Harper & Row, 1970); Harry A. Bailey, Jr., *Negro Politics in America* (Columbus, Ohio: Charles Merrill, 1967); Jack R. Van Der Silk, *Black Conflict with White America: A Reader in Social and Political Analysis* (Columbus, Ohio: Charles Merrill, 1970); Herbert Storing, *What Country Have I? Political Writings by Black Americans* (New York: St. Martin's, 1970); and Lawrence H. Fuchs, *American Ethnic Politics* (New York: Harper & Row, Torchbooks, 1968), Chapters 8, 9, 11, and 12.

SPECIALIZED STUDIES

The Law

Whether used to enslave black people, to occasionally emancipate them, or to again repress them, law has been central to black political life in the United States. The literature in this field is immeasurable, but I can recommend a few selections: A good record of court decisions of great importance to black people is found in Richard Bardolph, ed., *The Civil Rights Record* (New York: Thomas Y. Crowell, 1970), in Charles Aiken, *The Negro Votes* (San Francisco: Chandler Publishing Co., 1965), and in Joseph Tussman, *The Supreme Court on Racial Discrimination* (New York: Oxford University Press, 1963). For a good summary of the handling of national voting-rights legislation in the federal courts, see Donald S. Strong's *Negroes, Ballots and Judges* (University, Ala.: University of Alabama Press, 1968). For a superb and lucid case study of the impact of civil-rights laws, see Frederick Wirt's study of Panola County, Mississippi, *Politics of Southern Equality* (New York: Adeline Press, 1970). A handy interpretation of the Civil Rights Act of 1964 is Stanley Fleishman and Sam Rosenwein's *The New Civil Rights Act: What It Means to You* (New York: Blackstone, 1964). A somewhat routine survey of major court decisions and civil-rights laws is found in Chapter 5 of *Freedoms, Courts, Politics: Studies in Civil Liberties* (New York: Prentice-Hall, 1965) by Lucius and Twiley Barker, Jr.; a more thoughtful examination of civil-rights laws, their limitations, and the many challenges they face is found in Morroe Berger's *Equality by Statute: The Revolution in Civil Rights* (New York: Doubleday, Anchor, 1967). For more documentation, see Donald O. Dewey's *Union and Liberty: A Documentary History of American Constitutionalism* (New York: McGraw-Hill, 1969), Chapters 8 and 16. For a provocative but legally technical discussion of the relation of the civil-rights movement to the First Amendment, see Harry Kalven, Jr.'s *The Negro and the First Amendment* (Chicago: University of Chicago Press, 1965). Several fine studies of the Fourteenth Amendment are available: A brilliant examination of the impact of the anti-slavery forces on the passage of that amendment is Jacobus Ten Broek's *Equal Under Law* (New York: Macmillan, 1965). Another study of the evolution of the amendment, which is more concerned with its legal intent, is Joseph B. James's *The Framing of the Fourteenth Amendment* (Urbana: University of Illinois Press, 1965). A very different scholarly tract in the research on the Fourteenth Amendment, one which asserts that the amendment gives white Americans no right to discriminate against blacks, is Lois B. Moreland's *White Racism and the Law* (Columbus, Ohio: Charles E. Merrill, 1970). A good and well-documented study of school desegregation cases is Albert B. Blaustein and Clarence Clyde Ferguson's *Desegregation and the Law: The Meaning and Effect of the School Segregation Cases* (New York: Random House, Vintage, 1962). A plethora of articles on law and the black political struggle exist, for which the reader should consult the bibliographies suggested at the end of this essay.

Political Parties

Among the most outstanding studies of political parties and black political life are: Hanes Walton, Jr., *Black Political Parties* (New York: The Free Press, 1971) and *The Negro in Third-Party Politics* (Philadelphia: Dorrance, 1969); Angus Campbell, "The Case for an Independent Black Political Party" [*International Socialist Review* 29 (January-February 1968): 39–55]; Samuel LuBell, "The Negro and the Democratic Coalition" [*Commentary* 38 (August 1964): 19–27]; Francis Fox Piven and Richard A. Cloward, "Dissensus Politics: Negroes and the Democratic Coalition" [*New Republic* 158 (April 20, 1968): 20–24]; and David R. Segal and Richard Schaffner, "Status, Party and Negro Americans" (*Phylon*, Fall 1968).

Urban Politics

The city has become the major battleground for black political struggle. On this, see the *Report of the Advisory Committee on Civil Disorders* (Kerner Commission) (New York: Bantam, 1968) and "The Cycle of Despair: The Negro in the City" (*Life*, March 8, 1968). The most definitive work on the black man in the city is found in St. Clair Drake and Horace Cayton's *Black Metropolis: A Study of Negro Life in a Northern City* (New York: Harcourt, Brace, 1951); Kenneth B. Clark's *Dark Ghetto* (New York: Harper & Row, 1965); and Allan H. Spear's *Black Chicago: The Making of a Negro Ghetto, 1890–1920* (Chicago: University of Chicago Press, 1967).

On strictly political aspects of black life in the city, see: "Negroes in City Politics," in Edward C. Banfield and James Q. Wilson's *City Politics* (New York: Harvard University Press, 1963), pp. 293–312; Martin Kilson's "Black Politics: A New Power" (*Dissent* August 1971); Leo F. Schnore and Harry Sharp's "The Changing Color of Our Big Cities," in Jeffrey K. Hadden, Louis H. Masotti, and Calvin J. Larson, eds., *Metropolis in Crisis* (Itasca, Ill.: Peacock, 1967); Jeffrey K. Hadden, Louis H. Masotti, and Victor Thiessen's "The Making of the Negro Mayors," and Nat Hentoff's, "A Mayor Tours the Ghetto," both in Leonard I. Ruchelman, ed., *Big City Mayors* (Bloomington: Indiana University Press, 1969); Paul H. Friesema's "Black Control of Central Cities: The Hollow Prize" (*Journal of the American Institute of Planners* March 1969), and Kenneth Miller's, "Community Organizations in the Ghetto," in Richard S. Rosenbloom and Robin Marris, eds., *Social Innovation in the City: New Enterprises for Community Development* (Cambridge, Mass.: Harvard University Press, 1969) pp. 97–108.

Community Organizations

The character of black political life is now highly organizational, and literature on this aspect of black political life is slowly accumulating. One penetrating case study of community organization is found in William Ellis's *White Ethics and Black Power: The Emergence of the West Side Organization* (Chicago: Aldine, 1969). A somewhat different view of organization is Arthur M. Brazier's *Black Self-Determination: The Story of the Woodlawn Organization* (Grand Rapids, Mich.: Eerdmans, 1969). On pressure-groups in black politics, see: Warren D. St. James, *The National Association for the Advancement of Colored People: A Case Study in Pressure Groups* (New York: Exposition, 1958); Arvarh E. Strickland, *History of the Chicago Urban League*

(Urbana: University of Illinois Press, 1966); "Black Priority" (*Saturday Review* November 15, 1969), the story of the creation of the National Association of Black Students; William H. Gulley, "Relative Effectiveness in Negro and White Voluntary Associations" (*Phylon* Summer 1963); Norman Jackman and Jack Dodson, "Negro Youth and Direct Action" (*Phylon* Spring 1967); Lewis M. Killian and Charles Grigg, "Negro Perceptions of Organizational Effectiveness' [*Social Problems* 11 (Spring 1964): 380–388]; James Allen McPherson, "And What Does That Mean?" [*Atlantic Monthly* 223 (May 1969): 78–84], an interesting study of the Blackstone Rangers of Chicago; Wilson Record, "American Racial Ideologies and Organizations in Transition" (*Phylon* Winter 1965); C. Eric Lincoln, *The Black Muslims in America* (Boston: Beacon, 1961); Gene Marine, *The Black Panthers* (New York: New American Library, 1969).

POLITICAL BIOGRAPHY AND AUTOBIOGRAPHY

A treasury of information and insight into black political life is stored in recent biographies and autobiographies of blacks who have been active or who are versed in black political activity. Although some social scientists contend that these sources tend to be unsystematic and anecdotal, they provide much proximity to the persons, places, and events important to black politics. Some of the works subsumed under the categories of biography or autobiography are not strictly either one. They focus more on the social and political aspects of a black individual's life than on his personal life and outlook. But they are nevertheless fundamental to the study of black political life.

Good capsulated information about black elected officials, particularly their reflections on self and position, is found in Mervyn Dymally, ed., *The Black Politician: His Struggle for Power* (Belmont, Calif.: Duxbury, 1971) and in Edward T. Clayton's *Negro Politicians* (Chicago: Johnson, 1964). For insights into individual black political styles, see Hanes Walton, Jr., and Leslie Burl McLemore's "A Portrait of Black Political Styles" (*The Black Politician* Fall 1970) and James Q. Wilson's "Two Negro Politicians: An Interpretation" (*Midwest Journal of Political Science* November 1960), pp. 346–369. Good human-interest stories on black elected officials can be found in Hans Massaquoi's "Michigan's Negro Mayors" (*Ebony* July 1967) and the editorial "First Negro Mayor Since Reconstruction" (*Sepia* October 1964).

Other brief portraits of black elected officials appear in: Judy Miller's "The Representative Is a Lady" (*The Black Politician* Fall 1969); Hazel Smalley's "Black Women Legislators Answer Questions" (*The Black Politician April 1971); Richard Harris's "Black Legislators and Their White Colleagues" (*The Black Politician* Fall 1970) and in the same issue of *The Black Politician,* Judy Miller's "California's Black Lady Legislator; and Claude Lewis's *Adam Clayton Powell* (New York: Fawcett, 1963).

More recent and elaborate black political autobiographies are Charles Evers's *Evers* (New York: World, 1971) and Shirley Chisholm's *Unbought and Unbossed* (Boston: Houghton Mifflin, 1970). Much recent work attempts to relate the lives of black elected officials to black political development. Examples of this school of scholarship are Hanes Walton, Jr.'s *The Political Philosophy of Martin Luther King* (Westport, Conn.: Negro Universities Press, 1971), Alex Poinsett's *Black Power Gary Style: The Making of Mayor Richard Gordon Hatcher* (Chicago: Johnson, 1970), and Kenneth C. Wienberg's *Black Victory: Carl Stokes and the Winning of Cleveland* (Chicago: Quadrangle, 1968).

Beyond the world of the black elected official there are many other autobiographical and biographical works which shed light on black leaders, black pressure groups, black political thought and strategy, and black civil-rights organizations. Among the more recent and important of these are Malcolm X and Alex Haley's *The Autobiography of Malcolm X* (New York: Grove 1964), George Jackson's *Soledad Brothers: Prison Letters of George Jackson* (New York: Random House, Vintage, 1971), Angela Davis and Bettina Aptheker's *If They Come in the Morning; Voices of Resistance* (New York: The Third Press, 1971), Eldridge Cleaver's *Soul on Ice* (New York: McGraw-Hill, 1968), W. E. B. DuBois's *The Autobiography of W. E. B. DuBois* (New York: International Publishers, 1968), and H. Rap Brown's *Die Nigger Die!* (New York: Dial 1969).

FURTHER SOURCES

Bibliographies

Elizabeth W. Miller, *The Negro in America: A Bibliography* (New York: Cambridge University Press, 1970).
Dorothy Porter *Working Bibliography on the Negro in the United States* (Ann Arbor, Mich.: University Microfilms, 1969)
Black Bibliography (Hayward: California State College, Department of Black Studies).

Periodicals

The Black Politician (955 South Western Avenue, Los Angeles, California 90006).
The Black Scholar (Box 908, Sausalito, California 94965).
The Black World (1820 South Michigan Avenue, Chicago, Illinois 60616).
The Journal of Black Studies (275 South Beverly Drive, Beverly Hills, California 90212).
Newsletter, (Joint Center for Political Studies, 1426 H Street N.W., Suite 926, Washington, D.C. 20005).
Black Panther News Service (Atlanta, Georgia).
Muhammad Speaks (2548 South Federal Street, Chicago, Illinois 60616).
Black Review of Political Economy (New York, New York).

Organizations

Black Congressional Caucus (1122 Longworth Building, United States House of Representatives, Washington, D.C. 20515).
The College for Struggle (637 Gough Street, San Francisco 94102).
National Conference of Black Political Scientists (Political Science Department, Atlanta University).
Institute of the Black World (673 Beckwith Street, Atlanta, Georgia 30314).
Joint Center for Political Studies (1426 H Street N.W., Suite 926, Washington, D.C. 20005).
Urban Affairs Institute (955 South Western Avenue, Los Angeles 90006).

NOTES

1. For works mentioned in this category, I am indebted to the bibliography of Franklin's *From Slavery to Freedom.*

Index of Persons

Alexander, Clifford, Jr., 239, 245
Allen, Ivan, Jr., 138
Andrews, George, 81

Bassett, Ebenezer Don Carlos, 45
Beale, Howard K., 126
Beasley, Daniel, 70–104
Bentley, Frank, 73
Blackwood, George D., 128n
Blalock, H., 8–9, 19n
Bond, Julian, 3
Bradford, Lawrence W., Jr., 237
Brewer, John, 110
Brimmer, Andrew F., 238, 239, 245
Brooke, Edward W., 236
Brown, H. Rap, 166
Brown, Willie, 3
Brownell, Herbert, Jr., 137
Bruce, Blanche K., 40
Bryant, William B., 242
Bunche, Ralph, 125

Cain, Richard H., 40
Callaway, Howard H., 251
Carmichael, Stokely, 166
Clement, Kenneth W., 239
Cheatham, Henry P., 41
Chisholm, Shirley, 3
Church, Robert R., 47, 249
Cleaver, Eldridge, 179
Clark, Kenneth, 23
Clarke, Joseph S., 83
Cobbs, Price., 19n
Comer, James, 222n
Conyers, John, Jr., 50
Coser, Lewis, 120

Crum, William, 54
Cuffe, Paul and John, 36
Cuney, Norris Wright, 48, 53

Daley, Richard, 188, 229
Dargans, Louis Maxienne, 236
Dawson, William L., 48, 50, 62
Davis, Christine Ray, 237
DeLarge, Robert C., 40
De Priest, Oscar, 28–29, 48, 49, 50, 54
Dewey, Thomas E., 60–61, 138, 146
Diggs, Charles C., Jr., 50
Dodd, Thomas J., 22
Donovan, James B., 129n
Douglas, Paul, 72, 82, 84
Douglass, Frederick, 23, 45, 46, 125, 218, 244–245
Du Bois, W. E. B., 49, 56, 59, 60, 218
Dymally, Mervyn, 3, 248
Dyson, Wheeler, 100–101

Easton, David, 7, 19n
Edwards, Alfred L., 240
Edwards, G. Franklin, 239
Elliott, Robert B., 40
Evans, Ahmed, 16

Farmer, James, 237
Folsom, James E., 69
Folsom, Marion, 129
Freeman, Frankie Muse, 239
Frink, Bettye, 74–104

Galamison, Milton, 129n
Gallion, Macdonald, 74, 77
Garent, Henry Highland, 25

271

INDEX

Garvey, Marcus, 125, 218
Gibbons, Sam M., 236
Goldwater, Barry, 106, 121, 142–144, 220
Gomillion, Charles G., 69–104
Gordon, Walter A., 242
Grady, Henry Woodfin, 43, 133
Graham, William, 246
Granger, Shelton B., 239–240
Gray, Fred, 82
Gregory, Dick, 229
Grier, William, 19n

Haralson, Jeremiah, 40
Harris, Julian, 55
Harris, Patricia, 238
Hastie, William Henry, 242, 245
Hatcher, Richard, 3
Hawkins, Augustus, 50
Hayes, Rutherford B., 28, 42–43
Higginbotham, Leon, 242
Hoffman, Abbie, 178
Hoffman, S., 19n
Holloway, H., 19n
Holt, R. T., 19n
Hubbard, Charlotte M., 239
Hughes, Emmett John, 31
Hurst, Bishop, 59
Hyman, John A., 40

Ingram, Rosa Lee, 61

Jackson, Samuel C., 239
Jefferson, Thomas, 24
Jenkins, Howard, Jr., 239
Johnson, Andrew, 37
Johnson, Frank, Jr., 76–77
Johnson, James Weldon, 57, 59, 218
Johnson, Lyndon B., 142–144, 238, 244
Johnson, Mordecai W., 49
Jones, Raymond J., 158
Jordon, Vernon, 191

Kardiner, A., 19n
Katzenbach, Nicholas, 112
Kennedy, John F., 23, 123, 139–142
King, Martin Luther, Jr., 164
King, Martin Luther, Jr. Mrs., 140
King, Martin Luther, Sr., 140

La Follette, Robert M., 57, 59
Lamb, Gerald A., 246
Langer, William, 83
Langston, John M., 41
Lincoln, Abraham, 36–37
Livingston, E. P., 74
Lockard, Duane, 168

Long, Jefferson F., 40
Long, Norton, 19n, 109
Louis, Joe, 60
Lubell, Samuel, 249
Lynch, John R., 40

McCree, Wade Hampton, Jr., 242
McMillan, John L., 236
Maddox, Lester G., 18, 138, 220, 251
Malik, Charles, 228
Marshall, Thurgood, 156, 230, 234, 238, 242, 245
Martin, Louis, 252n
Matthews, Eunice, 236
Meier, A., 219
Miller, J. D. B., 23
Miller, Thomas E., 41
Mitchell, Arthur, 29, 49, 50
Mitchell, Frank V., Jr., 237
Mitchell, William P., 67–104
Monypenny, P., 20n
Moon, Henry Lee, 44, 61, 135
Morton, Ferdinand Q., 48
Morton, Thruston B., 83, 138, 141
Motley, Constance Baker, 242
Murray, George W., 41
Myrdal, Gunnar, 23, 47, 189

Nash, Charles, 40
Newton, Huey P., 176
Nix, Robert N. C., Jr., 50
Nkrumah, Kwame, 4

O'Hara, James E., 41
Overton, Watkins, 249
Ovesey, L., 19n

Paine, Rowlett, 249
Parsons, James B., 242
Patterson, John, 68–104
Pickens, William, 58, 59
Pinchback, P. B. S., 26, 39, 42
Pitkin, Hannah, 192
Powell, Adam Clayton, 22, 41, 50, 84, 157, 236, 237
Prosser, Gabriel, 46

Rainey, Joseph H., 40
Randolph, A. Philip, 60, 62
Raney, Wayne, 100–101
Ransier, Alonzo J., 40
Rapier, James T., 40
Revel, Hiram R., 40
Reynolds, Grant, 62
Richardson, Bobby, 187
Richardson, Scovel, 242

INDEX

Robeson, Paul, 125
Robinson, Spottswood W. III, 242
Rogers, Grady P., 68, 74–104
Roosevelt, Franklin Delano, 127, 136–137, 144–145
Roosevelt, James, 82, 84
Roosevelt, Theodore, 53–57
Roucek, J., 8, 19n
Rowan, Carl T., 230, 245
Royko, Mike, 229
Rustin, Bayard, 45

Schattsneider, E. E., 144
Schlesinger, Arthur, Jr., 23
Schuyler, George, 220
Scoble, Harry, 193
Silberman, Charles, 128n
Singleton, Pop, 218
Slaughter, Roger C., 138
Smalls, Robert, 40
Smith, Alvin D., 220
Springram, Joel, 56
Stevens, Harold A., 248
Stevens, Thaddeus, 25, 26
Stokes, Carl B., 237
Sumner, Charles, 25
Sylvester, Edward C., 240

Taylor, Hobart, 245
Taylor, Glen H., 60
Thurmond, J. Strom, 138
Trotter, Monroe, 218
Truman, Harry S., 50, 61, 127, 138, 163
Truth, Sojourner, 46
Tubman, Harriet, 46
Turner, Benjamin S., 40
Turner, H. M., 218
Turner, Nat. 25, 46, 117

Vardaman, James K., 35
Varner, William, 68–104
Vesey, Denmark, 46, 117
Villard, Oswald Garrison, 54, 58

Wallace, George C., 106, 219, 220
Wallace, Henry A., 60–63, 138
Waner, John, 229
Waring, J. Waites, 243
Warren, Earl, 139
Washington, Booker T., 49, 52, 54, 66, 125, 154, 218
Washington, Walter, 156
Watson, Barbara, 240
Watson, James L., 242
Weaver, George L. P., 239
Weaver, Robert, 156, 234, 238, 245
Weber, Max, 227
Wells, Josiah T., 40
Weltner, Charles, 251
Wert, Robert J., 212
Westerfield, Samuel Z., Jr., 239
White, George H., 41
White, Theodore H., 141
White, Walter, 60
Wilkins, Roy, 45, 106, 244
Willis, A. W., 235
Wilson, James Q., 19n, 170, 172n
Wilson, Woodrow, 48
Wingate, Livingston, 236
Wirth, L., 19n
Wood, Robert H., 42
Woodward, C. Vann, 126
Wright, Jonathan J., 39–40

X, Malcolm, 205

Young, Whitney, 45

PB-5923-810-SB
5-09

POLITICAL SCIENCE
HISTORY

Lenneal J. Henderson, Jr. is Assistant Professor of Sociology and Government and Director of Ethnic Studies at the University of San Francisco. He has taught, among other places, at Xavier University in New Orleans, Howard University in Washington, D.C., and St. Mary's College in Moraga, California, where he was also Assistant Dean of Students. He is the author of a number of articles on black political life and thought.

Also of related interest from Chandler...

Lynn B. Iglitzin, **Violent Conflict in American Society** (Spring 1972)
Matthew Holden, Jr., **The White Man's Burden** (Fall 1972)
Matthew Holden, Jr., **The Politics of the Black "Nation"** (Fall 1972)

ISBN-0-8102-0426-2